Challenging Approaches to
Academic Career-Making

Bloomsbury Higher Education Research

Series Editor: Simon Marginson

The Bloomsbury Higher Education Research series provides the evidence-based academic output of the world's leading research centre on higher education, the ESRC/RE Centre for Global Higher Education (CGHE) in the UK. The core focus of CGHE's work and of The Bloomsbury Higher Education Research series is higher education, especially the future of higher education in the changing global landscape. The emergence of CGHE reflects the remarkable growth in the role and importance of universities and other higher education institutions, and research and science, across the world. Corresponding to CGHE's projects, monographs in the series will consist of social science research on global, international, national and local aspects of higher education, drawing on methodologies in education, learning theory, sociology, economics, political science and policy studies. Monographs will be prepared so as to maximize worldwide readership and selected on the basis of their relevance to one or more of higher education policy, management, practice and theory. Topics will range from teaching and learning and technologies to research and research impact in industry, national system design, the public good role of universities, social stratification and equity, institutional governance and management, and the cross-border mobility of people, institutions, programmes, ideas and knowledge. The Bloomsbury Higher Education Research series is at the cutting edge of world research on higher education.

Advisory Board:
Paul Blackmore, King's College London, UK; Brendan Cantwell, Michigan State University, USA; Gwilym Croucher, University of Melbourne, Australia; Carolina Guzman-Valenzuela, University of Chile, Chile; Glen Jones, University of Toronto, Canada; Barbara Kehm, University of Glasgow, UK; Jenny Lee, University of Arizona, USA; Ye Liu, King's College London, UK; Christine Musselin, Sciences Po, France; Alis Oancea, University of Oxford, UK; Imanol Ordorika, Universidad Nacional Autónoma de México, Mexico; Laura Perna, University of Pennsylvania, USA; Gary Rhoades, University of Arizona, USA; Susan Robertson, University of Cambridge, UK; Yang Rui, University of

Hong Kong, Hong Kong; Pedro Teixeira, University of Porto, Portugal; Jussi Valimaa, University of Jyvaskyla, Finland; N.V. Varghese, National University of Educational Planning and Administration, India; Marijk van der Wende, University of Utrecht, The Netherlands; Po Yang, Peking University, China; Akiyoshi Yonezawa, Tohoku University, Japan.

Also available in the series:
The Governance of British Higher Education: The Impact of Governmental, Financial and Market Pressures, Michael Shattock and Aniko Horvath
Changing Higher Education for a Changing World, edited by Claire Callender, William Locke, Simon Marginson
Changing Higher Education in India, edited by Saumen Chattopadhyay, Simon Marginson and N.V. Varghese
Changing Higher Education in East Asia, Simon Marginson and Xin Xu
Higher Education, State and Society, Lili Yang
The Governance of European Higher Education, Michael Shattock and Aniko Horvath
Challenging Approaches to Academic Career-Making, Celia Whitchurch, William Locke and Giulio Marini
Universities and Regions, Michael Shattock and Aniko Horvath

Forthcoming in the series:
Online Learning Futures, Eileen Kennedy and Diana Laurillard

Challenging Approaches to Academic Career-Making

Celia Whitchurch, William Locke and Giulio Marini

BLOOMSBURY ACADEMIC
LONDON • NEW YORK • OXFORD • NEW DELHI • SYDNEY

BLOOMSBURY ACADEMIC
Bloomsbury Publishing Plc
50 Bedford Square, London, WC1B 3DP, UK
1385 Broadway, New York, NY 10018, USA
29 Earlsfort Terrace, Dublin 2, Ireland

BLOOMSBURY, BLOOMSBURY ACADEMIC and the Diana logo are trademarks of
Bloomsbury Publishing Plc

First published in Great Britain 2023
Paperback edition published 2025

Copyright © Celia Whitchurch, William Locke and Giulio Marini, 2023

Celia Whitchurch, William Locke and Giulio Marini have asserted their right under the
Copyright, Designs and Patents Act, 1988, to be identified as Authors of this work.

For legal purposes the Acknowledgements on p. xviii constitute an extension
of this copyright page.

Series design by Adriana Brioso
Cover image © Setthasith Wansuksri/EyeEm/Getty Images

All rights reserved. No part of this publication may be reproduced or transmitted
in any form or by any means, electronic or mechanical, including photocopying,
recording, or any information storage or retrieval system, without prior permission in
writing from the publishers.

Bloomsbury Publishing Plc does not have any control over, or responsibility for,
any third-party websites referred to or in this book. All internet addresses given in this
book were correct at the time of going to press. The author and publisher regret any
inconvenience caused if addresses have changed or sites have ceased to exist,
but can accept no responsibility for any such changes.

A catalogue record for this book is available from the British Library.

A catalog record for this book is available from the Library of Congress.

ISBN: HB: 978-1-3502-8253-7
PB: 978-1-3502-8257-5
ePDF: 978-1-3502-8254-4
eBook: 978-1-3502-8255-1

Series: Bloomsbury Higher Education Research

Typeset by Newgen KnowledgeWorks Pvt. Ltd., Chennai, India

To find out more about our authors and books visit www.bloomsbury.com
and sign up for our newsletters.

During the writing of this book, our first author, Celia Whitchurch, lost two close friends and colleagues, to whom the book is dedicated:
Diana Linden 1944–2019
Judith Taylor 1946–2021

Contents

List of Figures	x
List of Tables	xi
Series Editor's Foreword	xii
Notes on Authors	xvii
Acknowledgements	xviii

1	The Changing Parameters of Academic Work	1
2	Academic Career Trajectories and Aspirations	23
3	The Study and Early Findings	47
4	The Significance of Career Scripts	69
5	The Rise of the *Concertina Career*	91
6	Negotiating Misalignments and Disjunctures	109
7	Whither the Academic Profession?	131
8	Rethinking Academic Careers in a Post-Pandemic World	153

Appendix 1: *Survey Questionnaire*	179
Appendix 2: *Topic Guide for First Round of Interviews, Autumn 2017 to Spring 2018*	187
Appendix 3: *Topic Guide for Second Round of Interviews, Autumn 2019 to Spring 2020*	189
References	191
Index	211

Figures

2.1	Academic faculty (excluding atypical) by employment function, proportions, 2010–11 to 2019–20	27
2.2	Change in academic contracts, 2010–11 to 2019–20	28
7.1	Adjunct activities around the academic core of disciplinary teaching and research	143
7.2	The collective drift from a disciplinary focus, including cross-disciplinary and disciplinary applications, towards a focus on teaching and research in practice settings, and to extended academic activities	144

Tables

2.1	Academic Faculty by Employment Function, Selected Years 2010–11 to 2019–20	25
2.2	Academic Faculty by Academic Employment Function and Contract Level, 2017–18	34
2.3	Previous Employment Experience Outside Higher Education, by Current Academic Employment Function	38
2.4	Origin and Preferred Destination of Survey Respondents by Current Academic Employment Function	40
2.5	Comparison of Averages by Intention to Leave the Higher Education Sector	41
2.6	Prediction of Intention to Leave Higher Education	43
3.1	Employment Category of Academic Faculty Interviewed in the First and Second Round of Interviews	51
3.2	Levels of Seniority of Academic Faculty Interviewed in the First Round of Interviews, Additional Numbers in Each Category at the Second Round of Interviews and Total Numbers in Each Category at the Second Round of Interviews	52
3.3	Typologies of *Mainstream*, *Portfolio* and *Niche* Approaches to Roles and Careers, and Associated Domains	59
4.1	Description of *Institutional*, *Practice* and *Internal Scripts*	72
4.2	Categorization of Dominant *Career Scripts* of Individuals after First and Second Round of Interviews	73
6.1	Examples of Activity System Components in *Formal* and *Informal Institutional Economies*	126
7.1	The Shift Towards More Open-Ended Approaches to Roles and Careers	145

Series Editor's Foreword

Challenging Approaches to Academic Career-Making is the seventh title in the Bloomsbury Higher Education Research book series. This series brings to the public, government and universities across the world the ideas and research evidence being generated by researchers from the ESRC/OFSRE Centre for Global Higher Education.[1] The Centre for Global Higher Education (CGHE), a partnership of researchers from six UK and five international universities, is the world's largest concentration of expertise in relation to higher education and its social contributions. The core focus of CGHE's work, and of the Bloomsbury Higher Education Research Series, is higher education, especially higher education in the changing global landscape.

Each year the mega topic of 'higher education' seems to take on greater importance for governments, business, civil organizations, students, families and the public. Much is at stake. The role and impact of the higher education sector is growing. More than 235 million students enroll at tertiary level across the world, four-fifths of them in degree programmes. Over 40 per cent of school leavers now enter tertiary education each year, though resources and quality vary significantly. In North America and Europe, that ratio rises to four young people in every five. Universities and colleges are seen as primary locations of personal opportunity, social and geographical mobility and the development of whole communities. Almost three million new science papers are codified as part of the global literature each year, and the role of research in industry and government is expanding everywhere.

Higher education has become central to social, economic, cultural and political life. One reason is that even while serving local society and national policy, higher education and research are especially globalized in character. Routine cross-border movements of students, academics and researchers, knowledge, information and money help to shape not only nations but the international order itself. Until the pandemic broke out in early 2020, more than six million students changed countries in order to enroll in their chosen study programme, and two years later the world is returning to those kind of numbers. A quarter of all published research papers involve joint authorship across national borders. In some countries fee-based international education is a major source of export revenues. Some other countries are losing talent in net terms each year. However, capacity building in higher education and research is spreading across the world, and this is modifying earlier patterns of 'brain drain'.

The global higher education landscape is changing with compelling speed, reflecting larger economic, political and cultural shifts in the geo-strategic setting. Though research universities in the United States (especially) and UK remain strong in comparative terms, the worldwide map of power in higher education is becoming more plural. A larger range of higher education practices, including models of teaching/learning, delivery, institutional organization and system, will shape higher education in future. Anglo-American (and Western) norms and models will be less dominant, and will themselves evolve. Rising universities and science in East Asia and Singapore are already reshaping the flow of knowledge and higher education. Latin America, South East Asia, India, Central Asia and the Arab nations have a growing global importance. The trajectories of education and research in sub-Saharan Africa are crucial to state-building and community development.

All of this has led to a more intensive focus on how higher education systems and institutions function and their value, performance, effectiveness, openness and sustainability. This in turn has made research on higher education more significant – both because it provides us with insights into one important facet of the human condition and because it informs evidence-based government policies and professional practices.

CGHE opened in late 2015 and is currently funded until October 2023. The Centre investigates higher education using a range of social science disciplines including economics, sociology, political science and policy studies, psychology and anthropology, and uses a portfolio of quantitative, qualitative and synthetic-historical research techniques. It maintains ten primary research projects, variously of between eighteen months and eight years' duration, as well as smaller projects, and involves about forty active affiliated individual researchers. Over its eight-year span, it is financed by about £10 million in funding from the UK Economic and Social Research Council, partner universities and other sources. Its UK researchers are drawn from the Universities of Oxford, Lancaster, Surrey, Bath, Bristol and University College London (UCL). The headquarters of the Centre are located at Oxford, and there are large concentrations of researchers at both Oxford and UCL. The current affiliated international researchers are from Hiroshima University in Japan, Shanghai Jiao Tong University in China, Lingnan University in Hong Kong, Virginia Tech in the United States, and Technological University Dublin. CGHE also collaborates with researchers from many other universities across the world, in seminars, conferences and exchange of papers. It runs an active programme of global webinars that regularly engages participant audiences of 50 to 200 people a week and each year runs a well-attended online conference on higher education issues.

The Centre has a full agenda. The unprecedented growth of mass higher education, the striving for excellence and innovation in the research university sector and the changing global landscape pose many researchable questions for governments, societies and higher education institutions themselves. Some of these questions already figure in CGHE research projects. For example, what are the formative effects on societies and economies of the now much wider distribution of advanced levels of learning? How does it change individual graduates as people – and what does it mean when half or more of the workforce is higher educated and much more mobile; and when confident human agency has become widely distributed across civil and political society in nations with little state tradition, or where the main experience has been colonial or authoritarian rule? What does it mean when many more people are becoming steeped in the sciences, many others understand the world through the lenses of the social sciences or humanities, and a third group are engaged in neither? And what happens to those people left outside the formative effects of higher education?

What is the larger public role and contribution of higher education, as distinct from the private benefits for and private effects on individual graduates? What does it mean when large and growing higher education institutions have become the major employers in many locations and help to sustain community and cultural life, almost like branches of local government while also being linked to global cities across the world? And what is the contribution of higher education, beyond helping to form the attributes of individual graduates, to the development of the emerging global society?

Likewise, the many practical problems associated with building higher education and science take on greater importance. How can scarce public budgets provide for the public role of higher education institutions, for a socially equitable system of individual access, and for research excellence, all at the same time? What is the role for and limits of family financing and tuition loans systems? What is the potential contribution of private institutions, including for-profit colleges? In national systems, what is the best balance between research intensive and primarily teaching institutions, and between academic and vocational education? What are the potentials for technological delivery in extending access? What is happening in graduate labour markets, where returns to degrees are becoming more dispersed between families with differing levels of income, different kinds universities and different fields of study? Do larger education systems provide better for social mobility and income equality? How does the internationalization of universities contribute to national policy and local societies? Does mobile international education expand opportunity or further stratify societies? What are the implications of new populist tensions between national and global goals, as manifest, for example, in the tensions over Brexit in the UK and the politics of the Trump era in the United States, for higher education and research? And always, what can national systems of higher education and science learn from each other, and how can they build stronger common ground?

In tackling these research challenges and bringing the research to all, we are very grateful to have the opportunity to work with such a high-quality publisher as Bloomsbury. In the book series, monographs are selected on the basis of their relevance to one or more of higher education policy, management, practice and theory. Topics range from teaching and learning and technologies, to research and its organization, the design parameters of national higher education systems, the public good role of higher education, social stratification and equity, institutional governance and management, and the cross-border mobility of people, programmes and ideas. Much of CGHE's work is global and comparative in scale, drawing lessons from higher education in many different countries, and the Centre's cross-country and multi-project structure allows it to tap into the more plural higher education and research landscape that has emerged. The book series draws on authors from across the world and is prepared for relevance across the world.

CGHE places special emphasis on the relevance of its research, on communicating its findings, and on maximizing the usefulness and impacts of those findings in higher education policy and practice. CGHE has a relatively high public profile for an academic research centre and reaches out to engage higher education stakeholders, national and international organizations, policymakers, regulators and the broader public, in the UK and across the world. These objectives are also central to the book series. Recognizing that the translation from research outputs to high quality scholarly monographs is not always straightforward – while achieving impact in both academic and policy/practice circles is crucial – monographs in the Book Series are scrutinized critically before publication, for readability as well as quality. Texts are carefully written and edited to ensure that they have achieved the right combination of, on the one hand, intellectual depth and originality, and, on the other hand, full accessibility for public, higher education and policy circles across the world.

Simon Marginson
Professor of Higher Education, University of Oxford
Director, ESRC/OFSRE Centre for Global Higher Education

Note

1 The initials ESRC/OFSRE stand for the Economic and Social Research Council/Office for Students and Research England. Part of the original ESRC funding that supported the Centre for Global Higher Education's research work was sourced from the Higher Education Funding Council for England, the ancestor body to the OFS and RE. Research England continues to provide financial support for the research.

Notes on Authors

Celia Whitchurch is Honorary Associate Professor at IOE, UCL's Faculty of Education and Society, University College London, UK. She has conducted projects for the UK Leadership Foundation and Higher Education Academy, and was latterly Principal Investigator on the CGHE project on which this book is based. Earlier monographs include *Reconstructing Identities in Higher Education: The Rise of Third Space Professionals* (2013) and *Reconstructing Relationships in Higher Education: Challenging Agendas* (2017). She was founding Editor of the Association of University Administrators journal *Perspectives: Policy and Practice in Higher Education* and was subsequently Editor of the Society for Research into Higher Education journal *Higher Education Quarterly*. She has given keynote presentations in Australia, Hong Kong and across Europe.

William Locke is Honorary Professorial Fellow of the University of Melbourne Graduate School of Education, Australia, where he was Director of the Centre for the Study of Higher Education. Previously, he was Director of the Centre for Higher Education Studies at IOE, UCL's Faculty of Education and Society, University College London, UK. He was also Deputy Director of the ESRC/OFSRE CGHE. He is founding joint Editor of the Society for Research into Higher Education journal *Policy Reviews in Higher Education*. He has published widely and has given keynote presentations at conferences in North America, Australia, China, Japan and throughout Europe.

Giulio Marini is Lecturer (Teaching) at the Social Research Institute, IOE, UCL's Faculty of Education and Society, University College London, UK. Previously he was Research Associate at the CGHE at University College London, and a postdoctoral researcher at Scuola Normale Superiore (Italy), CIPES (Centre for Research in Higher Education Policies, Portugal) and the National Research Council (Italy). He has served as Associate Editor for the *European Journal of Higher Education* for the last three years. He is active in the topic of careers in higher education and employability of doctoral holders.

Acknowledgements

This book draws on a study entitled The Future Higher Education Workforce in Locally and Globally Engaged HEIs, conducted between 2016 and 2020. This was one of a suite of projects undertaken by the UK Centre for Global Higher Education, an international research centre based at the University of Oxford and University College London. We wish to gratefully acknowledge the support of colleagues at the Centre, in particular Professor Simon Marginson (Director) and Professor Claire Callender (Deputy Director). We also wish to acknowledge, with thanks, funding support from the Economic and Social Research Council (UK), the Office for Students (UK) and Research England (UK) (grant reference ES/M010082/1). Finally, we are indebted to those institutions and colleagues within them who willingly gave their time to participate in the interviews for the project. The interviews produced rich accounts of the lived reality of working in higher education in the years up to January 2020, for which we are immensely grateful. Without them this book could not have been written.

1

The Changing Parameters of Academic Work

Introduction

This book describes the outcomes of a four-year study, from 2016 to 2020, entitled 'The Future Higher Education Workforce in Locally and Globally Engaged Higher Education Institutions'. Although the empirical work of the study was funded for, and conducted in, the UK, it was set in the context of a large international literature on the academic profession, and was one of a suite of projects undertaken across multiple countries by the UK Centre for Global Higher Education (CGHE), an international research centre based at the University of Oxford and University College London. Most of the projects involved analysis of countrywide higher education systems and governance (see Callender et al. 2020; Chattopadhyay et al. 2021; Marginson and Xu 2022; Shattock, Horvath and Enders 2022; Shattock and Horvath 2021) and took a top-down approach. By contrast, the study that is the subject of the book primarily took a bottom-up approach, to explore ways in which contemporary academic faculty, across an increasingly diverse workforce, are making their careers by negotiating institutional processes and structures in ways that move beyond the duality of boundaried (with an emphasis on structures) and boundaryless (with an emphasis on agency) careers. It draws on the notion of career scripts to show how the career paths of individuals are informed by personal strengths, interests and commitments (represented by *Internal scripts*), and by activity associated with professional practice (represented by *Practice scripts*), as well as by formal career structures (represented by *Institutional scripts*). Hence, scripts are both internally and externally generated. *Internal* and *Practice scripts* have in turn led to new forms of activity, drawing on both *formal* and *informal institutional economies*, which are used as a metaphorical framework in relation to the production, exchange and consumption of academic or associated activity. Whereas the *formal economy* is represented by, for example, promotion criteria and career pathways, the *informal economy* is represented by personal initiatives, and professional relationships and networks, that may be unique to the individual.

Furthermore, a longitudinal dimension to the study demonstrates how roles and careers are being reshaped in ways that connect the university with a broadening range of constituencies, and how fluid identities are being created. This distinguishes it from other studies offering fixed typologies that represent a snapshot at a specific point in time. Arising from the influence of *Internal* and *Practice scripts*, faculty are stretching space and time constraints in a concertina-like process. The concept of the *concertina career* has been developed, therefore, to demonstrate ways in which, in the same way as the musical instrument expands and contracts in music-making, the process of career-making expands and contracts in relation to the different spaces that individuals find themselves in, over extended time periods. Therefore, the direction and tempo of an individual academic's career may not follow the linear pathway assumed by institutional career templates. Moreover, although there is a significant literature on early career faculty, there is less written about academics in mid-career, on which this text focuses.

With a view to achieving greater clarity in relation to the different stages of a career, UK institutions have, in recent years, been increasingly specific in defining progression criteria and milestones. However, these are, in turn, subject to interpretation by individuals as they seek 'personal growth and social and intellectual contributions'(McAlpine 2010: 2). These two factors influence individual approaches to careers, and although not necessarily incompatible, they hint at the tension between institutional rubrics and the actual process, and experience, of career-making for the individual. The impact of this tension on the way in which individuals enact their careers demonstrates that notions of fixed, linear career models tend to disguise the reality that the progression of an individual may involve detours (therefore a spatial dimension) and a disruption of standardized timelines (therefore a temporal dimension) (Whitchurch, Locke and Marini 2021). This process also reflects observations about professional life more generally, and 'the necessity of constructing new images of professionalism' (Noordegraaf 2016: 803), with a greater separation between the concept of a profession collectively, as an exclusive grouping of people, and of the members of it, who may have individual and sometimes unique trajectories (Freidson 1994). In the application of these ideas to higher education, the study on which this book is based thereby shines a light on 'more connective forms of professionalism', encompassing 'new professional relations and repertoires' (Noordegraaf 2016: 803).

The text goes on to explore the extent to which individuals are making their own accommodations and adaptations to the policy landscape at both national and institutional levels, how they do this, and the impact on their roles and career paths. What emerged were significant elements of misalignment with formal provisions, and a tendency by individuals to make use of *informal institutional economies* in developing bespoke trajectories, despite efforts by institutions to modify their employment frameworks, for example, in relation to career tracks and promotion criteria.

The UK Higher Education System

At the macro level, the UK higher education system represents what has been termed an *internal*, as opposed to an *external*, academic labour market (Musselin 2005, 2009). This development has had an impact on, for example, levels of competition between individual institutions and groups of institutions, and also on an emergent division of labour in research-oriented institutions, in which distinct career pathways have been established, focusing on research, teaching and/or service. This is in contrast to other European systems, which are traditionally externally driven, in that governments define and dictate the main regulations underpinning the working arrangements of academic faculty. In the UK, the internal academic labour market is characterized by strong autonomy at the institutional level, giving discretion in recruitment, promotion and progression procedures. This in turn influences the degree of agency that is assumed by sections of institutions, such as faculties and departments, and also by individuals, both local managers such as deans and heads of department, and academic faculty themselves. The UK system thereby reflects 'efforts to be intentional, to plan, and to construct a way forward given constraints… expected or unexpected…' (McAlpine and Amundsen 2016: 4). Environmental uncertainties and pressures have in turn led to creative interpretations of institutional rubrics, stimulated in part by an expanding range of experiences and expectations of academic faculty; porous boundaries with local, national and international communities; the requirements of professional practice; and expanding networks of relationships via social media.

On the one hand, employment of academic faculty and professional categories of staff in the UK higher education system is characterized by a single-pay spine, negotiated between the Universities and Colleges Employers Association (UCEA), representing the universities as employers, and the University and

College Union (UCU), representing faculty and professional staff as employees. National negotiations are responsible for comparable pay and conditions. On the other hand, the system as a whole can also be seen as a collection of heterogeneous employers within which individuals may find different opportunities, not only in terms of career pathways, linked, for example, to traditional teaching-plus-research, teaching-only and research-only tracks, but also in relation to the flexibility and autonomy available to the individual academic. Thus, academic careers in the UK have tended to be more fluid than has been the case in some parts of continental Europe and the United States. In these countries, formal tenure track models have operated, with strict qualification requirements for a tenured post (Pietilä 2017).

Other countries have four-stage models of doctorate, postdoctoral work, independent researcher/lecturer and professor (League of European Research Universities [LERU 2014]). The latter model broadly corresponds to practice in the UK, where academic tenure was abolished for new or promoted posts in 1988. Individuals appointed to a lectureship would have an expectation of proceeding to a senior lectureship (in some institutions, titled 'associate professor'), and possibly a professorship, in due course. Unlike in, for example, the United States, where liberal arts and community colleges are focused on teaching, all UK universities aspire to a teaching and research profile, even if the latter is geared towards the applied and practitioner side. As a first stage in their careers, those individuals who progress directly from doctoral work are likely to be appointed on a fixed-term research or teaching-only appointment, although those having research appointments may undertake some teaching, and those having teaching appointments may undertake some – usually unfunded – research. In both cases, the aim is usually to obtain experience with a view to progressing to an open-ended, as opposed to a fixed-term, teaching and research appointment (Locke et al. 2016). Within these arrangements, individuals are required to distinguish themselves by meeting progression criteria in the same way as they would in tenure track systems.

Each institution in the UK has its own structures and processes for implementation, for example, in relation to the organization of disciplinary activity and promotion and progression criteria, and there are also opportunities for different individual profiles and career paths to develop, although these may not necessarily be planned with precision. Individuals, therefore, are able to exercise agency depending on departmental conditions, promotion processes, work-life considerations, transparency, person-department fit, professional development resources and collegiality (Corbin, Campbell and O'Meara 2014).

On the one hand, UK institutions have been influenced by government policy, linking individual performance review to the contribution of individuals to the national Research Excellence Framework (REF) and (predominantly in England) the Teaching Excellence Framework. On the other hand, institutional progression criteria have expanded to encompass a range of activities, including, for example, employability agendas and public engagement. This has led to 'a trend toward a more individual management of academic careers replacing the more collective treatment of a supposedly homogeneous group' (Musselin 2013: 29). However, the interpretation and practice of formal requirements at local faculty, school and departmental levels (also referred to as 'middle management'), offering *ad hoc* adaptations of institutional policy, should not be underestimated in 'making things happen'. The study therefore enabled institutional and individual aspects of academic and associated activity to be viewed in parallel. Consideration is also given to ways in which individuals are motivated at different times in their lives and careers, and in relation to other aspects of their lives, such as caring responsibilities and work-life balance.

National UK policy, in particular the introduction of the REF, and the associated priority accorded to the impact of research, as well as the Teaching Excellence Framework, has been seen to represent a push for productivity, made visible by quantifiable research output, societal impact and student satisfaction scores (Clarke and Knights 2015; Clarke, Knights and Jarvis 2012; Leisyte 2016; Mingers and Willmott 2013; Reale and Marini 2017). It therefore also provides an overarching framework for the positioning of individuals and the decisions they take. While there is a body of literature that sees these developments as being counter-productive for individuals (e.g. Erickson, Hanna and Walker 2020), others review ways in which individuals are managing contemporary environments by 'search[ing] out and enact[ing] counter spaces' (Jones et al. 2020: 12). As a result, there have been calls for more research to understand ways in which individuals adopt 'meandering pathways' (Jones et al. 2020: 12), amid 'competing logics' (Pietilä and Pinheiro 2020), in response to the conditions in which they find themselves (Harland et al. 2015; Hartman and Darab 2012; Knights and Clarke 2014; Robinson 2016; Shams 2018). The study described in the following chapters contributes to this by demonstrating ways in which individuals, while acknowledging stressors, find ways of self-managing by creating new spaces, timescales and approaches, and taking a holistic view of work-life balance. They are therefore not simply adapting to the conditions in which they find themselves (Pietilä and Pinheiro 2020) but also actively modifying and expanding these via their day-to-day practice.

A significant literature also identifies the difficulties of co-ordinating a diversifying range of academic faculty, highlighting the fact that universities are never likely to be become 'complete organisations … with a well-defined identity, a hierarchical structure and capacity for rational action' (Seeber et al. 2015: 1450) (see also Franco-Santos, Rivera and Bourne 2014; Kallio et al. 2016; Kenny 2017; Reale and Marini 2017; Sousa, de Nijs and Hendriks 2010). These authors suggest that professional values and practices are likely to be blended with organizational requirements in different degrees in different institutions. This literature calls for further research on how this balance between institution and individual might be achieved. In response, the study described in this book contributes to understandings of ways in which individuals manage this process, in accordance with their own predilections and life courses. Universities and those within them are also working in times of intense uncertainty and turbulence, with potential for discontinuity and breakdown in expectations and aspirations. During the course of the study, this was demonstrated in the UK by the industrial action in the spring and summer of 2018 over early career insecurity, workloads, pay and pensions, in which the turnout and length of industrial action were unprecedented (Marini 2023 forthcoming). These conditions are likely to be exacerbated by the impact of the coronavirus pandemic and the UK's withdrawal from the European Union (Locke and Marini 2021; Marini 2019). The longitudinal dimension of this study enabled consideration to be given to innovative ways in which academic and associated staff cope with this turbulence and carve out opportunities for themselves. In particular, the study explored ways in which individuals negotiate misalignments and disjunctures between formal institutional requirements and the day-to-day enactment of roles. It goes on to consider the implications for careers and for the characteristics of the profession as a whole, and how these might be changing, drawing comparisons with trends internationally.

The Academic Profession

Although the diversification of the student body has been well documented in recent years (Belfield et al. 2018; Claeys-Kulik, Jorgensen, and Stöber 2019; Crawford et al. 2016; Keohane and Petrie 2017; Stevenson et al. 2019; Universities UK 2019), the consequent diversification of the academic workforce has been less so, despite significant implications for both academic faculty and institutions. This diversification is exemplified by the fact that significant numbers of faculty come into higher education from other sectors, that external activity has influenced faculty profiles across the range of disciplines, and that there is, therefore, a variety of entry and exit points to and from a career in higher education. As argued elsewhere (Gordon and Whitchurch 2010; Locke 2012, 2014; Locke, Freeman, and Rose 2018; Locke et al. 2016; Whitchurch 2018; Whitchurch and Gordon 2013, 2017; Whitchurch, Locke and Marini 2019, 2021), significant numbers of faculty have worked in business and industry and non-governmental organizations; others have strong links outside academia, for example, with professional bodies; and others use their academic work as a basis for building a portfolio that could provide a bridge to another type of career. An expansion of roles associated with academic activity within higher education institutions, such as supporting student employability, community engagement, equity and diversity or running online programmes, is also evident. Academic faculty therefore act not only as repositories of disciplinary knowledge but also foster exchange with other forms of knowledge and practice, often in a bridging role. Some individuals enter higher education employment later in their careers, and some move in and out of it. As a result, the hold that disciplines have had traditionally on academic communities has loosened significantly, as the role of institutions has grown in importance within marketized higher education systems. Increasing interdisciplinarity, the predominance of teaching over research in many academics' workloads, and demands for relevance have resulted in disciplinary boundaries, as described by Becher and Trowler (2001) and Henkel (2000), becoming more permeable. They are also weakening as real-world problems demand interdisciplinary solutions, including knowledge from across the sciences, but also from the human disciplines. The concept of the discipline is also being stretched by professional practice. Thus, even those individuals who want to advance in what might be regarded as relatively boundaried disciplines, with less obvious practical applications, are encouraged to think about how they could align their activity to real-world purposes.

Furthermore, large data sets provided by the UK Higher Education Statistics Agency (HESA) data, while they help to map the sector, do not necessarily reflect this day-to-day reality, particularly in relation to the specialization of roles, career trajectories and pathways. For example, the data show that the proportion of those academics who both teach and research has declined to below 50 per cent and the use of teaching-only contracts has increased (Locke, Freeman and Rose 2018). However, in practice, many of those on teaching-only contracts seek to undertake some kind of research, often unfunded and/or consisting of pedagogical research, often referred to as the scholarship of teaching and learning, or SoTL

(Fanghanel et al. 2016). Similarly, those on research-only contracts are likely to seek teaching experience by undertaking some lectures. This puncturing of the formal parameters of roles has been accompanied by an increase in fractional or part-time appointments, sometimes tied to specific income streams, and leading to a so-called casualization of the workforce. These developments have helped to break down assumptions about the traditional linear academic pathway of PhD completion, postdoctoral position(s), a permanent lectureship and promotions building on this. Individuals enter and leave the profession at different stages and with different levels of qualification. Those from the health professions, for example, who have been incorporated into universities in the past thirty years, often come in without a doctoral qualification, which they then seek to complete as part-time students. At the same time, a broadening of roles within institutions, to include activities associated with student outcomes, community engagement and research impact, have resulted in corresponding attempts to widen promotion and progression criteria. As a result, an academic career can no longer be claimed to be 'a linear and, to large extent, a predictable process' (Kwiek and Antonowicz 2015: 58).

Thus, it is apparent that broad-brush trends identified in contemporary literature on the academic profession and the UK HESA data sets can be belied by individual experiences and even contractual arrangements. Not only do individuals interpret and modify the structures within which they find themselves, but they also create bespoke spaces and pathways. Increasingly, interactions with, for example, professional practice and external settings may mean that this is an iterative process, with more scope for discretion on the part of individuals than is necessarily recognized in formal procedures. It would therefore appear that there has been considerable movement since 'stabilities at the core of academia, in the production, reproduction and negotiation of conceptions of knowledge of programmes of work over time … make it hard to change academic values and practices by the imposition of new purposes and structures from different policy and cultural arenas' (Henkel 2000: 251). Furthermore, although considerable attention has been paid to the insecurity experienced by early career academic faculty (Curtin, Malley and Stewart 2016; McAlpine, Amundsen and Turner 2014; Sutherland 2017; Locke, Freeman and Rose 2018; Locke et al. 2016), definitions of 'early career', and the timescales associated with this, are less well understood. Thus, some individuals may remain in postdoctoral positions until their forties or later, and others who come into higher education at a later stage, may be 'early career' in the sense of taking up a lectureship in their forties or fifties. Understandings about career timescales have therefore been disrupted, and there can be significant issues for those in mid-career, who may have choices to make about, for example, work-life balance and future possibilities, at a time when they may also have increased financial and family responsibilities.

Furthermore, the international study of the Changing Academic Profession suggested that the age at which academics in the UK obtain their first full-time higher education employment is increasing (Teichler, Arimoto and Cummings 2013; Teichler and Cummings 2015). In part, this may be a result of the increasing requirement for a doctoral qualification, although the average time taken to achieve this seems to have reduced (Galaz-Fontes and Scott Metcalfe 2015). Uncertain working conditions, limited opportunities and variable career trajectories for those starting out in academia appear to be extending the term of academic apprenticeship in many countries (Finkelstein et al. 2015). As a consequence, early career academics are not finding the security and predictability they had been led to expect (Locke, Freeman and Rose 2018). Indeed, there is a strong perception that new faculty are taking longer to establish their careers and that, rather than intentionally choosing a career in academia from the start, more doctoral students and postdoctoral researchers are considering their options in both academia and other sectors.

On the one hand, some authors have noted an erosion of autonomy and a sense of de-professionalization as well as the increasing length of time taken to achieve a balanced teaching and research role (Brew 2015; Clegg 2010; Gupta, Habjan and Tutek 2016). On the other hand, others have suggested a reorientation of approaches to roles (Kolsaker 2014; Scott 2014; Teichler, Arimoto and Cummings 2013), in which other options may be available to individuals with experience of academic employment, such as policy work with professional bodies or non-governmental organizations, generating different career paths and opportunities (Teichler 2017; Waaijer 2015). Alongside these narratives of diversification, it has also been noted that individuals are likely to actively 'plan, and … construct a way forward [within] given constraints' (McAlpine and Amundsen 2016: 4). They do this by navigating the structures within which they find themselves, such as job descriptions, promotion criteria, workload models, performance management practices and research evaluation processes. In turn, Degn (2018) suggests that sense-making for individual academics increasingly focuses on locale within an institution. In the study that is the subject of this book, the inclusion of the voices of a range of academic faculty at different stages of their careers has enabled a better understanding to be achieved of an increasingly complex relationship between faculty and their institutions, and how this can lead to accommodations of mutual benefit. This relationship is described in terms of the interaction between *formal* and *informal economies*, driven by *Institutional, Practice* and *Internal scripts*.

The complexities of the current environment, including the effects of local and global market conditions, alongside the diversification of the workforce, has engendered responses both from institutions, to create more flexible conditions (Whitchurch and Gordon 2013, 2017), and from individuals in adjusting their approaches to roles and careers (Whitchurch 2018). The international literature on the academic profession reflects these two interrelated aspects of academic work – that is, the organization of work within institutions and the personal experience of individuals who work in academia. It can be broadly categorized across a spectrum of countries according to a range of foci:

a. Broad-brush employment trends (fixed-term, open-ended, part-time, casual) represented by large data sets collected via survey instruments (Baruch 2013; Galaz-Fontes et al. 2016; Kwiek 2019; Machado Taylor, Soares and Teichler 2017; Siekkinen, Pekkola and Carvalho 2019).
b. The responses of individuals, particularly early career faculty, to less certain conditions and the increasing pressures of academic life, including performance review (Archer 2008; Franco-Santos, Rivera and Bourne 2014; Gornall et al. 2014; Jones et al. 2020; Marini 2019; McAlpine 2010; McAlpine and Amundsen 2016; Ortlieb and Weiss 2018; Rosewell and Ashwin 2019; Ylijoki and Henriksson 2017; Ylijoki and Ursin 2013; Yudkevich, Altbach and Rumbley 2015).
c. The impact of career structures at national levels, including the use of tenure track arrangements and market mechanisms such as the UK Research Excellence Framework (REF) and the knowledge economy (Coates and Goedegebuure 2010; Enders and de Weert 2009; Marini 2017; Musselin 2013; Pietilä 2017; Pietilä and Pinheiro 2020; Strike and Taylor 2009; Watermeyer and Tomlinson 2021).
d. Career typologies focusing on the individual, including the concept of the kaleidoscope career (Mainiero and Sullivan 2006), suggesting that the individual has multiple considerations when making decisions about their career (Baruch 2013; Sullivan and Baruch 2009), which can involve 'intersecting identities' (professional, personal and relational) (Pifer and Baker 2016: 192).
e. The interaction between individuals and institutional structures, and the degree of agency that they are able to exercise, for example, via 'boundaried' and 'boundaryless' approaches (Barnett and di Napoli 2008; Dany, Louvel

and Valette 2011; Djerasimovic 2021; Dowd and Kaplan 2005; Glaser and Laudel 2015; Kaulisch and Enders 2005; Leisyte and Hosch-Dayican 2016; Ortlieb and Weiss 2018; Siekkkinen and Ylijoki 2021; Siekkinen, Pekkola and Carvalho 2019; Whitchurch 2018; Ylijoki 2013). It is apparent from this literature that whatever type of career framework academic faculty work within, the way that individuals interact with institutional structures is a common theme that crosses national boundaries (Whitchurch, Locke and Marini 2021).

More specifically, and since the 2007 multi-country Changing Academic Profession (CAP) study (Locke 2011), there is increasing evidence internationally of a greater fluidity in academic work and of the impact of it crossing over into areas such as educational development, student support, research enterprise and public engagement (Carli and Tagliaventi 2022; Green and Little 2017; Groark and McCall 2018; Janke 2019; Stoltenkamp, van de Heyde and Siebrits 2017; Veles and Danaher 2022). This in turn has led to the creation of what have been termed third space environments (Behari-Leak and Le Roux 2018; Bossu and Brown 2018; Fink-Hafner and Dagen 2022; McIntosh and Nutt 2022; Schuck, Kearney and Burden 2017; Veles 2022; Whitchurch 2013, 2018, 2023a [forthcoming], 2023b [forthcoming]), in which multidisciplinary teams of academic faculty, and professionals with specific expertise and/or research and teaching experience and qualifications, work together, either permanently or for a defined period, on projects that not only enable and enrich academic endeavour but are also increasingly critical to contemporary institutions. It is against this background that the UK experience can be placed in the wider context of changes in the academic profession internationally, particularly in other English-speaking countries.

Against this background, the book builds on and updates earlier work by the authors on the diversification of the academic profession, including changing roles and identities, the emergence of teaching-only roles, the impact of more market-oriented approaches to higher education, issues for early career academics and the appropriateness of formal career development initiatives (Locke 2012, 2014; Locke, Freeman and Rose 2018; Locke et al. 2016; Whitchurch 2018; Whitchurch and Gordon 2013, 2017; Whitchurch, Locke and Marini 2019). Other recent studies of the academic profession in expanded higher education systems internationally have identified a continuing diversification (Fumasoli, Goastellec and Kehm 2015; Kwiek 2019), leading to a range of experiences at different stages of a career (Balbachevsky 2017; Crozier 2017; Frølich et al. 2018; Holcombe and

Kezar 2018; Machado-Taylor, Soares and Teichler 2017; Marini 2019; Rosewell and Ashwin 2019; Teichler 2017; Webber 2018), including at times a sense of invisibility or lack of academic identity (Siekkkinen and Ylijoki 2021). However, existing literature tends not to account for ways in which individuals may play with, or even push the boundaries of formal career pathways, for example, by being opportunistic, focusing for the time being on what needs to be done for the next promotion, negotiating a different balance of activity or creatively interpreting what they find in human resource policies. Thus, there would appear to be a spectrum of approaches from which individuals may develop strategies that will serve them not only for a range of purposes that includes career advancement but also for the satisfaction of cultivating personal strengths and interests.

The study on which this book is based, therefore, drilled down to obtain a fine-grained account of the lived experience of academic faculty over a three-year period. Two rounds of interviews were conducted between autumn 2017 and spring 2018, and between autumn 2019 and spring 2020, in eight higher education institutions across the UK. The focus of this book is on forty-nine academic faculty not having senior management roles such as pro-vice-chancellor, thirty-nine of whom agreed to be interviewed in the second round. This enabled the career trajectories of a range of people, in different types of institution, to be explored, including the impact of multiple entry points to higher education employment; the balance of activity in relation to teaching, research and associated academic activity; the interface with professional practice; and future career intentions. It not only illustrated how the workforce has diversified in relation to type of employment contract, entry and exit points and an increasing range of activity associated with disciplinary work, but also the variability in academic, professional and personal spaces that individuals occupy, and modifications over time in the tempo and pace of individual careers. This was contrary to what might be expected from fixed job descriptions and linear career models, and provided scope for exploration of, for example, ways in which individuals address misalignments and disjunctures arising from institutional policies and frameworks.

This process led to a deeper understanding of factors influencing the career trajectories of faculty in UK higher education who are involved in academic work, including those not on academic contracts, with a focus on mid-career faculty in a variety of roles and career trajectories. This mid-career group, as distinct from those in their early careers, is under-researched (Zacher et al. 2019). Furthermore, although much of the international literature on academic work assumes that academics are pursuing, or attempting to pursue, what might be seen as a 'traditional' academic career, the study demonstrated that this type of career is by no means universal. This multi-stranded approach, incorporating a longitudinal dimension which highlighted movements in individual trajectories, distinguished this study from other literature in the field, in particular those based on large statistical data sets.

Conceptual Framing

The text is framed conceptually by the interrelationship between *formal* and *informal institutional economies*, driven by the interaction between the *Internal* and *Practice scripts* of individuals, on the one hand, and *Institutional scripts* on the other, leading into the concept of the *concertina career*. This moves beyond earlier descriptions in the literature of academic careers based on the duality of structure and agency, and of boundaried and boundaryless careers, using the concept of an evolving morphogenesis, as defined by Archer (2000), to explain the process of individual career-making. The qualitative data are explored and explained within this conceptual framework.

Formal and *Informal Institutional Economies*

In the text, the terms *formal* and *informal institutional economies* are used as a metaphorical frame to refer to the production, exchange and consumption of academic or associated activity to which a value is ascribed. Such values may differ between institutions according to their focus in relation to, for example, the balance of teaching and research, local mission or international reach. The *formal institutional economy* could be said to be represented by, for example, contracts of employment, promotion and progression criteria, performance management and review, disciplinary and departmental affiliations and work allocation models. By contrast, the *informal institutional economy* could be said to be based on understandings that are not necessarily articulated, relating to, for example, the value of networks, mentorship, one-to-one advice, self-profiling, social media, personal disciplinary or allied interests and work-life balance. Whereas the *formal economy* is more visible and quantifiable, for example, via a measurable accumulation of publications, grants, teaching awards and management or 'good citizenship' roles, the *informal economy* is articulated via individual preferences, relationships, values and priorities, which, if recorded at all, may appear in personal development plans, which are likely to be confidential and thus hidden.

Both economies were apparent in relation to the investment of individuals in their work and future careers. Activity within the *informal economy* may, in turn, lead to individual and local solutions within the *formal economy* and its associated structures, enabling practice to influence policy over time. Although prestige may accrue from either *formal* or *informal economies* (Blackmore 2016), the accounts from the study demonstrated a schism whereby the *formal economy*, with associated markers of esteem, tended to be seen as a pragmatic necessity for employment and the *informal economy* as something that nurtures, supports and reinforces the individual's sense of self, thus ways in which 'academics serve as more than just employees' (Yudkevich, Altbach and Rumbley 2015: 1).

The *formal economy* of institutions could be said to be influenced by more market-oriented approaches as described by authors such as Galaz-Fontes et al. (2016), Santoalha, Biscaia and Teixeira (2018) and Musselin (2013, 2018), linked to the desire of governments across the globe that universities contribute to national socioeconomic goals. In the UK, this shift included, more specifically, a focus on impact in relation to research, formally defined in the 2014 Research Excellence Framework (REF) as 'an effect on, change or benefit to the economy, society, culture, public policy or services, health, the environment or quality of life, beyond academia' (REF 2014). In turn, institutions have translated the policies of successive governments into more variable contractual arrangements, including markers of progress and esteem such as job profiles, conditions of service and progression criteria. Such approaches play to assumptions that the motivations of individuals are primarily economic and competitive, geared principally to financial rates of return. Such assumptions underplay other possible motivations such as satisfaction with, and comfort in, a role, balance of activity, a sense of security and work-life balance considerations. To this end, *informal institutional economies* are drawn upon by individuals to modulate core employment considerations and facilitate individual preferences. In practice, multiple factors are likely to influence individual approaches to roles and careers, both concurrently and over time, with those assumed by labour market economics comprising only one element, albeit a basic one, that is to provide material benefits. However, individuals may vary in the extent to which they are able to modulate their approach, depending on the factors available to them across the *informal institutional economy*.

Institutional, *Practice* and *Internal* Career Scripts

The study developed the concept of career scripts primarily driven by institutions (Dany, Louvel and Valette 2011; Duberley, Mallon and Cohen

2006; Garbe and Duberley 2019) by incorporating the concepts of *Internal* and *Practice* (as well as *Institutional*) *scripts*. Thus, *Institutional* career scripts represent objective markers of individual positioning in relation to a career, such as progression pathways, promotion criteria and expected timelines. *Practice scripts* reflect activity associated with professional allegiances and requirements external to the university, not only in the classic professions but also in fields such as health and social care, humanitarian work, the media and business and industry; and *Internal scripts* reflect drivers such as personal strengths, interests and commitments, as well as what is considered to be an acceptable work-life balance. Individuals are likely to undertake, on an ongoing basis, a cost-benefit analysis of their activities in relation to the three types of script, the balance of which may change over time and according to circumstances. While *Institutional scripts* play into the *formal institutional economy*, *Internal scripts* are more likely to draw upon, and contribute to, the *informal economy*. Although *Practice scripts* may to some extent play into formal requirements in relation to, for example, the teaching of professional subjects such as health and social care, they may also enable new forms of associated activity to develop such as outreach work, particularly if the individual has a desire to progress community agendas, regionally or internationally. Both *Internal* and *Practice scripts* are likely, therefore, to contribute to a creative interpretation of roles and career paths.

From Boundaried and Boundaryless Careers to the Concept of Morphogenesis

In the application of career theory to higher education, approaches to career-making have tended to be broadly characterized in one of two ways: firstly, positional careers in which individuals rely on institutional structures such as promotion criteria and career tracks, and are therefore 'boundaried' (Dowd and Kaplan 2005); and secondly, non-positional careers that are 'boundaryless' (Arthur and Rousseau 1996; Dowd and Kaplan 2005) or 'protean' (Ortlieb and Weiss 2018), incorporating activity outwith institutional parameters. The 'boundaried/boundaryless' view of careers is reflected in theories of identity focusing on the interaction between individuals and the institutional structures in which they find themselves (Delanty 2008; Henkel 2000; Leisyte and Hosch-Dayican 2016; Ylijoki 2013). The research extended this theorization by utilizing Archer's concept of 'morphogenesis', in which the construction of identity has been seen as a cycle of interactions whereby the individual moves from passive to active mode, not only by interacting with the social structures that he or she occupies, but also in dialogue with himself or herself (Archer 2000). In Archer's terms, primary agency might be said to represent the initial position of an individual who, on appointment, accepts a career pathway represented in the job description that forms part of their contract. By extension, the passive enactment of a career would involve the reproduction of practice by adhering to established institutional progression criteria and pathways, in Archer's terminology, the condition of 'morphostasis'. However, in practice, career-making is likely to involve not only the individual's interaction with fixed structures, but also their interpretation of a role, or series of roles, in the light of factors such as their strengths, and their personal and professional interests and relationships. This distinguishes them from other individuals with similar contracts. The study therefore modulated the binary dichotomy of boundaried and boundaryless careers by developing the concepts of *Internal* and *Practice* (in addition to *Institutional*) career scripts to more fully represent the three-way interaction implied in the process of morphogenesis, so as to achieve a more nuanced picture of career-making over time.

Content and Structure of the Book

The chapters that follow explore how, in practice, individuals are able to progress within contemporary institutional environments, making these work for them, thereby demonstrating that navigating an academic career is not an either/or choice in which an individual 'plays by the institution's rules' or fails. It is likely to be a more dynamic situation in which choice is contingent upon, but not necessarily constrained by, structures, and is likely to arise from individual interactions between *Internal*, *Practice* and *Institutional scripts*. The longitudinal dimension of the study enables career movements to be tracked, together with variables such as discipline and institutional type, so as to capture the dynamism of this process.

Chapter 2 starts by giving an overview of the UK academic profession, reviewing key characteristics of the UK academic workforce at the time the study was undertaken, between 2016 and 2020. It considers the limitations of the data sets collected from universities by the Higher Education Statistics Agency (HESA) and in the definitions used. It also draws on a survey distributed during 2019 to all faculty in four of the eight case study institutions where interviews were undertaken. As well as providing a larger sample to draw on, the results of the survey offered indications about whether previous employment experiences of academic faculty were indicators of current career trajectory and future career intentions. The chapter explores the options open to academic faculty in a range of roles, including the aspiration to move from a teaching-only or a research-only role to a combined teaching and research role, and/or a middle or senior management role, in order to gain career advancement. Respondents to the survey also indicated whether they had an intention to leave employment in higher education and whether their preferred destination would be in the private, public or charitable sectors. The survey offered indications of an increasing diversity of career trajectories in UK higher education, and how these are constructed and managed in different institutions. This chapter therefore provides a broad context for the findings from the interviews in Chapters 4–6.

Chapter 3 sets out the parameters of the study across eight higher education institutions in the UK, including the questions that guided the study, and describes how the two-year, longitudinal dimension enabled an exploration of approaches that individuals took to their roles and careers, both simultaneously and over time. It shows how the interview data, from a range of academic faculty in different types of institution, in different disciplines, and at different career stages, was analysed. It goes on to describe the categorization of *Mainstream*, *Portfolio* and *Niche* approaches to roles and careers, identifying their characteristics, and showing how these are likely to affect individuals' interactions with four spatial domains that influence contemporary roles and careers: the disciplinary, the organizational, the external/community, and the internal/motivational (Whitchurch, Locke and Marini 2019). It demonstrates that the three approaches to roles are not mutually exclusive, and considers a fluidity that was apparent between approaches over the two-year period between the two sets of interviews. The chapter goes on to consider variables affecting the categorization of the three approaches: discipline, institutional type, gender and career stage, and to link the three approaches to *formal* and *informal institutional economies*.

Chapter 4 develops the initial categorizations described in Chapter 3, using the concepts of *Institutional, Practice* and *Internal scripts* to explain the fluidity of approaches to roles during the course of a career. Thus, people may be influenced by different scripts simultaneously, or at different stages of their career, according to their own set of circumstances and the value that they place on the different scripts. The three scripts are described in detail, *Institutional scripts* representing the formal requirements and timelines associated with progress in an academic career, *Practice scripts* reflecting the iteration between individuals and a range of professional environments across both public and private sectors, and *Internal scripts* focusing on personal strengths, interests and values that are unique to the individual. These scripts therefore represent an advance on the static categorization of *Mainstream*, *Portfolio* and *Niche* approaches to roles and careers described in Chapter 3. The three scripts are then framed theoretically in the context of Archer's (2000) theory of morphogenesis, so that the interplay between individual and institution becomes multifaceted during the process of career-making, as individuals not only interact with institutional structures but also incorporate new forms of activity, influenced by personal and professional activities and relationships outside the institution.

Chapter 5 develops the concept of the *concertina career* as a metaphor to demonstrate ways in which academic faculty may maintain more than one approach to a career, both simultaneously and over a period of time, suggesting that fixed templates and models to be found in institutional policies and in the literature do not fully explain the lived experiences of individuals. The concept characterizes the way in which an individual's activities may expand and contract, both across spaces represented by different commitments and relationships and over time, thereby influencing the direction and tempo of a career. The chapter demonstrates how the spatial parameters of a career are being stretched in two ways, firstly through the emergence of new forms of work around disciplinary activity, and the need to achieve recognition of these for career credit. Secondly, it shows how, driven by *Internal* and *Practice scripts*, the shape of a career may stretch or compress over time, concertina-like, to accommodate, for example, professional allegiances and responsibilities, career moves in and out of higher education, and life events, thereby reflecting the lived experience of career-making as opposed to conforming to the assumptions underlying institutional career pathways. By contextualizing careers within the individual's own experience, the concept of the *concertina career* demonstrates how individuals shape their own careers, at different stages and to suit the different circumstances of their lives. Through interactions with others, individual approaches to career-making, driven by *Internal* and *Practice*, as opposed to *Institutional*, *scripts*, gather collective momentum and may ultimately result in the transformation of practice and even institutional policy. Individuals, through their own interpretation and/or extension of their roles, make constant adjustments over space and time, so as to create elasticity within formal career structures. Thus, the interplay between individual and institution becomes multifaceted during the process of career-making.

Chapter 6 considers misalignments and disjunctures between individuals' perceptions of their roles and institutional frameworks, including disciplinary affiliations, contractual arrangements, job profiles, progression criteria and workload models. It goes on to review the general impact of such misalignments and disjunctures, and ways in which individuals negotiate them, making decisions about their academic interests, career aspirations and other commitments on the basis of local situations. Some take a pragmatic stance to coping with disruptions to their plans and expectations. This can involve being opportunistic and repurposing activity to create a wider range of applications and options. Others find what they see as a safe space, focusing on a strength or interest in which they feel secure. Whatever approach is taken, a common factor in success is enlisting the support of local managers and mentors in helping individuals to align their profiles and skill sets with formal requirements, by massaging, translating and legitimizing what might be bespoke activity, so as to achieve a fit with institutional templates. It is noted that individuals are likely to rely on the *informal institutional economy* as a means of accommodating their activities within formal parameters, and a framework of activity theory (Engeström 2001) is used to demonstrate ways in which the two economies interact as individuals find ways of coping with the misalignments and disjunctures that they encounter day-to-day.

Chapter 7 reviews pointers for the future of the academic profession, highlighting a collective momentum towards more fluid approaches to roles and careers. In doing so, it considers the relationship of individuals to disciplines and to professional practice associated with disciplines, reviewing the different degrees of embeddedness that individuals have within the profession and the direction of travel for the profession as a whole. It suggests that in future it is likely to be influenced by a diversification and reshaping of disciplines, and an expanding hinterland for individuals, opening up academic activity to wider purposes, and at the same time expanding professional selfhood. The drift towards more fluid approaches to roles and careers is illustrated by a model demonstrating shifts in the professional formation of academic faculty. It is also noted that skills such as self-profiling, seeking and recognizing opportunities, and networking are increasingly evident in managing complex academic roles and career paths. Thus, formal, contractual relationships with an institution are likely to be underpinned by the development of 'soft' skills, and what might be seen as elements of 'soft' power, via relationships with colleagues, external networks and a variety of professional arenas. Finally, it is suggested that, on the one hand, the onus is on institutions to recognize and incorporate a broadening range of contributions associated with academic activity, in particular innovative work by individuals. On the other hand, it is also for individuals to explore spaces where they think they can add value and to be persuasive about these.

Chapter 8 suggests that many of the trends identified by the study may have been accelerated and become more pronounced during the Covid-19 pandemic, while new trends have emerged. However, academic faculty have developed strategies that will be useful to them in dealing with changing environments, particularly in harnessing *informal institutional economies* in dealing with formal requirements. Furthermore, the chapter suggests that faith in the *formal institutional economy* is likely to decline unless institutions begin to recognize and incorporate some of these changes and reward those who have taken essential initiatives in the face of major disruption associated with the pandemic. In particular, they need to acknowledge innovative work, such as the development of online and hybrid forms of teaching and learning, the advancement of interdisciplinary education and research, and the transformation of curricula to address global challenges. The book concludes by arguing that the elements of the *formal economy* – for example, contracts of employment, promotion and progression criteria, disciplinary and departmental affiliations, performance review, development processes and work allocation models – need to be reformed in order to realign with the lived reality of academic roles and careers in the mid-twenty-first century. To this end, it suggests that institutions may wish to pay attention to ways in which they can build resilience and trust within the workforce, by reviewing the nature of the psychological contract with both faculty and professional staff, and also with the communities that universities serve, both regionally and nationally.

Conclusion

The key themes of the book have been introduced in this chapter and will be further developed in later chapters. These include:

- the positioning of academic faculty who have extended the traditional teaching, research and knowledge exchange nexus with new forms of academic activity associated with, for example, the student experience and community engagement;
- the morphogenetic relationship between individuals, their interpretation of roles, their personal and professional commitments and the processes and structures of their institutions, driven by *Internal* and *Practice*, as well as *Institutional*, scripts;

- the spatial and temporal dimensions of career-making by a diversifying academic workforce within the framework of *formal* and *informal institutional economies*;
- ways in which individuals deal with misalignments and disjunctures between the two institutional economies;
- the effect of such developments on ways in which academic faculty express themselves as professionals;
- changing characteristics of the academic profession as a whole in the light of these developments; and
- some indicators for the future of the implications of these changes.

2

Academic Career Trajectories and Aspirations

Introduction

This chapter considers key characteristics of the UK academic workforce at the time the study was undertaken, between 2016 and 2020, prior to the Covid-19 pandemic, and against this background draws on the survey undertaken at four of the case study institutions during 2019. It is significant that, given the major contribution of academic faculty to higher education and the work of higher education institutions, there have been only limited attempts to grasp the key structural characteristics of the UK academic workforce, or how these have changed over time (Wolf and Jenkins 2020; 2021). Those that exist rely heavily on the extensive data collected from institutions by the Higher Education Statistics Agency (HESA) (e.g. HESA 2021), but there are limitations in the definitions used and ways in which these are interpreted in the faculty records submitted by institutions. Nevertheless, this data set represents the most comprehensive source of information available (Locke 2014). Analysis of this dataset provides a more detailed map of the broad trends identified in Chapter 1, prior to the Covid-19 pandemic.

Via the survey, the chapter also provides a more detailed exploration of the options open to academic faculty in a range of roles, including the aspiration to move from a teaching-only or research-only position to a traditional teaching and research role and/or to a middle or senior management role, in order to gain career advancement within the academy. Respondents to the survey also indicated whether they had an intention to leave employment in higher education and whether their preferred destination would be in the private, public or charitable sectors. The results of the survey offer insights as to whether the previous employment experiences of academic faculty are indicators of current career trajectory and future career intentions. Together with the review of key characteristics of the academic workforce, it provides a broad context for the fine grained analysis of the forty-nine interviews conducted in the study, described in Chapters 3–7, locating these in-depth findings against broad-brush patterns and trends in employment conditions. More specifically, this chapter demonstrates the impact of the UK Research Excellence Framework (REF) and a more market-oriented higher education system generally on institutional structures and strategies (which we term the *formal economy*), within which individuals are working.

Academic Employment Functions and Conditions up to 2020

This section of the chapter focuses on changes in academic employment functions and conditions, underlying reasons for these developments and specific issues affecting the ability of individuals to develop their careers. Overall, there had been a substantial increase (42,335 or 23.4 per cent) in the total number of academic faculty, especially from 2010–11 onwards, to 223,525 in 2019–20. The majority of these additional faculty were employed on teaching-only or research-only contracts, and only 7.9 per cent of the increase during that decade was accounted for by those expected to both teach and research. However, these broad categories need to be unpacked in order to understand more about how the academic workforce developed during this period. Moreover, this data points to an increasing division of labour and sense of fragmentation, putting pressure on the concept of a 'unitary profession' and a common experience of being a member of a singular academic community, thus informing the rationale for the study described in the following chapter.

First, the increase in the numbers and proportions of faculty in roles that are variously described as 'teaching-only' or 'teaching specialist', 'teaching fellow', 'education focussed' or similar. Between 2010–11 and 2019–20, these increased by 61.2 per cent, from 45,005 to 72,540. Table 2.1 shows that the proportion of all academic faculty (excluding atypical faculty) with contracts described as teaching-only had increased, from 24.8 per cent in 2010–11 to 32.5 per cent in 2019–20. As a proportion of those who actually teach (in other words, excluding research-only faculty and those in senior academic management positions who neither teach nor research), this has increased from 32.2 per cent of those who taught in 2010–11 to 42.5 per cent in 2019–20. Initially, this growth was more noticeable in 'other pre-1992 universities' (Locke 2014; Locke et al. 2016), but since the 2014 REF exercise, the increase in teaching-only faculty has been mainly in research-intensive Russell Group universities and

Table 2.1 Academic Faculty by Employment Function, Selected Years 2010–11 to 2019–20

	2010–11		2013–14		2016–17		2019–20	
	No.	%	No.	%	No.	%	No.	%
Teaching-only	45,005	24.8	52,575	27.1	56,130	27.1	72,540	32.5
Teaching and research	94,760	52.3	94,480	48.6	100,165	48.4	98,085	43.9
Research-only	40,740	22.3	45,580	23.5	49,085	23.7	51,510	23.0
Neither teaching nor research	685	0.4	1,605	0.8	1,490	0.7	1,390	0.6
Total	181,190	100	194,235	100	206,870	100	223,525	100

Source: HESA 2012, 2015, 2018 and 2021.

particularly in business and health and other professional disciplines (Wolf and Jenkins 2020, 2021). Second, there has also been an increase in the number of faculty on research-only contracts, from 40,740 in 2010–11 to 51,510 in 2019–20, but this has been in line with the overall increase in faculty. Research-only faculty accounted for 23 per cent of all faculty in 2019–20, compared with 22.5 per cent in 2010–11. Again, these are predominantly employed in research-intensive universities.

Those on teaching-only and research-only contracts are more likely to have worked in higher education for less than ten years, be young and female (Locke et al. 2016). They are paid less than those on teaching and research contracts, with 93 per cent of those full-time faculty who earned less than £34,189 in 2019–20 coming from these two categories, including 68 per cent who were on research-only contracts (HESA 2021).

The working conditions and levels of support for teaching-only faculty on part-time and/or fixed-term contracts have been the subject of a number of recent studies (Bryson 2013; Crimmins 2017; Lopes and Dewan 2014; Loveday 2018). The following issues are most commonly reported:

- heavy teaching and marking workloads
- workload allocation that does not allow sufficient time for preparation, marking and student support
- lack of access to office space for meetings with students and colleagues, lack of space to store materials and resources
- lack of access and time for continuing professional development opportunities

- lack of time for the scholarship required for providing a research-based education
- minimal involvement in more substantive educational activities, such as course review, curriculum and assessment design and innovation
- lack of access to relevant institutional funding schemes for developing learning and teaching
- few opportunities for developing leadership skills and experience.

While there have been efforts in some institutions to provide support and professional development for part-time and fixed-term teaching-only faculty in their teaching roles, there are a lack of examples of systematic, evidence-based university-wide approaches to training and supporting this group in their teaching roles (however, see Baik, Naylor and Corrin 2018; Broadbent, Brown and Goodman 2018; Goodman et al. 2020; McComb, Eather and Imig 2021; and Whitton, Parr and Choate 2021, for recent examples from Australia).

It is worth repeating from earlier studies (Locke 2014; Locke et al. 2016) that these data only include those faculty members whose contracts specifically state that they are only employed to teach. There is considerable evidence from the case study institutions in several of these studies that some of those on teaching and research contracts are also being directed to conduct less or no research (or are receiving less or no funding or time allocation for research) and so effectively undertaking teaching-only *roles*, despite their contractual status. This confirms the results of previous surveys of faculty (Copeland 2014; University and College Union (UCU) unpublished). In addition, it seems reasonable to assume (as mentioned in Chapter 1) that, in an effort to improve their chances of eventually obtaining a teaching and research position – the ultimate goal of many early-career faculty – some of those in teaching-only roles are likely to continue their research when they can, and many of those on research contracts will be seeking to gain experience of teaching as opportunities present themselves. This demonstrates some of the limitations of this general data set.

In contrast to the increase in teaching-only positions, the proportion of faculty who are expected to both teach and research has fallen from 52.3 per cent of the total in 2010–11 to 43.9 per cent in 2019–20, with a decline in absolute numbers since 2016–17. So, significantly fewer than half of all faculty are now in what have long been regarded as 'traditional' academic posts. This echoes similar trends in the United States (Finkelstein et al. 2016) and in Australia and Canada (Australian Higher Education Industrial Association [AHEIA], Faculty Bargaining Services [FBS] and Universities and Colleges Employers' Association

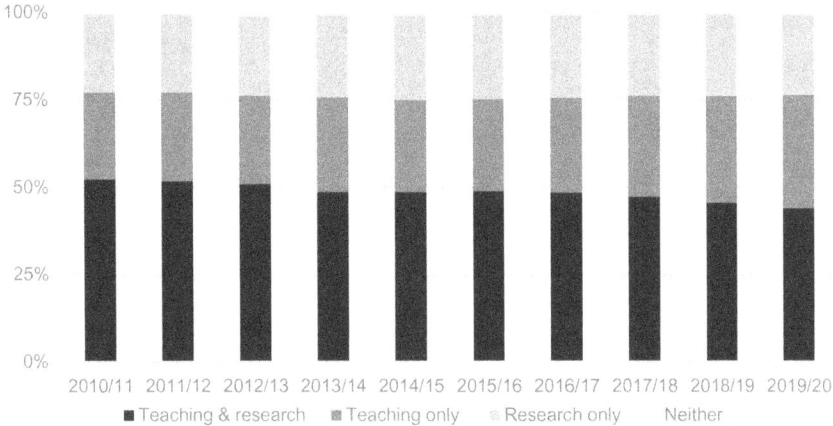

Figure 2.1 Academic faculty (excluding atypical) by employment function, proportions, 2010–11 to 2019–20
Source: HESA 2012–21.

[UCEA] [AHEIA, FBS and UCEA 2015]), where this decline in core faculty positions is, perhaps, even more marked. In addition to these faculty, there were 66,165 'atypical' faculty in 2019–20, and this is a reduction of 15.5 per cent since 2010–11. These are individuals who are generally on non-permanent contracts for short, one-off, or 'as-and-when' tasks, and their work was equivalent to 5,190 full-time posts (HESA 2021). Figure 2.1 summarizes these key changes in the profile of UK faculty in the past decade.

There are other important characteristics of these categories of academic faculty. Although teaching-only faculty are predominantly part-time (68.5 per cent in 2019–20), in the past few years there has been a growing proportion who are full-time, rising from 24.5 per cent in 2014–15 to 31.5 per cent in 2019–20. Also, historically, most of this category of faculty were fixed-term. However, the majority of teaching-only faculty in 2019–20 were on open-ended/permanent contracts, and this proportion increased from 45.7 per cent in 2014–15 to 55.7 per cent in 2019–20, a growth of 70.2 per cent in five years. These two trends give rise to a situation where more than a quarter (26 per cent) of teaching-only faculty are now on full-time, open-ended/permanent contracts, compared with 19.8 per cent in 2014–15. With a slight increase in the high proportion of teaching and research faculty in full-time and open-ended/permanent positions since 2014, this means the majority (56 per cent) of those who teach are in relatively secure positions. However, less than a third (32 per cent) of those on research-only contracts are on open-ended/permanent contracts, as the majority of these positions are funded from fixed-term research project funding. Figure 2.2 summarizes these trends.

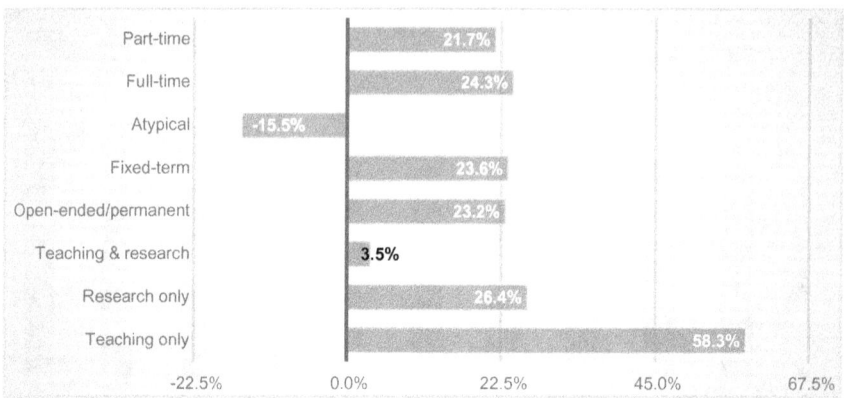

Figure 2.2 Change in academic contracts, 2010–11 to 2019–20
Source: HESA 2012, 2021.

Underlying Reasons for These Developments

Part of the explanation for these developments lies in many institutions' responses to increases in numbers of students, following the UK Coalition Government's reforms to policy and funding that led to the trebling of tuition fees in England from 2012 and the removal of the cap on the numbers of domestic and European Union students from 2014 onwards. Together with an increase in the volume of international (non–European Union) students, this has required substantial investment in teaching capacity across the sector. Also, given the volatility in the recruitment of students, and the huge growth in some Russell Group universities (leading research-intensive universities in the UK), it is helpful to human resources managers if additional academic faculty are part-time and fixed-term, offering flexibility and room for manoeuvre during unpredictable times. Teaching-only faculty can more easily be recruited on a part-time and fixed-term basis, as and when student numbers warrant this for a particular programme. Institutions are also responding to the increased emphasis on 'student satisfaction' and 'the student experience' as evidenced by the National Student Survey, and are mindful of their staff-student ratios, as a result of the growing marketization of higher education and competition for students.

These trends also seem to be partly driven by the periodic research evaluations – the Research Assessment Exercise (RAE) in 2008 and the REF exercises of 2014 and 2021 (Locke 2014; REF 2014; Wolf and Jenkins 2020, 2021). It appears that many of the larger research-intensive universities have reduced the number of their academic faculty who would be eligible for submission to the REF in order to increase their 'research intensity' rankings. This meant appointing new faculty on teaching-only, rather than teaching and research, contracts. It also meant moving those already in open-ended/permanent teaching and research positions who were deemed no longer 'research active' to teaching-only contracts. This appears to have led to the acceleration of growth in both teaching-oniy and research-only faculty in the years leading up to the REF 2014, followed by a slowing of this growth in the years immediately afterwards. These trends seemed to have been given further impetus in 2016 by the review of the REF chaired by Lord Stern (Department for Business, Education, Innovation and Skills [DBEIS] 2016), which prompted the decision to include all 'research-active' faculty in the 2021 REF, rather than allowing institutions to select those to be submitted, as in 2014. This decision was immediately followed by a decline, not just in the proportion of faculty on teaching and research contracts but also in their absolute numbers, as already mentioned.

According to a recent study by Wolf and Jenkins (2020, 2021), this trend is not so noticeable in post-1992 universities, where research and research funding is less of a focus and there are fewer advantages – and even some disadvantages, in terms of attracting academic faculty – of teaching-only contracts (Wolf and Jenkins 2020, 2021). In some pre-1992 universities, it may be that fixed-term teaching-only appointments are made in order to free up permanent faculty to undertake research projects or complete publications arising from these. However, it also seems that these trends are only partially the outcomes of purposeful institutional policies and plans. Wolf and Jenkins' (2021) respondents from several case study institutions denied any central strategic direction to replace teaching and research positions with teaching-only faculty. Indeed, their study highlighted 'the limited extent to which these changes are even understood, let alone scrutinised or fully evaluated by senior management teams or, therefore, by the Academic Boards and Senates, or the University Councils and Courts, which have responsibility for governance and academic standards. This should be of concern to the entire university community' (Wolf and Jenkins 2021: 15–16).

Moreover, according to a recent survey of human resources directors by the UCEA, it seems that many UK universities have more difficulty recruiting academic faculty to teaching and research posts below professor level (e.g. lecturer, senior lecturer and reader) than to teaching-only or research-only positions (UCEA 2019). Those disciplines more likely to report difficulties recruiting at this level included medicine, dentistry and health, and science, engineering and technology, with administrative and business studies not far behind. The reasons given for the difficulty were candidates not meeting the required standard of research outputs and not matching the particular subject specialism sought, which, in certain fields, may be possessed by only a small pool of faculty worldwide (UCEA 2019). This may be partly caused by a reluctance by pre-1992 universities to recruit to a traditional teaching and research position anyone who is unlikely to enhance the academic department's performance in the REF. Instead, it may be preferable to recruit a fixed-term, and even part-time, teaching fellow to meet the immediate demand caused by additional student recruitment than to commit to a member of faculty who may not deliver longer term on research outcomes. UCEA respondents reported that recruitment to teaching-only and research-only roles was less problematic across all subjects (UCEA 2019).

In most pre-1992 universities – Russell Group and other – academic faculty who research have often been given lower teaching loads and periodically offered paid sabbaticals for research and writing. While this made these positions more expensive than their equivalent in post-1992 universities, it increased the quantity and quality of publications, and hence the research reputation of the institution, its standing in the global rankings and its attractiveness to international students. So, in the longer term, if a high-performing, productive researcher was recruited to a traditional faculty position, this could pay greater dividends in terms of both research and teaching income. However, it seems a balance was sought, so that the quality of students' learning experience was not reduced by the mass casualization of teaching, with lower salaries and higher workloads, which could have damaged the academic reputation of the programme and the institution. Some research-intensive universities have even developed policies to limit the circumstances under which fixed-term contracts are used for the employment of teaching fellows, including maximum grading levels (e.g. University College London [UCL] 2020).

This, in turn, highlights the importance of demonstrated research excellence – and, in particular, highly cited publications and research income – in the progression to senior faculty positions in UK universities. Nevertheless, the role of 'professor' was held by only 10.2 per cent of all faculty in the UK in 2019–20, and even if those in 'other senior' faculty positions are added – such as head of school or department, many of whom would also be professors – this only accounts for another 2.7 per cent of faculty. The 194,600 (87.1 per cent of) faculty in the UK in 2019–20 who were not professors or 'other senior' faculty were made up of teaching assistants, research assistants, lecturers, research fellows, teaching fellows, senior lecturers, senior research fellows, principal lecturers and principal research fellows. Some research-intensive universities have adopted the titles 'assistant' and 'associate professor' in place of 'lecturer' and 'senior lecturer' in order to align with such nomenclature in North America and attract more recruits from that region as well as expanding the 'professoriate' in the UK beyond those who are full professors.

Specific Issues Affecting Career Progression

There is also a significant under-representation of women faculty at higher levels, particularly at the professorial level, where only 28 per cent of positions were held by women in 2019–20 when women made up 47 per cent of all faculty (excluding atypical) (HESA 2021). In 2012–13, when the currently used definition of professor was adopted, this figure was 22 per cent, so some progress has been made but from a low base. Women also made up 56 per cent of those faculty who work part-time, 54 per cent of those who have part-time fixed-term contracts, 54 per cent of those on zero-hours contracts, 53 per cent of faculty on teaching-only contracts, 51 per cent of hourly paid faculty and 49 per cent of those who are on all fixed-term contracts – all above what would be a representative proportion. Of those full-time faculty who earned £45,892 or above in 2019–20, only 39 per cent were female, and of those who earned £61,618 or above, this figure was just 31 per cent. This is despite the Athena Swan Charter which was established in 2005 to recognize work undertaken to achieve gender equality, including addressing barriers to women's career progression.

Concerns have also been expressed about the progress of early career academics/faculty (ECAs) and an apparent extension of the time taken by individuals to establish themselves in the profession. Several studies have confirmed that ECAs no longer appear to be a homogenous group, following a linear path from undergraduate and masters study through postgraduate research, a postdoctoral position and into full-time permanent employment as a lecturer in higher education (Locke, Freeman and Rose 2018; Renfrew and Green 2014). They are experiencing a 'portfolio' or patchwork initial career, reflecting the broad shifts described here (Whitchurch, Locke and Marini 2021). In part, this is due to an expansion in the numbers of doctorates obtained, on the basis of a belief in government that a large number of people with high qualifications will provide a competitive advantage for the economy on a global scale (Kehm, Freeman and Locke 2018). In some disciplinary areas, such as the humanities and social sciences, this has resulted in an oversupply of PhDs (Locke, Freeman and Rose 2018). However, a doctorate is a necessary, but no longer a sufficient, condition for admission to an academic career, such that decisions as well as selection processes have shifted into the 'postdoctoral' phase (Kehm, Freeman and Locke 2018). The difficulty of following a linear path into academia seems to be the source of considerable disappointment and frustration among ECAs. To quote one survey respondent from another study, 'National and institutional policies – and, particularly, institutional practices – have yet to catch up with these shifts' (Locke, Freeman and Rose 2018: 63). Again, there appears to be a gender dimension to this, with ECAs reporting a lack of transparency in promotion and recruitment processes, and a lack of female mentors and role models in academia.

Concerns about opportunities for career progression for those in teaching-only, research-only and other specialist roles led many universities, especially the research-intensive institutions, to introduce new promotion pathways alongside the traditional academic track for those who both teach and research. Their aim was to achieve parity of esteem between the different pathways. These policies usually included more explicit criteria for the reward and recognition of, for example, teaching and supporting students' learning, and sometimes aimed to identify what counts as evidence of good-quality teaching. A 2019 UCEA study found that two-thirds of the 87 higher education institutions surveyed had teaching-focused pathways in place, and that 86 per cent of these aimed to facilitate the progression of teaching-only faculty through to professor. The remaining schemes stopped at reader or senior lecturer levels. A similar number of respondents to the UCEA survey had introduced research-only pathways, but a higher proportion of these extended to professor. A much smaller proportion (31 per cent) of the higher education institutions surveyed had pathways focussing on leadership and innovation. The introduction of a Knowledge Exchange Framework in England (UK Research and Innovation [UKRI]/Research England 2021) to parallel the Research and Teaching Excellence Frameworks may result in similar pathways for this area of university activity.

Some of the problems with efforts to 'bolt on' new career tracks in this way to the traditional faculty career path have already been identified (Cashmore, Cane and Cane 2013; Locke 2014; Locke et al. 2016; Rothwell and Rothwell 2014). These include:

- different job titles to the 'mainstream' faculty career path, such as 'professorial teaching fellow' or 'enterprise professor', which mark them out as somehow limited or even inferior to the traditional 'professor' in a particular academic discipline on a teaching and research contract;

- individuals being locked into a specialist pathway which restricts their opportunity to change their focus – this is especially the case for those accepting a teaching-only contract who, at a later stage in their career, might wish to move to a teaching and research role;
- a lack of clarity and precision around how the 'alternative' career tracks operate and, in particular, what counts as evidence of high-quality teaching, leadership or knowledge exchange and engagement activity; and
- new initiatives which do not stimulate broader change in institution-wide policies and practices – for recruitment and promotion, in particular – which are themselves embedded in a dominant organizational culture and collective mindset that is unlikely to embrace or implement the reforms fully.

The design of the study that will be described in Chapter 3 aims to explore ways in which individuals are addressing such issues in progressing their careers.

These may be some of the reasons why, despite these initiatives, the proportions of teaching-only and research-only faculty in senior academic positions remain very low and, conversely, these categories of faculty make up the bulk (81 per cent) of the lower contract levels of lecturer (Lecturer A in pre-1992 universities) and teaching or research assistant (96 per cent), as shown in Table 2.2. The majority of faculty at senior lecturer (Lecturer B in pre-1992 universities) and above are on teaching and research contracts, and these still predominate (94 per cent) among professors. If the alternative career tracks are successful in promoting alternative career trajectories, it would appear that this is only the case among the more junior ranks during the early stages of academic careers.

From this analysis, it seems that, on academic employment function, gender, ECAs and contract levels, even the best efforts of UK universities to achieve a 'level playing field' and equality of opportunity have foundered on the broader, macro developments in the academic workforce, and more generally in UK higher education, and on the traditions and culture of the academy itself. The elements of the *formal economy* within institutions – contracts of employment and job descriptions, criteria for recruitment, promotion, progression and reward, the processes for allocating academic work, the measurement and management of performance and so on – have, at least partially, frustrated some individuals' attempts to carve out successful, lifelong academic careers. Thus, even pre-Covid-19, in an environment that was, for some, increasingly competitive, precarious and insecure, those seeking to enter and prosper in

Table 2.2 Academic Faculty by Academic Employment Function and Contract Level, 2017–18

Contract level (and total)	Teaching and research (%)	Teaching-only (%)	Research-only (%)
Head of school (4,785)	87	10	3
Professor (20,780)	94	3	3
Senior (pre-92)/principal (post-92) lecturer, reader (29,725)	81	13	6
Lecturer B (pre-92), senior lecturer (post-92) (54,810)	67	20	13
Lecturer A (pre-92), lecturer (post-92) (70,260)	19	41	40
Research assistant, teaching assistant (25,615)	4	54	42

Source: Adapted from UCEA 2019: Table 5, page 27; original source: HESA 2019 (Based on headcount. Job titles are indicative only. Contract levels definitions can be found at https://www.hesa.ac.uk/collection/c17025/combined_levels).

academia were already needing to be pro-active and strategic in pursuit of this (Finkelstein et al. 2015; Locke, Freeman, and Rose 2018). As will be shown in later chapters, this has led some individuals to develop highly personalized trajectories and create bespoke opportunities for themselves.

The Survey

As part of the study on which this book is based, an online survey was conducted in the spring and summer of 2019 in the four case study institutions that were willing to participate: one pre-1992 university, two post-1992 universities and one post-2004 university. The survey aimed to investigate career trajectories and aspirations in higher education, asking recipients about their previous and current experiences of working in other employment sectors, the balance of their current academic work activities, their key professional relationships and future career aspirations. The survey questionnaire for each case study institution was drafted on the basis of the findings from the analysis of the first phase of interviews. This consisted of the same questions for each case study institution, although some were translated into the common terms used in each institution, where appropriate. The information gathered added to institution-specific HESA data by shedding light on where academic faculty had worked before entering higher education, both within and outside higher education institutions; the extent to which individuals contemplated leaving higher education; and, if so, where they thought they might move to. Future intentions were then subject to multivariate analyses using different variables, for example, current academic employment function, current working conditions, number of years employed in higher education, whether or not they had a PhD, sex and age. Destinations outside higher education included public (and, specifically, other education sectors), private and charitable organizations. The survey instrument is included in Appendix 1. The sample size was 440 fully usable responses.

Background and Context

The international study of the Changing Academic Profession (CAP) in 2007 (Locke 2011) asked some similar questions to this 2019 survey. These had also been asked in the Carnegie Foundation for the Advancement of Teaching international survey of 1992 (Altbach 1996; Boyer 1994) and give some historical context to the survey findings: Within the past five years, have you considered a major change in your job? And did you take concrete actions to make such a change?

- to a management position in your higher education/research institution
- to an academic position in another higher education/research institute within the country
- to an academic position in another country
- to work outside higher education/research institutes

In 2007, over three-quarters of the UK survey respondents had considered making a major change (Locke and Bennion 2011), which was much higher than the average of 45 per cent across all nations in the study (Galaz-Fontes et al. 2016). Of these, the fewest (13 per cent) had considered changing to a management position in their higher education institution, and even fewer (8 per cent) had taken concrete action to achieve this. Thirty per cent had considered an academic position in another UK higher education institution, and most of these (a quarter of all respondents) had taken action. Almost as many had considered an academic position in another country, but far fewer had done anything about this. A greater proportion (37 per cent) had considered working outside higher education, but, again, fewer (11 per cent) had taken action. So, despite fewer 2007 UK respondents expressing greater satisfaction with their current job than in 1992, and with the overall UK job satisfaction ratings being low compared with other nations in the CAP study, only one in ten respondents had actually taken specific steps to find work outside higher education.

Contemporary turnover rates for academic faculty in the UK are low in comparison with other similar professions. In 2017–18, the median resignation rate in individual institutions was 8 per cent of all faculty and 5 per cent of those on open-ended contracts (UCEA 2019). However, these generic figures mask wide variations in turnover according to age, gender and type of contract, with a particularly high turnover among research faculty due to the use of fixed-term contracts, which particularly affects early career faculty (Gandy, Harrison and Gold 2018). The proportions of those resigning were much lower among teaching and research faculty than those on both teaching-only and research-only contracts, and also lower in pre-1992 universities than in post-1992 universities. In a 2019 survey of human resources directors by the UCEA, retention was not seen as a significant problem. UCEA's report continues,

> While individual tactics such as counter-offers are occasionally used, HEIs [higher education institutions] appear to be thinking about retention more strategically and holistically. Specifically, this means a focus on career pathways and workforce planning to give academic faculty members a recognisable and achievable career pathway without having to move to a different institution. Recognition awards are also becoming more popular in order to recognise achievements both on an individual and team basis. (UCEA 2019: 25)

Common strategies for retaining faculty reported in the UCEA survey included:

- career pathways, particularly for early career academic faculty
- a contribution supplement to enhance the salary of a member of faculty
- support for faculty seeking Fellowship of the Higher Education Academy or nomination for a National Teaching Fellowship
- investment in professional development programmes, particularly leadership and management
- provision of research funds or research support
- salary benchmarking exercises
- focusing on employee engagement
- use of market supplements
- accelerated consideration of promotion cases
- health and well-being initiatives
- opportunities for flexible working

It is in this context that the responses to the survey are reported and analysed.

Responses to the Survey

There were 536 responses from the four institutions. Percentages in the following categories are as follows, although they do not necessarily add up to 100 per cent as respondents could choose the 'prefer not to reply' option. The respondents self-identified as 277 female and 183 male. From the total, 284 were British, 57 came from the EU and 29 from outside the UK (EU excluded). A PhD or a professional doctorate was held by 345 of the respondents. Based on age, 27 were less or equal to 30 years old, 266 were between 31 and 50 years old, 162 were between 51 and 65 and 7 were above 65. Respondents were distributed among the following disciplinary fields as defined by the HESA: medicine, dentistry and health (116); administrative, business and social studies (111); education (85); engineering and technologies (76); biological, mathematical and physical sciences (62); humanities, language-based studies and archaeology (38); design, creative and performing arts (32); and architecture and planning (8). They self-attributed to the following categories of posts: 147 lecturers, 154 senior lecturers, 24 readers and 48 professors; 64 in research-only posts, 33 in teaching-only posts, 30 in middle and senior manager posts and 57 working in academic services.

Previous Employment Experiences

Survey respondents were asked whether they had worked in sectors or industries other than higher education and for how long. The results were analysed according to their current academic employment function, in other words, whether they were teaching and research faculty, on research-only or teaching-only contracts, or faculty who neither taught nor researched, for example, because they were in senior executive positions. As Table 2.3 shows, teaching-only faculty were far more likely than other faculty to have had experience of working in other sectors and particularly other education sectors, such as further education or secondary education. More than half of the teaching-only respondents had worked in the private sector. Further analysis confirmed that teaching-only faculty had spent more time on average in other sectors than other types of academic faculty. Research-only faculty were less likely than all faculty who taught to have worked in other sectors or industries, but that could be because they moved directly from a doctorate to a research fellow post. Overall, as the chi-squared tests highlight, it was a respondent's previous employment, especially in other non-higher education sectors, that appeared to have greatest influence on which academic career track they were likely to find themselves in at the time of the survey.

Table 2.3 Previous Employment Experience Outside Higher Education, by Current Academic Employment Function

		Teaching and research	Research-only	Teaching-only	Neither teaching nor research	Total
Any non–higher education sector	No	25.07	31.75	4.00	3.33	*21.66*
	Yes	74.93	68.25	96.00	96.67	*78.34*
	Total	100.00	100.00	100.00	100.00	*100.00*
	Chi-squared					Pr = 0.000
Other education sector	No	81.32	81.4	73.61	65.52	*78.9*
	Yes	18.68	18.6	26.39	34.48	*21.1*
	Total	100.00	100.00	100.00	100.00	*100.00*
	Chi-squared					Pr = 0.142
Private sector	No	52.38	51.16	43.06	44.83	*50.12*
	Yes	47.62	48.84	56.94	55.17	*49.88*
	Total	100.00	100.00	100.00	100.00	*100.00*
	Chi-squared					Pr = 0.505
Non–education public sector	No	73.99	69.77	66.67	68.97	*71.94*
	Yes	26.01	30.23	33.33	31.03	*28.06*
	Total	100.00	100.00	100.00	100.00	*100.00*
	Chi-squared					Pr = 0.617

Career Aspirations in the Next Five Years

Survey participants were asked what their career aspirations were in the next five years. This question included the following options:

- continuing on the same academic career pathway
- continuing on a different academic career pathway, research and teaching, research-only or teaching-only
- taking on a professional role and/or contract, for example, in relation to teaching and learning, online learning, widening participation and engagement

- taking on management responsibilities such as principal investigator, head of department or pro-vice-chancellor
- working outside the higher education sector, in the private, public or charitable sectors or
- withdrawal from the labour market altogether.

An Origin-Destination Matrix

From their answers, it was possible to construct an origin-destination matrix of respondents by career track and type of industry, which is represented in Table 2.4. The origin is the respondent's current academic contract, and the destination is their declared intention to apply for specific positions either within or outside higher education. More respondents (45 per cent) aspired to work in the traditional academic teaching and research role than any other option, although some other preferences were indicated. Middle management, such as head of department, or senior management, such as dean or pro-vice-chancellor roles, were also mentioned by a significant proportion (16 per cent), reflecting a growing option for career progress within academia. This pathway does not necessarily preclude the traditional academic role, as some managerial positions often imply a professorial/reader status. In some (18 per cent) of the cases, faculty declared an intention to change industry, especially opting for the private sector (13 per cent), followed by the public sector (8 per cent) (some respondents were open to both options). Other roles in higher education that do not involve teaching or research, such as public engagement or knowledge exchange, were also relatively popular (11 per cent), whereas teaching-only and research-only contracts were less frequently mentioned.

Overall, it seems that respondents tended to prefer to remain on their current career track (the percentages for this option are shown in italic in Table 2.4). In almost 70 per cent of cases, teaching and research faculty wished to remain in this role. Nearly 59 per cent of those in research-only roles preferred to continue on this type of contract, whereas 45 per cent of teaching-only faculty wanted to remain. Teaching-only and research-only faculty tended to indicate an interest in more options than other faculty, perhaps demonstrating a feeling that they ought to consider a wider range of options for their career because their own current employment circumstances were less secure or less likely to continue beyond the five-year horizon specified in the question.

Table 2.4 Origin and Preferred Destination of Survey Respondents by Current Academic Employment Function

	Origin				
Destination	Teaching and research	Teaching-only	Research-only	Academic, non-teaching nor research	Total
Teaching and research	69.96	24.00	22.22	6.67	44.53
Teaching-only	3.02	45.33	1.59	0.00	7.19
Research-only	6.87	0.00	58.73	0.00	9.69
Neither teaching nor research	9.89	26.67	9.52	30.00	11.09
Middle/senior manager	14.29	17.33	25.40	16.67	16.17
External employment	15.38	25.33	25.40	20.00	18.23
Private	10.99	21.33	17.46	10.00	13.16
Public	6.87	6.87	12.70	16.67	8.08
Charitable	3.30	9.33	11.11	13.33	5.64

Note: Column totals may exceed 100 per cent because respondents could select more than one option

Intention to Leave the Higher Education Sector

It is also possible to explore those factors which may have led survey respondents to declare an intention to leave higher education, focusing on the 18 per cent of respondents (see Table 2.4) who indicated at least one destination outside higher education, including those who were keen to leave higher education for another sector. Table 2.5 presents some of these possible circumstances, analysing averages by the dependent variable 'Would you work outside the higher education sector during the next five years?' Those who wanted to leave higher education were more likely to have already worked outside the sector before taking up their current employment, although the difference is not statistically significant (84 per cent compared with 77 per cent), and the numbers of respondents were not large. Those who wanted to leave had also spent slightly less time working in higher education (9.9 years compared with 10.2 years), although this difference is very small. Potential leavers were also more likely to have a PhD (58 per cent compared with 48 per cent).

Table 2.5 Comparison of Averages by Intention to Leave the Higher Education Sector

	Intention to leave higher education		t test
	No	Yes	(p)
Experience in non–higher education environment (1 Yes)	0.77273	0.83505	0.0873
Experience in higher education (years)	10.2	9.9	0.2839
Education: PhD (1 Yes)	0.47882	0.57732	0.0370
Work hours (weekly)	42.9	41.1	0.0281
Extra function (1 Yes)	0.36868	0.44330	0.0870
Overtime	113.3%	118.2%	0.0218
Function = Teaching and research	0.70805	0.57732	0.0061
Function = Teaching	0.12874	0.19588	0.0430
Key relationship = Dean	0.25441	0.13402	0.0058
Sex (1 Male)	0.35309	0.47917	0.0113
Age	46.4	44.2	0.0267
Studying (1 Yes)	0.28608	0.21650	0.0846

In terms of weekly working hours, those wanting to leave higher education worked slightly less than other respondents: almost two hours fewer per week. This might be because those faculty with a full-time contract were more satisfied than those with a fractional contract. This group of potential leavers was also more likely to be working overtime (expressed as a percentage of their actual weekly hours over the required time to be worked derived from the fraction of their full-time contract). Table 2.5 shows that potential leavers on average worked 18 per cent longer hours than required compared with 13 per cent of respondents who were not considering leaving higher education. Leavers were also more likely to have been asked to carry out activities that were not formally part of their employment contract (44 per cent compared with 37 per cent). They were also more likely to have not had a traditional faculty teaching and research role and, in particular, to be currently in teaching-only positions.

Survey participants were also asked about their key relationships, internal and external to their university. Among the options available, the most relevant key relationship was that with the respondent's dean. Those who did not select their dean as a key relationship were more likely to be considering leaving higher education. This may suggest the need to have good relationships with middle managers in order to wish to continue to work in higher education, at least in the respondent's current institution. More males than females and younger respondents wished to leave higher education, but those who were still studying were less likely to seek an exit. This latter finding suggests that those respondents acquiring qualifications while working as faculty are doing so in order to progress their academic careers rather than to move to another profession. This is likely to be because the majority of the institutions surveyed were less research-intensive universities, so those faculty studying for a PhD or a professional doctorate may have been doing so to comply with institutional policies on the minimum qualifications expected of academic faculty. Overall, and understandably, potential leavers seemed less satisfied working in higher education in comparison with those who did not declare a desire to leave the sector.

These bivariate analyses take us only so far in understanding the survey respondents' career aspirations. In order to explore the factors most influencing the intention to leave higher education, a multivariate analysis was undertaken. Table 2.6 presents the results of a logistic regression using the same variables as in Table 2.5 as predictors. The findings indicate that those survey respondents most likely to indicate an intention to leave higher education were younger males who had a PhD as their highest qualification and did not indicate their deans as a key relationship. This latter factor does not necessarily mean that such a relationship was lacking or negative. It could suggest, however, that it may be important for such senior academic leaders to be actively supportive of early- and mid-career faculty for their successful continuation in the profession. This was corroborated by the qualitative responses to the questionnaire, in which external networks and mentors were also mentioned as being significant in this respect.

The highest coefficient in the analysis was found in the variable relating to the extent to which respondents were working beyond the hours indicated by the fraction of their contract (including full-timers). Also a factor in expressing an intention to leave higher education, but to a smaller extent, was whether the respondents undertook activities that were not formally part of their contract. As in the bivariate analysis, those who were studying for a higher degree or professional qualification did not appear to want to leave higher education. Interestingly, factors such as having worked outside higher education, the length of time working in higher education, the amount of hours worked per week

Table 2.6 Prediction of Intention to Leave Higher Education

	Coef.	Std. Err.	z	P>|z|	[95% Conf. Interval]	
Experience in other educational sector	-1.23424	0.473713	-2.61	0.009	-2.1627	-0.30578
Experience in higher education (years)	0.035867	0.033945	1.06	0.291	-0.03066	0.102397
Education PhD (1 Yes)	-1.05367	0.33198	-3.17	0.002	-1.70434	-0.403
Working hours (weekly)	-0.01774	0.017634	-1.01	0.314	-0.0523	0.016822
Extra functions (1 Yes)	0.626959	0.266879	2.35	0.019	0.103885	1.150032
Overtime	1.810501	0.680107	2.66	0.008	0.477516	3.143486
Function = Teaching and research	-0.68559	0.345023	-1.99	0.047	-1.36182	-0.00936
Function = Teaching-only	-0.22625	0.44624	-0.51	0.612	-1.10087	0.648364
Key relationship = Dean	-1.06352	0.377422	-2.82	0.005	-1.80325	-0.32379
Sex (1 Male)	1.015741	0.275981	3.68	0.000	0.474828	1.556653
Age	-0.04788	0.01913	-2.5	0.012	-0.08537	-0.01038
Studying (1 Yes)	-0.84279	0.365301	-2.31	0.021	-1.55877	-0.12682
_cons	0.265241	1.187821	0.22	0.823	-2.06285	2.593328

Logistic regression Number of obs = 440
LR chi2(12) = 52.87
Prob > chi2 = 0.0000
Log likelihood = -190.93871 Pseudo R2 = 0.1216

and different academic employment functions were not significant variables that might explain the choice to leave this sector.

Overall, in the universities surveyed, the female respondents were less likely to indicate an intention to leave higher education. This may be because they enjoyed some degree of work-life balance not guaranteed in other employment sectors. Those who had worked in other education sectors were also less likely to indicate an intention to leave higher education, suggesting that the less research-orientated universities in the survey may suit some faculty. On the other hand, young PhD holders may not believe that such universities are the best they can aspire to. This could be a problem if non–Russell Group universities wish to build and improve their research reputations, if Russell Group universities attract the best early career researchers away from other types of higher education institutions.

Discussion of the Survey Findings

The relatively low number of survey responses from some case study institutions means that caveats should be applied to these findings and their interpretation. This places limitations on how differentiated the analysis can be. It has not been possible, for example, to disaggregate the responses by institution type and disciplinary affiliation or by specific characteristics, such as career stage or time in higher education. These limitations also prevented the development of a conceptual framework around career trajectories and aspirations which might add to the literature on academic job satisfaction, morale and intention to leave (e.g. Barnes, Agago and Coombs 1998; Gandy, Harrison and Gold 2018; Noor 2011). However, this analysis does add the dimension of whether the respondent has previously worked in an employment sector other than higher education and the broad nature of that sector. This is a dimension that is largely missing from previous studies which investigated the intention of faculty to leave their current position or the profession altogether (e.g. Gormley and Kennerly 2011; Rosser 2004; Ryan, Healy and Sullivan 2012) and enables a longitudinal appreciation of a broader range of career trajectories and aspirations, including a number of options for progressing a career within the academy. It also helps contextualize the in-depth interviews that are analysed in the chapters that follow.

The survey findings confirm the enduring attraction of a traditional faculty role that involves not only both teaching and research but also the declining likelihood of attaining one of these (as indicated earlier in this chapter). Nevertheless, a research-only role remains attractive predominantly for those already in that role, perhaps reflecting the primary status that research has in most UK universities. A research-only position may appeal to discipline specialists who are less attracted to other kinds of academic work, despite the often fixed-term nature of these positions, given their project-based funding. A teaching-only role was attractive to a smaller proportion of those respondents already on such a contract. This may be due to the employment conditions and perceptions of the limited prospects for career progress in these types of roles (see section 'Academic Employment Functions and Conditions up to 2020' earlier in this chapter). Despite these findings, there may be attractions to a specialist role which does not require an individual to balance the competing demands of teaching and research (see Collet 2021). Those survey respondents who were currently focusing on teaching were more likely to have worked in other sectors, not just in education but also in the private sector. This may have also broadened their appreciation of other career opportunities available to them.

The appeal of future employment outside of higher education, and especially in the private sector, expressed by some of the survey respondents is comparable with HESA data on actual leavers. In 2019–20, of those leavers whose destinations were known, significant proportions of both teaching-only and research-only faculty who left UK higher education were destined for the nation's private sector. Where this survey helps supplement the sector-wide, but generic, HESA data set is by showing the importance of an individual member of faculty's previous employment experiences, especially outside of higher education, in explaining the options open to them on leaving higher education. The HESA data also confirm the high proportion of higher education starters in teaching-only roles who have come from the UK private sector. Many of these may have worked in other professions, such as the law and media, before moving into higher education in order to teach a related vocational subject, as found among several of the interviewees in this study.

The survey also confirmed the prevalence of a long working hours culture in UK higher education (Morrish 2019; Sang et al. 2015; Wray and Kinman 2021). However, it supplemented this by asking about additional activities undertaken that were not formally part of the respondent's contract. Combined with information about workload allocation systems where these were applied, only a minority of respondents confirmed that these accurately represented the amount and range of work they undertook (see also Fumasoli and Marini 2022). This not only relates to wider issues about the management of academic work (Franco-Santos, Rivera and Bourne 2014; Graham 2015), but it also reflects promotions policies and criteria in universities which require an individual member of faculty to be performing above their current level in order to progress to the next career stage, unlike other professions and occupations, which more readily recognize potential in their promotions processes.

Conclusion

This review of trends in national data sets, and the survey undertaken as part of the study, provides a framework for the individual accounts arising from the interviews that are analysed in Chapters 4 to 7. The trends outlined above illustrate some of the constraints that appear to be imposed by *formal institutional economies*, and reflected in the collective data sets of movements in the sector, using nationally agreed definitions. However, such data sets do not and cannot be expected to offer detail of how individuals work with the national and institutional structures that they find themselves in, in order to achieve personal interests and ambitions, and what may be bespoke career paths. The aim of the study, therefore, was to achieve a more nuanced and qualitative account of the academic experience than was available from national data sets or the one-off survey instrument. It was felt that the picture was likely to be more uneven than indicated by broad-brush, quantitative data, in which a smoothing of trends was likely to belie day-to-day reality. To this end, Chapter 3 sets out the parameters and method of the study, which also had the advantage of re-interviewing respondents after a two-year period to gain an additional perspective.

3

The Study and Early Findings

Introduction

This chapter introduces the rationale for the four-year project on which this book is based and describes the three stages of the study between 2017–18 and 2019–20, including the two rounds of interviews and the survey in 2019. It goes on to describe the method and initial categorization of data after the first round of interviews. Building on earlier work by the authors, the aim was to seek to establish under what circumstances, and in what ways, individuals took cognisance of, and drew upon, a broader hinterland than, for example, institutional job profiles and career frameworks, represented by the *formal economy*. The chapter describes the initial categorization of respondents as having *Mainstream* (driven by structural considerations and timelines), *Portfolio* (focused on a cumulative gathering of experience, not necessarily aligned to formal institutional pathways) and *Niche* (focusing on developing an area of personal interest and/or strength) approaches to their roles. It relates these categories to four spatial domains: the disciplinary, the organizational, the external/community and the internal/motivational, and considers variables that appeared to affect these approaches, such as type of institution, discipline, gender and career stage. Finally, the limitations of such fixed categorizations in understanding changes that occur during the course of career-making are noted.

Rationale

Earlier work by the authors considered the relationship between academic roles and careers as pursued by individuals and the institutional frameworks within which they operated in relation to, for example, job descriptions, promotion and progression criteria, career pathways and professional development opportunities. Thus, Locke (2017) reviewed the implications of a more marketized environment, including the time pressures on roles and careers. Whitchurch (2018) identified more open-ended approaches to roles, and lower expectations of a positional career with clear milestones and criteria, particularly in the early stages, but increasingly in mid-career as well. Locke, Freeman and Rose (2018) went on to note the increasing length of time for early career researchers in the social sciences to achieve a permanent appointment, amid less stable working conditions, showing that this could no longer be assumed to be a homogeneous group pursuing a linear path from postgraduate research and a postdoctoral position to full-time permanent employment. Some people were also leaving academia, particularly those in the practice professions or with links to business and industry. Greater fluidity was evident between academic and associated activities undertaken by individuals, who might be employed on either academic or professional contacts, with responsibility, for example, for learning support, employability, equity and diversity or community engagement (Carvalho, Marini and Videira 2016; Whitchurch 2013). Whitchurch and Gordon (2017) further identified the importance of key relationships for individuals, as institutions tried to create more flexible employment models, which could also result in less certainty for individuals; and Locke et al. (2016), reviewing the professional development opportunities available to support academic careers, noted that there appeared to be a gap between the intentions professed by senior managers and the lived experiences of academic faculty and associated professional staff.

From earlier studies, it appeared that institutions were, to a greater or lesser extent, behind the curve in relation to changes that were occurring. The question therefore arose as to how individuals were not only coping with, but also actively managing the gaps between institutional policy and day-to-day practice; and more broadly, how individual initiatives were shaping the character of roles and careers, as well as the profession as a whole. The findings demonstrated a creativity on the part of individuals that was not necessarily evident in broad brush accounts of the composition of, or trends in, the profession, or in statistical data sets such as those published by the UK Higher Education Statistics Agency (HESA). Collectively, individuals were inspired by a range of factors, drawn not only from their discipline but also from professional practice, community engagement, family and other commitments, represented by the *informal economy*. As a result, formal job descriptions and institutional career frameworks appeared to be less and less aligned with the lived experience of academic faculty. Acknowledgement of this mismatch, and individual strategies for addressing it, turned out to be more widespread among academic faculty than anticipated (Whitchurch, Locke and Marini 2019, 2021).

However, despite acknowledgement in many cases of a lack of fit with formal requirements, there was also some sense of positivity associated with the pathways that individuals carved for themselves. Although this had been picked up on an individual basis in earlier work, it appeared that there was something of a groundswell in relation to a more self-reliant approach, and the researchers in this study were interested to discover whether there might be consistent patterns to this, within a conceptual framing of:

1. The identification of *formal* and *informal institutional economies* with which individuals interact to different degrees, undertaking a cost-benefit analyses in relation to career progression, professional allegiances, personal security and satisfaction, and the strength of the contribution that they feel they are able to make.
2. Ways in which individuals create and move into new spaces that may be unique to them.
3. Ways in which individuals actively manage time as well as being constrained by it.
4. The stretching of the academic experience, taking into account mid-career as well as early career faculty, pointing to the fact that the distinction between these two groups may not be as clear cut as has been assumed in the literature.

The study therefore combined the observation of trends in a diverse and mobile academic workforce with a demonstration of how individuals devise their own responses to situations that may, in general terms, be common to others, but in local terms are unique to them. It therefore provided the opportunity to review individual approaches to roles and careers, and ways in which these contributed to broader collective patterns. Although the following broad research questions guided the study on which this book is based, the method and process of analysis identified patterns in the relationship between institutional policy and individual practice, and picked up movements in the longitudinal elements of the data which were not anticipated at the outset of the study:

1. In what ways are academic roles and identities diversifying?
2. What are the implications for individuals and institutions, locally and globally?

3. What tensions and/or synergies arise from this diversification, for instance, between individual aspirations and institutional missions, structures and processes?
4. How are such tensions being managed and resolved in optimal ways for individuals and institutions?

Data Collection

Eight case study institutions were selected on the basis of:

- regional location, covering all four UK nations (five English, and one each from Scotland, Wales and Northern Ireland);
- institutional type, to ensure the range of non-specialist institutions was captured: (three pre-1992 Russell Group [leading research-intensive universities], two pre-1992 non-Russell Group universities, two post-1992 universities [former polytechnics prior to the Further and Higher Education Act 1992] and one post-2004 university [former College prior to 2004, when the requirement that non-university institutions held research degree-awarding powers before they could gain university status was dropped in England and Wales]); and
- disciplinary and faculty profiles.

The aim was to achieve a broad and balanced range of institutional profiles, across the four geographical regions of the UK. For the first round of interviews (autumn 2017 to spring 2018), in each of the case study institutions, the research team interviewed eight individuals, including the director of human resources, a pro-vice chancellor and six individuals undertaking academic work. In the latter group, the interviews included one individual with a teaching-only contract, one with a research-only contract, one with a learning support remit and at least one with a traditional teaching and research remit. The analysis of the interview material, because it is focused on the career development of individuals, is largely based on the forty-nine interviews with academic faculty not having senior management roles, such as pro-vice-chancellor, on the institutional management team, one of the institutions having offered seven rather than six interviewees. Included in these were a few individuals who were employed on professional services contracts and yet undertook teaching and learning or research-oriented roles, for example, supporting student learning or applications for research funding. The data arising from the study indicated that a total of

Table 3.1 Employment Category of Academic Faculty Interviewed in the First and Second Round of Interviews

	First round of interviews (2017–18)	Second round of interviews (2019–20)
Middle managers, e.g. heads of schools and departments	9	8
Teaching and research faculty	28	22
Teaching-only faculty	2	2
Research-only faculty	5	4
Learning support professionals	5	3
Totals	49	39

twenty out of the original forty-nine interviewees had worked outside higher education at some time during their working lives, in other sectors, or currently had dual roles (as for example in the health professions, law or media sectors).

Thirty-nine of the original forty-nine interviewees, that is, those not having senior management roles, agreed to be re-interviewed in the second round (autumn 2019 to spring 2020), as shown in Table 3.1.

The disciplinary profiles of the original group of interviewees were fifteen science, technology, engineering and mathematics (STEM), thirteen arts and humanities, and twenty-one social sciences. The preponderance of social science faculty reflects the expansion of the UK university system in the last thirty years or so to include applied subjects such as health education, criminology and marketing, particularly in the post-1992 universities.

The retention rate in the second round of interviews was 80 per cent, and the longitudinal dimension enabled exploration of the evolving perceptions of academic faculty about the progress of their careers. Of the ten people who were not re-interviewed, one had retired, and the others either did not respond to requests for an interview, declined or said that they did not have time, despite follow-up emails and phone calls. Four of these came from post-1992 universities, three from pre-1992 Russell Group universities, one from another pre-1992 university and two from the post-2004 university. They were, therefore, fairly evenly balanced across the range of institutions included in the study. Five out of the ten were in management positions at sub-institutional level, such as faculty or school dean, or head of department, and may have had more calls on their time, and six out of the ten were female.

Table 3.2 Levels of Seniority of Academic Faculty Interviewed in the First Round of Interviews, Additional Numbers in Each Category at the Second Round of Interviews and Total Numbers in Each Category at the Second Round of Interviews

	Total numbers in each category at first round of interviews 2017–18	Additional numbers in each category during second round of interviews 2019–20 as a result of promotions	Total numbers in each category at second round of interviews 2019–20
Professor (or equivalent)	8	4	7
Reader	8	1	6
Senior lecturer	11	6	12
Lecturer	16	3	10
Senior research fellow	0	1	1
Research fellow	6	0	3
Totals	49	15	39

Note: Some of those in the professor category had titles such as head of learning and teaching or academic development

The overall gender balance of academic faculty interviewed across the two sets of interviews was 65 per cent female and 35 per cent male. Of the thirty-nine individuals re-interviewed, fifteen, that is, just over one-third, had been promoted, as shown in Table 3.2.

At the first round of interviews, eight individuals were employed on fixed-term contracts, six as research fellows and two as lecturers. By the time of the second interviews, all but two of the respondents had established career positions. The two remaining were relatively settled in research roles which they felt could, if necessary, lead to a career outside higher education. Only two individuals were part-time, and although six were formally appointed to teaching roles, they spoke of conducting unfunded or minimally funded research. The average age of the interviewees was forty-five, therefore the focus was on those in mid-career. Five had some kind of management role at dean or head of department level. They therefore spanned what have been described as the later phases of a conventional career (Establishment [age 26–45] and Maintenance [age 46–65]) and were likely to have family responsibilities (Super 1992). As noted by Zacher et al. (2019) and Whitchurch (2018), those in mid- to later academic career stages have been neglected in the literature on the academic profession in comparison with those in the early stages of their careers.

Interviews

The questions to interviewees in the first round focused around their current range and balance of activity; relationships with the university, external partners and communities; any diversification of roles individually and collectively; any activities that were not formally specified in their contract with the employing university; and perceptions of possible future roles. The questions in the second round of interviews focused on changes that had occurred in the previous two years in relation to these themes, the reflections of individuals on developments in their roles and careers since then, and their thoughts on how their careers might develop in the short and longer term future. The aim was to gain a sense of trends in institutional policies and structures, and movements in the perceptions, aspirations and the agency of individuals, and to understand how the two interact. A key issue arising was the variability of individuals' approaches to roles and careers, both vis-a-vis the academic, professional and personal space available to them and to mutations over time. This was contrary to what might have been expected from fixed-job descriptions and linear career pathways, and provided scope for exploration of, for example, ways in which individuals addressed misalignments and disjunctures in organizational arrangements. The topic guides for the first and second set of interviews are included in Appendix 2 and Appendix 3.

Initial Categorization of the Data from the First Round of Interviews

The longitudinal study offered the opportunity to map approaches to academic roles and careers over a two-year period, drilling down to look for connecting factors in the way that individuals responded to institutional requirements and frameworks, in the light of the wider policy environment, perturbations in individual circumstances, and changes that might occur over time. This was contextualized in relation to the value placed on different activities by institutions and individuals, and, more specifically, what was perceived by individuals as being valued by their institutions. As a starting point, after the first round of interviews, the research team drew up a biographical profile of interviewees, both from a pro forma completed by respondents a week in advance of the interviews, and from the accounts of the individuals themselves. This included their current role and future aspirations. From this, *descriptive codes* were developed. These included:

- age
- gender
- nationality
- ethnicity
- qualifications
- discipline
- current post/role
- type of contract
- key relationships
- career trajectory (in and out of higher education).

These details gave a sense of where people had come from, where they were currently positioned, what their key relationships were and where they saw themselves going. They provided the basis later on for understanding variables in the narratives. Following a summary of factual details, significant aspects of the accounts were noted by the research team, for example, dissonance in understandings about processes for promotion, which activities were seen by individuals as valuable in career terms, or views about possible alternative career moves. Further analysis of the emergent data considered respondents according to their positioning in relation to institutional processes and structures, academic activity, their aspirations, and their involvement in expanding areas of work such as student support or community engagement. *Interpretive codes* were then developed for possible latent meanings, such as tension between individual aspirations and perceived career opportunities. These included:

- disciplinary activity
- balance of teaching and research
- associated activity, for example, in practice settings
- management activity
- relationships in which respondents were involved.

Thus, at a factual level, information was gathered about role histories, trajectories and transitions, and at an interpretive level around the relationship between individuals and institutional structures. During the analysis, consideration was also given to the degree of agency that individuals adopted in relation to their roles, and how individuals negotiated and managed these.

As a second step in the analysis, an overview was taken of overarching themes, and from these *pattern codes* were developed, to establish links or themes across respondents' accounts. These included, for example, approaches to roles and careers, understandings about the value placed on individual activities vis-a-vis institutional progression criteria, and about future prospects, including where the narratives told different stories (Miles and Huberman, 1994: 57). After the first round of interviews, individuals were initially mapped against existing broad-brush models of 'boundaried' and 'boundaryless' approaches to roles and career-making, according to the individual's dominant disposition (Archer 2008; Arthur and Rousseau 1996; Dowd and Kaplan 2005). The former, labelled *Mainstream*, were driven by structural considerations and timelines, undertaking a cost-benefit analysis of activities deemed to be most valuable in the light of, for example, promotion criteria. The latter, labelled *Portfolio*, focused on a cumulative gathering of academic and associated experience, internal and external to the institution, and were not necessarily aligned to formal institutional pathways (Whitchurch, Locke and Marini 2021). Pattern codes were developed in relation to these categories:

Pattern Codes Relating to *Mainstream* Approaches:

- awareness of structures (e.g. in understandings about roles, responsibilities and job descriptions)
- a linear approach to the career ladder
- awareness of career timescales and milestones
- learning from one's own and others' experience
- ability to modulate processes and systems.

Pattern Codes Relating to *Portfolio* Approaches:

- communication across internal and external boundaries with colleagues, peers, academic and professional colleagues
- translation/interpretation of working across disciplinary and institutional boundaries
- ease of movement across boundaries
- partnership and networking
- negotiation skills.

At this stage, two novel features became apparent, which provided the basis for further investigation:

Firstly, it became clear during the analysis that not all individuals fell into these two broad categories. There was significant evidence of individuals making a positive decision to focus on a specific area of activity that they shaped and moulded for themselves, so as to achieve a positioning that they found comfortable and rewarding. In a sense, this was their own, unique space, unlikely to be clearly represented in job descriptions or progression criteria. An additional, third category, labelled *Niche*, focusing on developing an area of personal interest and/or strength that was comfortable to the individual, which might nevertheless be developed for career purposes, was therefore created to describe individuals who adopted such an approach, either permanently or for the time being. This positioning, in which an individual effectively designed their local territory and, from that, their career pathway, has not been well represented in the literature. Such individuals were also likely to demonstrate a sense of service, for example, to their institution, academic colleagues, students and local and professional communities. Pattern codes were therefore devised relating to *Niche* approaches:

Pattern Codes Relating to *Niche* Approaches:

- focus on personal strengths/interests
- strongly held values; an ethical base
- service (e.g. to institution, academic colleagues, students and/or external clients)
- trusteeship (e.g. of programme standards, sources of help for students)
- knowledge exchange for collective/community purposes
- team working across a mix of functions/levels of seniority.

Secondly, it was clear that the majority of participants, after both the first and the second rounds of interviews, and whether interviewed once or twice, displayed characteristics of more than one type of approach. The original typology of three approaches to roles, therefore, represented dominant tendencies or dispositions, and individuals were placed in the category with which they appeared to have the strongest affiliation at the time of the first interview. However, across the original forty-nine interviewees, only seven displayed evidence of only one category, twenty-one of two and twenty-one of three. Thus, none of the three categories was mutually exclusive, and there appeared to be a desire by individuals to hold on to more than one approach to career-making, even though the emphasis might change at different points in time. There was therefore a danger of reification of the original fixed categories. Therefore, second order pattern codes were developed after the second round of interviews to identify shifts over time:

Second Order Pattern Codes

- changes in categorization
- reasons for this
- understandings of role/career success
- shifts in direction (disciplinary focus, new roles or orientations, personal life changes and/or intention to leave job or higher education)
- successes and disappointments.

The data gathered from both rounds of interviews was further analysed using Creswell's 'data analysis spiral' (Creswell 1998: 143), whereby data are revisited via processes of reading, describing, classifying, interpreting and representing, with continuous links made between these activities. The data were then mapped against possible variables, such as different types of institution and the career stage of the individual. This enabled 'semantic' (explicit, overt) and 'latent' (underlying, implicit) themes to be identified (Braun and Clarke 2013). The research method described above represented a process of exploration that yielded a more comprehensive picture of approaches to roles and careers than in the authors' earlier work, providing a framework for these in relation to the use of *formal* and *informal institutional economies*. It therefore helped to build a more sustained and dynamic picture across academic and associated spaces and over time, as well as of ways in which individuals sought to optimize their prospects, not only in relation to career-making but also in relation to individual satisfactions and securities. This process of analysis also enabled the analysis to be taken to a conceptual level around the disciplinary, organizational, external/community and internal/motivational spaces occupied by academic and associated staff, leading to a theorization of emergent spaces.

Framing and Categorizing the Data

After the first round of interviews, it was apparent that the three approaches were likely to influence the individual's interaction with four spatial domains: the *disciplinary domain*, representing academic knowledge; the *organizational domain*, representing institutional structures; the *external/community domain*, representing a spectrum of other activities with which an individual might be involved, such as professional practice or community engagement; and the *internal/motivational domain*, representing personal values and commitments, for example, to the pastoral care of students. The resulting framework demonstrates the reach of, and influences upon, contemporary approaches to roles and careers, shown in Table 3.3.

As stated above, although some individuals demonstrated characteristics of a single approach, others demonstrated the characteristics of two or more. therefore represents a heuristic device for the purposes of illustration, in which the three typologies represent dominant characteristics or dispositions affecting approaches to roles.

Mainstream Approaches

Academic faculty adopting *Mainstream* approaches had a strong awareness of structures and processes, as well as career timescales, expectations of roles and the likely impact of activity, as observed by Leišytė (2016) in relation to publication outputs. In Giddens' terms (Giddens 1990, 1991), their activity was principally influenced by the 'rules and resources' of institutional structures. They were likely to see themselves as advancing in a linear fashion within defined periods of time, and to use the structures in which they found themselves strategically, undertaking a cost-benefit analysis of different activities and making choices based on this. Some took a holistic view of the relationship between teaching and research, and the desirability of achieving an optimal balance between these:

> A lot of our teaching is genuinely research driven, in the sense that it's the book you're working on, you're talking about it with your students and they give you ideas that help shape what you write, so it's always seemed to be a very artificial divide and that's even before you address the question, whether that makes you a better teacher ..., but even if that wasn't true, I think [teaching] makes better research, which is often neglected in that nexus. (Professor, humanities, pre-1992 Russell Group university, interview 1)

Seeing synergy between the two activities might be regarded as a somewhat traditional view, dating from before the introduction of teaching-only positions in the UK.

Table 3.3 Typologies of *Mainstream*, *Portfolio* and *Niche* Approaches to Roles and Careers, and Associated Domains

Domains	Mainstream	Portfolio	Niche
	Instrumental/temporal/testing known system and parameters	Exploratory/temporal and spatial/testing new arenas of activity and parameters	Shaping known arenas of activity/spatial/creating own parameters/focus on service
Disciplinary	Teaching and research synergy International networks, conferences Reputational activity/impact Vertical networks	Teaching and/or research Practice locales Interdisciplinary/boundary crossing Innovation	Teaching and/or research Teaching and learning Areas of strength and intrinsic interest Pedagogic research
Organizational	Involvement in research assessment Teaching evaluation Funding sources Management activity Vertical networks	Horizontal, peer-group networks (cross institutional/external)	Horizontal, peer-group networks (local) Some unfunded activity Local colleagues/team
External/community	Funding sources (international/national/regional) Measured involvement in support of career goals	Business/professional/community networks (extended/virtual) Professional bodies Non-governmental organizations (NGOs)	Support networks Service to community, e.g. widening participation/outreach
Internal/motivational	Responsive in observing/optimizing structures (rewards, constraints) Cost-benefit analysis Satisficing if necessary to optimize career progress and minimize stress	Professional and vocational allegiances Proactive in creating new locales of action Spirit of exploration Hedging bets Exit plan if needed	Sense of vocation/service/personal satisfaction and of where strengths lie Internally value driven Work-life balance Satisficing if necessary to optimize work-life balance and minimize stress

Others took the view that a focus on either teaching or research would be likely to reap the most rewards, both in terms of satisfaction and financial security:

> I think that in terms of long-term job security, being a pure researcher is probably the best way to go, because if you have a sustained source of income ..., in terms of research grants, a steady cash flow, you will have a very long and happy career in academia. If you take on both responsibilities, teaching and research, your time is split and so your ability to be able to maintain that steady flow of income, it's much harder to do because you have that much less time. Then ..., if you're very effective at teaching, maybe, and the way in which the higher education system is moving that we're, you know, it's becoming a lot more focused on student experience, student satisfaction, because of the income that students generate and the fact that we're now becoming more of a service provider than an education facility ..., I guess there probably is a lot of career security associated with teaching-only as well. (Lecturer, science, pre-1992 university, interview 1)

The emergence of promotion pathways based on teaching and pedagogical research, although not seen as easy to achieve as a pathway that included research, made such a choice between teaching and research a possibility. Nevertheless, those taking a *Mainstream* approach were likely to rely on the *formal economy* of an institution, defining, and indeed calibrating, their roles and careers according to local frameworks and criteria. However, this could in some cases lead to stark choices, and sacrifices, in relation to the time commitments required to meet institutional goals for progression, as in the case of the following individual: 'The main sacrifice ... I've made, unconsciously ... is that I haven't been able to start a family, and now that's passed me by' (lecturer, social sciences, post-1992 university, interview 1).

Portfolio Approaches

Academic faculty adopting a *Portfolio* approach, while having cognisance of institutional norms and values, are likely to look beyond institutional boundaries to work with, for example, colleagues in practitioner environments, thereby developing professional capital elsewhere. This was commonly in order to enhance academic activity, develop opportunities and/or give themselves a safety net and possible exit plan if necessary. External networks could also prove helpful in making a contribution to impact agendas. As might be expected, a significant number of those adopting *Portfolio* approaches came from applied, practice- or business-orientated disciplines, with natural links outside the higher education sector, which they used to enhance their teaching and research profile. Furthermore, extended activity, along with the impact that resulting networks could bring, is seen in some disciplines and institutions as an important component of applications for progression:

> The professorial application is much more than just having a list of four star journal articles, there's a lot more to it in terms of individual profile and as I say externality … we look to support the economic prosperity of this region … In my heart I am a …, business practitioner turned academic, with the emphasis on business … I think if you've never experienced the cut and thrust of a private practice in business, I think it's a chink in a CV. (Reader, business, post- 2004 university, interview 1)

Other individuals took the initiative in including extended academic activity, for example, in the community:

> Outreach is something that I've always really enjoyed doing, so when I first started, the deputy head of department … saw that I was happy to be involved in this and so essentially, within a couple of months, handed it over to me … and there was money behind it, so I did essentially give myself probably more work because of that, so I wanted us to have things like summer schools and we didn't have any work experience opportunities and things like that, so I have created more things in that sense. (Teaching fellow, science, pre-1992 Russell Group university, interview 1)

In this case, because of the individual's interest and active agency, their head of department was willing to make discretionary space and time available to them.

Niche Approaches

As noted above, it was apparent that the *Mainstream* and *Portfolio* categories did not fully represent or explain the full range of approaches to roles and careers. A significant number of individuals highlighted factors associated with a desire to focus on their strengths and activity that they found rewarding as well as a need for a sense of security. This meant that they preferred to work within a space that they found comfortable and that, to a greater or lesser extent, they created for themselves. This could be influenced by personal strengths, interests and considerations of work-life balance, such as coping with periods of ill health, caring for family members and changes in circumstances such as a relationship break-up or finding a new partner.

A further *Niche* category was therefore developed for individuals for whom such considerations were dominant. This could represent a temporary or permanent positioning.

Academic faculty taking a *Niche* approach were also likely to be driven by considerations of service to students, colleagues and/or their professional communities. There was therefore a sense in which *Niche* academics might be seen as representing a vocation and dedication to a discipline: 'I think academia is a way of life, as opposed to a job, it's a life choice. It certainly worked out that way for me, and personal life is geared towards that as well really' (lecturer, social sciences, post-1992 university, interview 1). Others simply enjoyed what they were doing and had no sense of wanting to move on: 'I could be a research fellow for ten years, I'd probably be happy enough, I enjoy doing research and it's nice' (research fellow, social sciences, pre-1992 Russell Group university, interview 1). Those taking a *Niche* approach could also become involved in non-quantifiable, and to some extent invisible, activity such as pastoral care, a role that often fell outside workload calculations, and this could make them vulnerable in the sense of unconsciously opting out of credit bearing activity. Thus, 'it's something that … some people relish more than other people and it's something that … isn't completely clear cut what your pastoral role is and …, what you need to do to fulfil it and so on' (professor, science, pre-1992 Russell Group university, interview 1). *Niche* academics can therefore be useful to the institution in doing this 'unpaid' and sometimes unacknowledged work, although the narratives demonstrate that this does not necessarily position them as 'academic artisans' (Brew et al. 2018), particularly if this is something that they find rewarding.

Those taking a *Niche* approach, therefore, were likely to be motivated by intrinsic values such as a dedication to students and/or the local community, reflecting a desire to undertake work that was meaningful to the individual (Knights and Clarke 2014). They thereby distanced themselves to some extent from markers of impact or influence, and from being involved in the 'cultural reproduction' of the field (Bourdieu 1993). They tended to see their futures within the sector and to create their habitus within a segment of the academic field, staying within a space that was comfortable and felt secure. Positive aspects of teaching-only roles were thereby recognized by those who wished to undertake them. Some also saw themselves as reinforcing their position and eligibility for a lead role in, for example, the student experience or knowledge exchange, rather than necessarily being 'stuck'. A *Niche* approach to roles might also be seen as a response to disruptive influences and as a recovery position, although not necessarily in the sense of 'loss, alienation and retreat' (Locke and Bennion 2011), rather as a sense of fulfilment, focusing more on the present, at least for the time being, than on future pathways. Such individuals were therefore effectively creating their own space within the broad parameters of the *formal economy*, drawing upon the *informal economy* in order to do this. Thus, 'I want to be much more involved and much more networked with colleagues across higher education, I think that's where I want to really see my career developing and that doesn't necessarily equate to tangible career progression in terms of promotion' (senior lecturer, health science, post-1992 university, interview 2).

Limitations and Variables in the Initial Categorization

With the usual caveats about sample sizes, of the forty-nine faculty interviewed in the first round who were undertaking academic (as distinct from senior management team) roles, fourteen individuals (28 per cent) displayed characteristics that positioned them primarily as having a *Mainstream* approach, nineteen (39 per cent) as having a *Portfolio* approach and sixteen (33 per cent) as having a *Niche* approach. Those with a predominantly *Mainstream* approach, adopting what might be seen as normative assumptions about career paths in higher education, achieving certain milestones within certain timescales according to quality and volume of teaching and/or research output, were therefore in the minority. This might be seen as contrary to what might be expected, given the fact that institutions are expanding formal career pathways, for example, broadening criteria for promotion on the basis of teaching or knowledge exchange activity as distinct from research, and allowing for a focus on different activities at different times, thereby giving a broader range of formal career structures with which individuals might engage.

However, the three approaches were not mutually exclusive. In reality, people are likely to take different approaches at different stages of their career or in different roles and institutions, or move between approaches for specific purposes and according to circumstances. The lived reality is therefore both dynamic and complex, and the study provided a way of bringing into view underlying positionings that might not be visible when calibrated against formal frameworks of career paths or types of contract. This may involve an ongoing assessment by the individual of 'fit', for example, in relation to local environments, teams and policies. Of those demonstrating two categories of approach after the first round of interviews, *Mainstream* was the most represented (seventeen examples), with *Portfolio* (twelve examples) and *Niche* (thirteen examples) being evenly divided in a combination with *Mainstream*. *Niche* combined with *Portfolio* (four examples) was the least frequent combination, as might be expected, in that those spreading their interests more widely, whether permanently or for the time being, had less inclination to focus on a specific activity. Thus, each individual is likely have different drivers and priorities at different times, according to local circumstances and personal motivations.

After the initial categorization, consideration was given to four variables: institutional type, discipline, gender and career stage. However, the fact that there were five pre-1992 universities, two post-1992 universities and one post-2004 university in the sample, and that 65 per cent of respondents were female, mean that conclusions can only be seen as indicative.

Type of Institution

Eleven of the fourteen individuals (79 per cent) categorized as *Mainstream* were in the five pre-1992 universities. This suggests that they may be more likely to flourish in traditionally orientated institutional structures, in particular those related to career progression, with clearly defined steps on the ladder, and perhaps less scope for modification or adaptation of such requirements. To a lesser extent, thirteen of the nineteen (68 per cent) categorized as *Portfolio* were also clustered in the five pre-1992 universities, suggesting that there was more scope there for extended activity internally or externally. In turn, the fact that a significant proportion of *Niche* approaches (31 per cent) were to be found in Russell Group universities might be linked to the creation of teaching-only roles in these institutions from 2011 onwards so as to avoid 'diluting' scores in the UK Research Excellence Framework by including academic faculty who were not deemed 'research active'. Hitherto, all academic faculty would have been expected to undertake both teaching and research. Conversely, there have been fewer teaching-only roles created in the non-Russell Group pre-1992 universities (Locke et al. 2016), so that more individuals have the aspiration and opportunity to undertake some kind of research. Otherwise, *Niche* approaches were predominantly (56 per cent) in the post-1992 and post-2004 universities, which tend to be more teaching orientated, but also allow scope for research and scholarship, particularly in practice-based disciplines.

Discipline

Although disciplines have traditionally been fundamental to academic identity (Becher and Trowler 2001; Henkel 2000), differences in approach could be seen between disciplinary types. *Mainstream* approaches were concentrated in the sciences and humanities, with humanities featuring to a much lesser degree in relation to *Portfolio* and *Niche* approaches. This may not be surprising in relation to *Portfolio* approaches in that opportunities for the expansion of activity, for example, in business, the community or industry, may be fewer in the humanities. *Portfolio* and *Niche* characteristics were evenly distributed between the sciences and social sciences, perhaps reflecting greater opportunity for a spread of activity but also a significant amount of teaching and service-orientated activity, especially if individuals were not research active.

Gender

Even allowing for the fact that there were twice as many female as male interviewees in the study, the majority of individuals categorized as *Niche* were female. A number of justifications were offered for taking this approach, including feeling fulfilled in and enjoying their role, being able to achieve an acceptable work-life balance and a sense of security, rather than necessarily feeling confined by their role. A small majority of individuals with a *Portfolio* approach were also female. These findings corroborate those of González Ramos, Fernández Palacín and Muñoz Márquez (2015), that women tended to focus on activity that is diversified, and that men were more likely to focus on 'scientific production', i.e. elements of a *Mainstream* approach. The categorization also reflects to some extent 'output-driven' (corresponding with *Mainstream*) and 'adaptive flexible' (corresponding with *Portfolio*) patterns of career development of women noted by Fritsch (2016).

Career Stage

As might be expected, those nearer the beginning of their careers, in research- or teaching-only roles, tended to adopt *Portfolio* or *Niche* approaches, depending on how able or inclined they were to develop a profile outside the precise parameters of their job description. Few saw themselves as being on a secure career ladder at this stage. Lecturers tended to be clustered in the *Mainstream* and *Niche* categories. In the first case, this suggests that they saw themselves as having their foot on the first rung of the ladder, with reasonable expectations of progression. In the second case, they had either adopted a *Niche* role by design, because they found satisfaction in a specific role, or because they had not yet found ways of developing the role. Some individuals had in practice progressed to senior lecturer/reader via a *Niche* role, although some developmental activity was likely to have been undertaken to move up the career ladder. There were no professors categorized as *Niche*, which is not surprising as they would be likely to have had to meet certain *Mainstream* criteria and/or had a portfolio of activity to progress to a professorial level. However, it may be that, as more people are appointed to chairs on the basis of teaching and other non-research-related achievements, this could change.

However, the three categorizations in this chapter, and therefore any variables associated with them, suggest a reification of positions when in practice they represent a dominant approach at any point in time. As will be shown in Chapter 4, each individual's positioning is likely to reflect an iteration between different career scripts, one of which may dominate, then another, reflecting a situation that is fluid and subject to ongoing adjustments and mutations. As a result, the situation at any point is likely to be more nuanced than suggested by a direct association of variables with the three categorizations.

Conclusion

This chapter provided an overview of the rationale for, and method adopted in, the four-year study that is the subject of this book, together with a description of the outcomes of the first round of interviews in 2017–18. The initial categorization of interviewees as *Mainstream*, *Portfolio* and *Niche* is significant because it demonstrates that approaches to roles can be characterized not only by, for example, type of contract, or a focus on teaching, research or other forms of academic activity, but also by individual circumstances, motivations and the way that roles and careers are interpreted and enacted. Thus, a *Mainstream* approach involves a careful calculation of how institutional processes, in the form of, for example, promotion criteria, might be used most effectively for individual purposes, in a considered interaction with institutional structures. A *Portfolio* approach is characterized by an ongoing search for opportunities and possibilities, with a greater emphasis on personal agency, extending outside institutional structures. In turn, a *Niche* approach involves the shaping of a space that is comfortable to the individual, in which existing structures may be adjusted and massaged according to preference, so that there is a sense in which the individual creates a bespoke environment. The three approaches demonstrate that, in different ways, academic faculty are not solely what Archer terms 'primary agents' (Archer 2000: 11), for example, in relation to institutional job descriptions and promotion criteria, but also 'actors' (Archer 2000: 261). However, in personifying their roles, individuals are not solely interacting with the structures in which they find themselves, but also developing and acting upon self-knowledge about their own strengths and priorities, as well as extending their activities, including relationships and networks that will support them. They are therefore expanding their interaction with the *formal institutional economy* into spheres represented by the *informal economy*.

Furthermore, the initial categorizations of *Mainstream*, *Portfolio* and *Niche* represented a snapshot in time, and therefore gave a static picture of what is, in reality, a dynamic process of career-making that evolves for each individual in the light of experience. Nor did these categorizations capture choices and decision-making that take place on an ongoing basis, or ways in which individuals are influenced in different degrees and at different periods by factors such as the perceived likelihood of achieving promotion, their relationships and networks, and considerations of personal strengths and interests. It therefore became evident that a longitudinal element would help to demonstrate shifts between categories, two or more of which could be exemplified by an individual, not only at a single point in time but also across the two-year period. In the second round of interviews, therefore, the work was extended to observe ways in which the categorizations might have changed over the two-year period and possible reasons for this. Drawing on this material, Chapter 4 considers how and why approaches to roles and careers may be adjusted, developing the concepts of *Institutional*, *Practice* and *Internal scripts* to illustrate the considerations that individuals take into account in making their careers.

4

The Significance of Career Scripts

Introduction

The longitudinal study described in Chapter 3 offered the opportunity to map approaches to academic roles and careers over a three-year period between 2017–18 and 2019–20. In this chapter, the concepts of *Institutional*, *Practice* and *Internal scripts*, as drivers of careers, are developed to explain the fluidity of allegiances to and shifts between the original *Mainstream*, *Portfolio* and *Niche* categories. The scripts offer a rationale for the ways in which individuals respond to institutional requirements and frameworks, wider practice environments and perturbations in their individual circumstances. This is contextualized by the value placed on different activities by individuals and what is perceived by them as being valued by their institutions. More generally, it is demonstrated that, in practice, people may hold different scripts simultaneously or at different stages of their career, moving between approaches for specific purposes and according to circumstances. This chapter therefore advances understanding of the diversification of the academic workforce, offering a more nuanced picture than that provided by, for example, classifications of employment status such as fixed-term, part-time and teaching- or research-only contracts; the duality of a structure and agency framework; or the original fixed categories of *Mainstream*, *Portfolio* and *Niche*.

The Shift to Career Scripts

The second round of interviews enabled a shift from the static, one-dimensional typology described in Chapter 3 to one that was more dynamic in capturing the momentum of a career. Arising from the initial categorization of respondents as *Mainstream*, *Portfolio* and *Niche*, the study drew on the notion of *career scripts* to show how the roles and careers of individuals were informed by personal strengths, interests, and personal and professional commitments, as well as by formal institutional career structures, so that scripts were internally, as well as institutionally, generated. This process built on earlier career theory, based on international studies, whereby organizations such as universities are seen as providing career structures, as a 'road map' in the form of entry and progression points; and individuals are seen as having agency to manage the way in which they interact with this 'road map', according to their interpretation of institutional "career scripts" (Dany et al. 2011; Duberley et al. 2006; Garbe and Duberley 2019). Such scripts outline different ways of making a career, for example, via a focus on research, teaching and/or academic management, the balance of which may shift over time (Baruch 2004). However, they are based solely on institutional descriptors of, and formal prerequisites for, a career. Thus, in the UK, institutions have been influenced by government policy, for example, linking individual performance review to the contribution of individuals to national Research Excellence and (predominantly in England) Teaching Excellence Frameworks, although *Institutional scripts* have also expanded to encompass a range of activity, including, for example, improving the student experience, employability agendas and community engagement. In general terms, this has led to 'a trend toward a more individual management of academic careers replacing the more collective treatment of a supposedly homogeneous group' (Musselin 2013: 29). Nevertheless, *Institutional career scripts* represent public markers of individual positioning, as opposed to the more subjective *Internal* or *Practice scripts* of individuals.

The extension of the concept of *Institutional career scripts* to include *Practice* and *Internal scripts*, neither of which are likely to be clearly represented in formal job descriptions or progression criteria, helped to explain the increasing fluidity of approaches to careers across space and time. This approach adds another dimension to the binary categorizations of academic careers as 'boundaried' or 'boundaryless' (Dowd and Kaplan 2005), and of *career scripts* as being solely defined by the institution (Dany et al. 2011; Duberley et al 2006; Garbe and Duberley 2019). From examination of the narratives in the study, it became apparent that those able to think of their careers in a 'boundaryless' way were likely to have roles as professional practitioners in other fields, which nevertheless could have an influence on the individual's teaching and research. Practice environments that were represented included not only the health and caring professions, but also, for example, the law, the media, the probation, career and social services, business and industry, and activity in humanitarian settings. *Practice scripts* therefore focused on responsibilities and allegiances to the requirements of professional activity outside the university and associated networks. In turn, *Internal scripts* focused on personal strengths, interests and values that were unique to the individual, including, for example, a dedication to improving the student experience, caring and family responsibilities, and a desire for an optimal work-life balance. The concepts of *Institutional, Practice* and *Internal scripts* were therefore developed to achieve greater precision in understanding the drivers behind the process of career-making, as described in Table 4.1.

The second round of interviews provided an opportunity to review how the *career scripts* of individuals might change over time. The categorization of individuals after both sets of interviews is summarized in Table 4.2. A general shift can be detected from *Practice scripts* to either *Institutional* or *Internal scripts* as the dominant script over the two years between the first and second rounds of interviews. There would seem to be two pathologies represented here: firstly, a more settled status, reflected in *Institutional* and *Internal scripts*, as people achieve the next career move or decide to focus on favoured activities; and secondly, a focus on building an academic profile while maintaining work in practice settings, at the same time as retaining the latter as a future option if necessary. *Internal scripts* were also being used in some instances to build a future case for promotion, an example being the development of employability skills in the curriculum. The shift away from *Practice scripts* could also have reflected perturbations in the environment between 2017 and early 2020, evidenced by (1) the UK University and College Union (UCU) industrial action in the spring and summer of 2018 over early career insecurity, workloads, pay and pensions; (2) the requirement for evidence of impact in research in the 2020 Research Excellence Framework; and (3) the gradual introduction of the UK Teaching Excellence and Student Outcomes Framework in England from 2017. All these factors may have diverted attention away from external commitments for the time being, towards immediate requirements by the university, such as the development of impact statements, the completion of research databases and adjusting lecture programmes in response to student feedback.

The study therefore extended understandings of contemporary practices of academic career-making by demonstrating that 'boundaried' and 'boundaryless' approaches to careers, as described in the literature, are not mutually exclusive, and may coexist and/or shift over time, as individuals fashion both *Internal* and *Practice scripts* according to their own preferences, choices and opportunities. These scripts enable them to circumnavigate *Institutional scripts* by drawing on their own resources, including extended

Table 4.1 Description of *Institutional*, *Practice* and *Internal Scripts*

Type of career script	Characteristics	Associated activity	Goal(s)/outcomes
Institutional	Closely aligned to formal institutional promotion criteria and timelines Institutionally driven (e.g. progression pathways, promotion criteria)	Pursuit of activities likely to lead to promotion, whether in teaching, research or other specified areas Being strategic, even political, with a view to quantifiable career outcomes and impact Undertaking a cost-benefit analysis of individual activities	Timely promotion on institutional career progression pathway(s)
Practice	Externally driven (e.g. professional practice, health and business/industry) Interdigitate with institutional career pathways Fully or partly outside the institution	Exploratory activity on the basis of practice considerations and professional networks Translational function bringing practice considerations into teaching and research	Creation of options for the future, including possible exit plan
Internal	Script internally generated, based on e.g. personal interests, values and strengths Likely to be oriented towards service and/or personal comfort zone	Pursuit of activity related to personal values, interests and strengths Development of relationships, networks, value-added in relation to, for example, the student experience, improved work-life balance	Personal security and satisfaction Massaging of institutional career scripts and progression pathways Bespoke career trajectories

Table 4.2 Categorization of Dominant *Career Scripts* of Individuals after First and Second Round of Interviews

	Categorization of dominant career scripts of individuals after second interview (2019–20)				
Categorization of dominant career scripts of individuals after first interview (2017–18)	*Institutional scripts*	*Practice Scripts*	*Internal scripts*	(No second interview)	Totals
Institutional	13	1	1	(3)	15(18)
Practice	4	2	6	(2)	12(14)
Internal	5	0	7	(5)	12(17)
Total	22	3	14	(10)	39(49)

disciplinary interests, activities in external work settings and personal strengths and commitments. In many cases, such scripts might be seen as a backup to formal frameworks, offering protection to the individual, for example, in relation to actual or potential career setbacks, work-life balance or a possible exit plan. They therefore offer the possibility of maintaining some equilibrium in what might be uncertain conditions. As one person said, 'I'm protecting myself by doing a little bit of everything … I love how I can do a little bit of research without a lot of pressure, how I can do teaching well, how I can still engage with the community and bring that into my teaching … I kind of just do my own thing' (senior lecturer, social sciences, post-1992 university, interview 1). Thus, while *Institutional scripts* might be seen to offer material security, if they can be achieved, practice-based and internally generated scripts allow for an accommodation to current circumstances, at least for the time being, rather than a necessary prioritization of career advancement. Even individuals who felt that they were blocked for the time being in their career were making subtle adjustments to their balance of activity. Thus, disciplinary and wider activity profiles are unlikely to remain static but rather to mutate as a result of the influence of *Internal* and *Practice scripts*. Furthermore, the three scripts are likely to coexist for any individual, creating different emphases at different times and in different circumstances.

Theoretical Framing

The concept of career scripts has been developed to illustrate the way an individual's internal dialogues and professional allegiances can influence their decision-making and subsequent activity. It is framed theoretically by Archer's theory of morphogenesis (Archer 2000), whereby the construction of identity is seen as a cycle of interactions in which the individual moves from passive to active mode, in dialogue with him- or herself, and with the social structures that he or she occupies. In the context of the present study, academic faculty can be seen as positioned involuntarily, on appointment, as 'agents', within given structures represented by *Institutional scripts*. However, in enacting their roles, they are empowered by *Practice* and *Internal scripts* to become 'actors'. Thus, in Archer's terms, the 'agent' might be said to represent the initial position of an individual who, on appointment, accepts a role represented by a job description that forms part of their contract within a pre-defined career path. However, he or she only achieves their professional and academic identity 'by assuming a role and personifying it, by investing oneself in it and executing it in a singular manner' (Archer 2000: 11). The individual's interpretation of the role via *Practice* or *Internal scripts*, and thereafter a series of roles that comprise a career, therefore, distinguishes him or her from other individuals with similar job descriptions.

Archer's 'collectivities' of primary agents might be said to incorporate individuals who operate within formally stated parameters and criteria for career progression, for whom the *Institutional script* is the main driver, for the time being, or on a longer term basis. In Archer's terminology, this represents the condition of 'morphostasis', while a more interpretive approach, via *Practice* and *Internal scripts*, allows for the transformation of practice, which she describes as 'morphogenesis'. Thus, 'It is only when the morphogenetic scenario engages ... that collectively primary agents can cease to be the largely passive recipients of their positions in the social distribution of life-chances [*or formally stated requirements of a career pathway*] and can begin to play an active part in their shaping' (Archer 2000: 267; emphasis added). Under the condition of 'morphostasis', academic faculty would be subject to, for example, criteria enshrined in institutional promotion policies. Under the condition of 'morphogenesis', they would become actors, driven by *Internal* and *Practice scripts*, adapting ways in which such criteria might be met and persuading senior decision makers of the validity of new forms of activity. In practice, however, an individual who is, in Archer's terms, 'personifying' as well as 'animating' a role [*or career trajectory*] (Archer 2000: 288; emphasis added), and thus making their own contribution to it, is likely to be involved in a mix of the two forms of agency. In relation to a career, the 'animating' element could be said to be represented by adherence to formally prescribed benchmarks in *Institutional scripts*, and the 'personification' element as being driven by *Internal* and *Practice scripts*.

Academic faculty might be said, therefore, to have moved from being what Archer terms 'primary agents', that is, 'members of collectivities who share the same life [*or career*] chances' (Archer 2000: 11; emphasis added), positioned involuntarily within given career structures, to what she terms 'actors', who 'acquire their social identities from the way in which they personify the roles [*or sequence of roles in career-making*] they choose to occupy' (Archer 2000: 261; emphasis added). They do this through their own interpretation and/or extension of their roles, making continual adjustments over space and time, so as to create elasticity within formal career structures. These adjustments reflect ongoing micro-shifts by individuals, in particular their willingness to personalize career paths and to articulate their needs and aspirations to line managers. Thus, the interplay between individual and institution becomes multifaceted during the process of career-making, via the influence of *Practice* and *Internal scripts*. This process is, therefore, more complex than a dual structure and agency binary, involving new forms of activity that may in turn lead to the modification of institutional policy and practice more generally, although in the initial stages this may be implicit rather than explicit.

The following sections demonstrate how the three types of script influence the individual's career journey, leading to a mutability in individual positionings over time, as well as the potential for tensions at any single point. We have used Pen Portraits in these sections and throughout the book to give a fuller picture than might be offered by single quotations from the narratives of individuals. Through the Pen Portraits, we illustrate the range of approaches that may be taken by individuals, in some cases across the two sets of interviews, via different types of script, at various stages of their careers and according to a range of circumstances.

Institutional Scripts

Adherence to *Institutional scripts* represented a willingness by individuals to focus their efforts on achieving the formal requirements for career advancement, either on an ongoing basis or at a particular point in time. Such individuals were typified by thinking that led to pragmatic decisions about the balance and focus of their activity, prioritising those that were likely to be of most benefit in relation to the next role or promotion. This could involve not only negotiation with line managers but also a tactical approach, as illustrated by the following comments:

> I've just been given a lot more admin[istration] responsibility … so I tried to ask to drop some of those roles to take more time to do the research, but instead they said oh no, you need to do that too, do those roles even better to demonstrate your eligibility for promotion … [so] I'm going to be more selective in what I take on … in order to narrow down the time spent on [administration] and go back to the research. (Lecturer, science, pre-1992 Russell Group university, interview 1)

Such a cost-benefit analysis is likely to include taking cognisance of the value of (particularly) research, and its impact, in shaping the choice and emphasis of activity:

> Knowing how important funding is in terms of your promotion application success … I have made use of opportunities that are out there that probably I would not have applied for had I been doing my research just driven by my interest … [impact] has changed the way I'm now going to construct a particular project … not the kind of books that I would have written years ago … I made a conscious decision that I wanted … to reach … not just historians … [but] lots of different people. (Reader, humanities, pre-1992 Russell Group university, interview 1)

This individual had, therefore, subscribed to their *Institutional script* by making a positive decision to focus on research that carried greater weight in the eyes of a promotion committee, at the expense of personal interests. Thus, adherence to *Institutional scripts* could be said to represent acceptance of the status quo, in whole or in part, in the longer or shorter term, as well as a level of confidence in the institutional system. If necessary, this could involve a suppression of personal inclinations or interests, at least for the time being.

The following Pen Portrait illustrates someone early in their career, who had had an initial spell in industry, who was focused on meeting the criteria required to advance in a career in higher education up to retirement, and therefore was following closely the *Institutional script*:

Pen Portrait 1

So in five years' time, I'd like to be senior lecturer. I've taken on a number of additional responsibilities within the university voluntarily to support … the way in which we do things …, so I've taken on some management roles and that's part of the personal career progression that's associated with promotion to senior lecturer … I've had a year at this now, a year and a couple of months …, we're beginning to really develop data, which will, I'm sure, lead to some good outputs and some further inputs … So, as the career develops, I think my teaching is already excellent, the student feedback I get is always top, so I see no reason why I wouldn't be senior lecturer in five years' time and … promotion to senior lecturer on research would be how I would want to be promoted, because I think my research is powerful …, I have the benefit of being young … I've achieved a lectureship at the age of 28, so I have a long career 'til I retire probably at 65, hopefully … I would hope to achieve a professorship, if it's not here, somewhere else … I know often people have to move through their career because, for whatever reason, they need to move on and I would be prepared to do so …, to allow me to achieve my own goal, which is I would like a chair…

A lot of people see the draw of going to work for a big company as being a big salary, but what they don't realise is that there's very little job security, so is it really that big a salary, if you only go and work for them for six months and then they make you redundant … In academia, there's not such a big salary, but there is … comparable job security, shall we say, and …, as long as you're not passive and you don't just sort of …, sit back and just let it happen, and as long as you're a fighter and you work hard, then you do have the potential for a nice, long, happy career in this game, I think. So, that's why I would certainly stay in academia and I feel very privileged to do the job that I do, although I grumble sometimes, everyone does, it's a deep privilege to be able to do what I do and …, obviously I work for the university, obviously I have a line manager here and I have targets and expectations that I have to meet, but …, I can achieve those targets and drive the work in the direction that I want to take it and it's all down to my intellectual freedom and that is just invaluable.

… the things that I do, the things that I've taken on, I do them because I want to do them and because I know that they will be useful to the university as a whole, to the environment that we're in … it contributes to the society of the university and that's the reason why I wanted to do it, because it … injects something back into the community of the university … and I hope that that will be recognised …, as a valuable contribution to the university, but …, I want to be promoted on my research, not on that, so I do that because it's useful and valuable, but it's not my focus … The way in which … academic

> promotion works is you have to be proficient in all aspects of your job, but outstanding in one particular area and you're promoted on that one particular area, so when I say I want to be promoted on research, what I mean to say is that my research meets that outstanding standard and that everything else is good enough to ..., for me to be awarded that promotion ... I'm on a fixed term contract, all staff in this school are hired on a fixed term contract for five years, which is then, after three to five years, when you have a sustained evidence of effectiveness at the job, you would then be put on ... a permanent contract, so that's relatively standard within this school ... but really ... I'm not concerned about the continuing appointment, I think I am effective at my job and I think I'm certainly going to continue to be effective at my job ... my focus is that promotion. (Lecturer, applied science, pre-1992 university, interview 1)

This person displayed confidence in the *Institutional script* and knew precisely what they were required to do in order to meet the promotion and progression criteria that would enable them to develop a career in higher education. They therefore prioritized their research as their promotion 'route', while undertaking service contributions such as student support and a significant amount of management and administration, to round out their contribution. Although they were primarily focused on the *Institutional script*, it was their *Internal script* that provided them with the focus and determination to meet the requirements, having weighed up considerations such as, for example, a career in industry. It could also be that later on in their career their dedication to the *Institutional script* might be modified, for example, if they acquired family responsibilities.

At the same time, another individual at a different university showed that it was possible to push the boundaries in meeting system requirements for progression, gaining recognition for new approaches to data collection in the humanities as a marker of achievement within the existing promotion framework:

> I was at the cutting edge ... and my digital [work] also fed back into my teaching quite a lot. So, my career progression, although I've got a research record which I'm proud of and which I've defended, [is] actually, equivalent to several monographs, nonetheless, [has] a non-traditional element and my career has owed something to taking on these other roles on the basis of those experiences that have given me an institutional role, which I'm sure helped underpin my chair when I got it ..., so ... I suppose the two things that strike me about it is,

one, that doing the 'wrong' kind of research, given the kind of advice people tend to report being given with reference to REF [Research Excellence Framework], has not done me any harm ..., and actually I've been able to build a very different portfolio of research without that being an obstacle ... I've had to explain it, but I've been able to do so. (Professor, humanities, pre-1992 Russell Group university, interview 1)

This demonstrates how an *Institutional script* was, in practice, modulated by an individual's developmental work, driven by their *Internal script*, for which there was no precedent. Nevertheless, this person was working within given structures and had been successful in persuading promotion committee members that their work met existing criteria. Therefore, extended research interests could be used to progress within an *Institutional script*, depending on the individual's powers of persuasion and the willingness of senior colleagues to recognize new forms of activity. Much seemed to depend on individual assessments about what might be possible within formal structures associated with linear career paths and associated timelines.

Practice Scripts

Practice scripts were illustrated by individuals who maintained professional capital outside the university, commonly in order to retain credentials, skills and contacts; enhance academic activity; and/or provide a safety net or exit plan if necessary. In this context, it was significant that twenty of the forty-nine interviewees in the study had come in to higher education from a different sector. They were evenly spread across the four types of institution, showing that this was not solely the case in the more regionally and practice-orientated post-1992 institutions, thus:

pre-1992 Russell Group - five interviewees
pre-1992 - five interviewees
post-1992 - five interviewees
post-2004 - five interviewees.

As indicated above, *Practice scripts* were not limited to the classic professions such as medicine and law but also included people in applied, practice- and business-orientated disciplines. They had natural links and allegiances outside the higher education sector that were deep-rooted and integral to their professional existence, for example, in fields such as health and social care, journalism/

media, policing, the probation and career guidance services. Other individuals had close links with business and industry, charities and non-governmental organizations and were involved in developments associated with the digital environment, humanitarian work in the Third World, refugee education, the rehabilitation of offenders, child protection and charitable giving. This, in turn, provided interaction between academic activity and a range of settings and agencies, including technology companies and the creative industries, fostering the exchange of knowledge and practice.

Individuals for whom *Practice scripts* were dominant were likely to regard themselves as having options, as exemplified in the following Pen Portrait of an early career member of faculty in an applied science:

Pen Portrait 2

My role as the postdoc on the project for the whole consortium is to …, bring lots of different pieces of data from different PhD students and different projects and bring that into one place and look at policy relevant landscape designs for [plant-based industry] and work with the … industry to improve [plant] landscapes so that they can …, let's say maximise conservation and environmental issues, but also maximise [plant] profits at the same time, or at least, you know, not have the detriment of, so it's, yeah, palatable for the industry … I think academia is quite different … the industry is just one part of knowing how to speak to people, it's more the culture, especially in [plant producing country] …, learning that is more important and actually I did work in [plant producing country] for a few months, so I guess I was already familiar a little bit with the customs … so I manage … bringing the data into one place and then I manage my own aspects of my project in terms of working with the industry … I think a lot of [applied scientists] see themselves as academics who crossed the boundary into practice … there's more emphasis on impact case studies, which in our field, means being more practice-oriented … so … if it's not applied, if it's not relevant for [applied science] and it's just a high impact factor paper, I'm not interested … I see myself as an academic, but only sort of 50% academic … (interview 1). It's a combination of research and impact work … [the] main bulk of my research that I'm doing … is [in third world country] … that would be more like meetings and workshops and sort of focus groups and things like that and to a degree, my work in [second third world country] is a similar thing, sort of meetings, workshops, focus groups … for example, these research partners and government agencies that I help in [third world country] ... I'm essentially keeping up trust. If they say, oh, you know, we don't have anybody to make this map, can you do it, because ... the President wants to see it tomorrow morning, you know, I do it because I know that it's going to help my research ultimately go in the right direction and it's keeping that trust going, which is really important in [third world country], so there are bits and bobs that are not represented directly ... I also try and support, you know, undergrad[uate] students beyond what I have to, or master's students beyond what I have to. A lot of them come to me and say ..., 'can you help, are there any opportunities ..., I want to volunteer in a tropical forest' and so I'll put them in touch with the right people and stuff like that. (Research fellow/lecturer, applied science, pre-1992 university, interview 2)

The fact that this person did not self-identify entirely as being a member of the academic profession affected their worldview beyond purely *Institutional scripts*, and, in particular, their confidence about gaining employment outside higher education in the future, for example, in industry or a non-governmental organization (NGO). Some individuals with these types of backgrounds worked part-time in higher education and part-time elsewhere: 'Sometimes you have to make a choice if you're having two careers, you can't always do both to the full extent that you would like ... But maybe that's not such a bad thing because the two can bumble along quite nicely together and complement each other in some ways as well' (senior lecturer, humanities, post-2004 university, interview 1). Others went further and kept open the possibility of a future career in another sector, including the private sector, which was a clear motivating factor for the following individual, both as a possible exit strategy if needed as well as a more lucrative option, thus:

[Academic] research doesn't pay as much as industry ... I can definitely see myself going out of academia ... I quite like the idea that I could go there eventually, I mean I'd need more project work and more experience if I did do it, but it's always nice to have that card in your hand ..., you can go elsewhere, you can stay, you've got options. (Research fellow, social sciences, pre-1992 Russell Group university, interview 1)

Practice scripts therefore involved extended interests and calculations of success beyond the *formal economy* of an institution, either temporarily or permanently, for example, by assessing the value of experience in external settings and developing lateral networks. This could also offer a confidence to succeed outwith *Institutional scripts* and eventually take an individual in a different direction.

A variation on this was an opt in/opt out approach, moving back and forth between high-earning and high-comfort roles over time, assuming that these were unlikely to be combined in one post:

> For the money I'm getting here now, it's fine, I mean, I don't have children …, I don't have family commitments, so I can live pretty well and travel and do things with the money I earn … also I value that I'm happy with the job and I think that's important, because …, you can earn a lot of money and then be miserable and …, it doesn't compensate …, or maybe … I can work for …, a couple of years in a very profitable job and kind of save a lot and then move back again to maybe a less profitable one, with better conditions …, I mean …, like, let's do a bit of sacrifice for a couple of years. (Research fellow, social sciences, pre-1992 Russell Group university, interview 1)

The implication for this person, motivated by the fact that their disciplinary background meant that they could move into a policy or think tank environment, as well as by lifestyle considerations, was that they could move out of higher education from time to time but also return at a later date. They would, thereby, avoid being completely locked in to institutional progression pathways and have the freedom to pursue a self-directed career.

Internal Scripts

Internal scripts contextualize the idea of a career within the broader framework of a person's sense of themselves, as expressed through strengths, interests, relationships and aspirations. In Archer's terms, they represent the 'I' in an individual's interaction with *Institutional scripts*; in their relationships with colleagues, family and professional networks; and in providing the stimulus to personalize career-making. They run through all the narratives to a greater or lesser extent and also reflect Bhabha's (1994) concept of 'splitting', whereby people accommodate to the formal institutional economy for the time being, while at the same time modulating their activity as far as they can to accommodate other considerations. *Internal scripts* therefore represent a process of negotiation with given conditions (representing Archer's 'me' (Archer 2000)), as exemplified by the following train of thought:

> I am … doing something that I don't dislike … I've got kids, I need to be home, it's convenient, this university is five miles away from where I live, I can be a big fish in a small pond here, the money is good for what I have to do, I don't have any management responsibilities … you dig a trench for yourself, so people know who you are, so in the way people know me here, they know what I do, my strengths and weaknesses. (Reader, social sciences, post-2004 university, interview 1)

Therefore, this person placed a premium on security, convenience and being comfortable in their current situation. It was a holistic view contextualizing their immediate role for the time being within a range of factors in their life.

A number of individuals mentioned that an academic career differs from many other careers in that advancement is likely to involve applying for promotion within one's own institution, without a change of role as such, as opposed to applying for an entirely new post within their home institution or elsewhere. Promotion, therefore, is likely to represent development of an existing role rather than a change to an entirely new one. Individuals are more likely to move either before they have an open-ended post, i.e. when they are still on fixed-term contracts in early career, or if they are headhunted at the professorial level for a specific set of skills and knowledge, particularly in relation to research. This means that scope for mobility, with a view to finding a more congenial *Institutional script*, may be limited, and individuals are therefore more likely to try to massage the situation in which they find themselves. This process is likely to occur via the adoption of *Internal scripts*, and in the study such scripts focused, in particular, on individuals' specific strengths and interests, their desire to maintain a sense of security and equilibrium, and lifestyle considerations, as follows:

Playing to Strengths and Interests

The teaching/research nexus was frequently cited as an example of individuals being influenced by their *Internal script*. There was a sense among some individuals that it might not be possible to undertake both teaching and research to the highest standards, with a preference to focus on one or the other, according to individual strengths, interests and the personal satisfaction derived from one or the other. Thus, in relation to teaching,

> 'a lot of people are very hung up on what their impact factors are and what their H index is and … all these sorts of things …, but for me …, what I care about is

the quality of experience for the students and the fact that they're going to learn something useful and they're going to graduate and go into the world of work and achieve something, and perhaps that's not doing my career any favours …, but to be honest with you, that's not what I'm in it for. I really get so much from being face-to-face with the students …, and I'm really passionate about helping them to become all they can'. (University teaching fellow, applied science, post-1992 university, interview 2)

Conversely, the following person focused on the intrinsic satisfaction they gained from research and in developing capacity in Third World countries:

I just see myself having a good research project in a research team and doing good … science and not just being … a lot about impact …, bringing master's students over from less developed countries …, capacity building, which we do a lot of here in our department and I'd want to be doing that, wherever I was based …, so just doing good science and at a career progression which probably wasn't amazingly quick. (Research fellow, applied science, pre-1992 university, interview 1)

This is in direct contrast to Pen Portrait 1, although they both had a dedication to research. There could be both practical and ideological reasons for a preference to focus on teaching or research, such as awareness that one's talents were greater as a teacher or as a researcher; a lack of success in achieving research funding; commitment to the social outcomes of teaching or research that would benefit, for example, underserved populations; and the personal satisfaction, and even excitement gained from one or other activity.

Maintaining a Sense of Equilibrium

Against the background of uncertainty associated with career insecurity, workloads, pay and pensions between the two rounds of interviews, as well as local issues in individual universities, 'satisficing' approaches were evident in many of the narratives, i.e. taking the view that things were good enough for the time being, therefore acceptable, even if the optimal scenario might not be available or even in view. Such narratives could also be driven by, for example, a perceived mismatch between the value accorded to research as opposed to teaching, or other developmental activity related to specific talents or interests such as community engagement or online learning. Such *Internal scripts* often involved a reframing of an individual's positioning when adherence to *Institutional scripts* did not seem possible, or had not gone to plan, for example, when an application for promotion had not been accepted, as in the following case:

> By being strategic and career oriented … I'd probably have more money than the majority of staff in this school … [but] I don't want to kill myself for the next 10 years before retirement …, do you want to be leaving your family for weeks on end and … it's a lifestyle thing … I'm at the stage where I'd rather be enjoying what I'm doing … you go to professor …, there's a lot of stress and pressure brought to bear, so you can almost fly under the radar if you're at a lower level. (Senior lecturer, applied science, pre-1992 Russell Group university, interview 2)

Similarly, work on applying for research funding, or writing an academic paper that had been rejected, could, with hindsight, be turned to advantage:

> I'm working a lot with younger colleagues who apply for grants and then they don't get it, they really feel frustrated, some of them almost feel, like, I'm never going to do this again, or when they don't get an article published, but I'm now of a stage when I think, well, it's not wasted, I can repackage it, or even in the process of doing it, I've met some interesting people, I've had some interesting connections and they may come in later, may be useful for something. (Professor, humanities, pre-1992 Russell group university, interview 2)

Such a rebalancing of thinking during the progress of a career could help to maintain a sense of equilibrium about things as they stood, although this did not necessarily preclude considering alternative options such as applying for new responsibilities or posts elsewhere.

Others had found what they saw as a safe space, where they could focus on personal strengths and interests, and preferred to remain there, working with, rather than against, the grain. Thus, the following individual did not want to leave a supportive environment for just this reason, including the existence of a helpful mentor:

> I'm happy working here … in this sector and … in a university … within this role, and my plan going forward, to keep developing myself, is to …, continue to apply for funding for pedagogic research and to collaborate … I've had someone from the school of education who's sort of mentored me informally …, I'm trying to … formalise that a bit more …, so that eventually I can become a sort of … prof[essor] of higher education type role … The thing that would motivate me to move would … not necessarily be better pay or promotion, but … the working conditions … In this role, I do have a lot of work to do, but I know how to manage it and I know that I've got supportive colleagues, so if I went

somewhere else … I don't know how supportive my line manager's going to be. (University teaching fellow, post-1992 university, science, interview 2)

Nevertheless, although this policy might work for the time being, it did not take account of possible future perturbations in the working environment, including changes of line manager.

Maintaining a Lifestyle and Work-Life Balance

A career trajectory was often seen in the context of a broader hinterland of commitments and responsibilities and of achieving an acceptable balance between these. As one individual, who had had a successful career but had experienced perturbations in relation to the career track embodied in an *Institutional script*, acknowledged, 'people get challenges personally. I had … caring responsibilities; a son with [mental health condition], and more recently … caring for elderly parents, and so some things simply have to be put on hold' (professor, social sciences, post-1992 university, interview 2). Nevertheless, they had ultimately obtained a chair by moving institution between the two rounds of interviews. The challenge of managing dual careers was also a common theme. A number of respondents also had partners who were academic faculty and, as one person said, 'We weren't quite sure whether our relationship would cope … with us both working full time' (senior lecturer, applied science, pre-1992 university, interview 1). A compromise could be for one individual, male or female, to focus on meeting the criteria and timelines of an *Institutional script*, at least for the time being, and for the other to take a more flexible approach. Such considerations also affected decisions about where to live and work, those with young families tending to favour being outside large cities, with easy journeys to work: 'Family is too important to me to commute …, so unless I was desperate, I wouldn't commute' (research fellow, applied science, pre-1992 university, interview 1).

The influence of *Internal* and *Practice scripts*

Internal and *Practice scripts* might therefore be seen as representing an iterative process in relation to *Institutional scripts*, with the aim of optimizing personal predilections and professional loyalties in a series of adjustments and modifications. This process may in turn put pressure on the *formal economy* of an institution if there is a groundswell of individuals expressing the desire for recognition of, for example, new and emergent forms of activity. *Internal* and *Practice scripts* can also generate tipping points whereby people weigh up the options and pathways available to them, including personal and professional considerations and resources, triggering decisions about, for example, where to focus their energies, whether to apply for promotion, whether to accept administrative or management roles and/or whether to try to move institution or sector. The duality of structure and agency between the individual and the institution therefore becomes more complex, involving a multiplicity of micro-decisions at any point in time.

The following Pen Portrait is an example of the role played by *Internal* and *Practice scripts* in interpreting and re-profiling a standard teaching and scholarship contract, as expressed in the terms and conditions of this person's *Institutional script*. The formal career path was seen as one of a number of strands in the individual's life, and as part of a broad hinterland of interests, without being the dominant element. Although it is an extreme example, it demonstrates how career development may result from the pursuit of individual interests, strengths and external practice in the community, leading to a serendipitous relationship with the *Institutional script*.

Pen Portrait 3

I did an undergraduate degree in science ... I then worked, as you do, for the probation service. I lived in a collective house, so we set up a building co-operative ... I worked as a carpenter for ... several years. Then I met my wife and went to live [abroad] ... and she brought me back to England, she wanted to do postgraduate studies and we ended up in xxxx, where I worked again as a carpenter, but ... self-employed ..., Then, through her contact with [the University of xxx], I heard about things that were going on ... and got involved in [applied science] education in local schools ... and then, through ... her contacts, I got onto a project on [applied science] education ... Through that, I did a masters in science and technology... policy ... Then ... my wife got a fellowship in [European country], we went and lived in [European country] for a year and then she got the job here ... and I looked around and I saw this [applied science institute] .... and it looked interesting and I walked in the door and who should be sitting there but my old ... lecturer from when I was an undergraduate ... Then ..., somebody left a research project, I took over that project and then sort of bumped along, always in a part-time role, and that was sort of partly decided on the back of my wife having a full-time job...

Then, through several bits of research, sort of part posts, I put up a[n] [applied science] education module on the master's programme and then the university put out a fees waiver to members of staff who wanted to do PhDs, so I signed up for a PhD and seven or more years later, after I'd become primary carer to [elderly relative] in the meantime, I ended up with a PhD. Some years later, a sympathetic head of school … made my job into … a part post but actually like a permanent post …, I'm up to a 0.5 now, but I've also done …, quite a lot of research projects in that time … And then through that process, I've come into a space where I've combined … a whole bunch of evening classes, I've done a[n] [arts and crafts] course …, I did a BTEC [Business and Technology Education Council qualification] … and so that's why I'd describe it as … a career through life, and then I've sort of come to a space where I've put up an undergraduate module …, so I'm trying to bring these ideas of creativity into that space … I teach [conservation project] …, so that's a nice thing to do … given all this employability, so it's demonstrating team skills etc … I'd describe myself as an educator … I see it as a process of facilitation and being a sort of creative producer in some ways … (interview 1).

I've just put in for promotion … to reader. I must maintain this unconventional role within universities, so they can't put me in a box …, I've kind of …, moved myself into a sort of sweet spot really … I was an associate artist in [local town] … And so I spent two days a week that year working with …, being mentored by professional artists … 2018 was a difficult year for me, because I lost [two family members] within the space of ten days and then …throughout the year, another ten people in my vicinity …, so it was, like, twelve people died in that year … also that was after …, I slipped down a ladder and fell off a balcony … and I could have easily died, so I had this sort of … near death experience and at the same time, I was being a sort of creative artist …, so it was really, it was very intense in many ways … I do feel stronger and a bit more resilient in many ways on the back of it … And also, it's made me …, less angst ridden about what I do here, you know, and if there's colleagues I don't get on with, it doesn't matter … and … how I engage with this space is rather, well, I feel much more relaxed …, I think the thing is, what I've learned, where I've come to since I last saw you is, I'm not particularly worried about the future so much, I'm comfortable where I am, I feel I've occupied a space where I do, I enjoy almost every aspect of the job, even though it's not a full job …, and then … I'm looking for opportunities to sort of engage and innovate … A lot of my promotion application was essentially saying, well, I've never been given any major administrative roles in this school …, therefore I've done all these other things … I'm a trustee of a couple of [charities] … my research funding applications are really essentially about trying to sort of facilitate community based conservation projects in other countries, and it's more about that practice than generating data that can be published ... the project work in [third world country] has been incredibly impactful... The feedback I get from students is amazing ..., I feel sort of that warm glow at times. More of a challenge to try and sort of consolidate that into ... how I might move to a senior HEA [Higher Education Academy] Fellowship ... , I'm not included in the REF [Research Excellence Framework], [although] actually, the [third world country] work ... could be a REF impact case study ... I hope to stay here for a while, finish the projects that I'm working on ..., we'll see and then ..., just step sideways and kind of carry on with ..., I do want to immerse myself more in creative practice, from a personal point of view. (Senior lecturer, applied science, pre-1992 university, interview 2)

This person described the relationship of their career trajectory to formal institutional requirements and structures (or *Institutional scripts*) as 'the Maginot line technique. I just walk around [it], like the Germans did'. Nevertheless, they ultimately achieved a readership after the second interview. Their holistic approach was supported by their promoting the fact that they were qualified to teach in certain areas, developing positive relationships with colleagues, their willingness to suggest new forms of activity for students, for example, in conservation projects, and by taking opportunities that arose, sometimes by happenstance. This person might not be seen as a typical career academic, but their somewhat idiosyncratic approach in creating a 'designer career', selecting activities that played to their strengths and developing a unique trajectory, ultimately worked for them within the formal system, and in gaining promotion. It is an open and honest account demonstrating the influence of dominant *Internal* and *Practice scripts*. In a sense, they were working from the outside in, rather than inside out. This represents an inversion of the relationship with *Institutional scripts* as a template or organizing framework, with guide marks for measuring progress in making a career. Although the career path described, and the extent of the influence of personal drivers, was unique among the interviews, there were elements of the same underlying processes in other respondents' accounts.

Conclusion

The development of the concept of *career scripts* yielded a more comprehensive picture of approaches to roles and careers than is available in the literature, including earlier work by the authors, allowing these to be conceptualized and explained within the framework of *formal* and *informal institutional economies*. The study also shed light on underlying considerations for individuals in their day-to-day activity and identified changes that occurred over a two-year time period. It therefore provided a more complex account than that suggested by a simple dichotomy of structure and agency, or of 'boundaried/boundaryless' approaches to roles. Moving beyond the influence of disciplinary considerations, and a calibration of interaction with institutional structures such as job descriptions or promotion criteria, the study reviewed ways in which individuals were able to massage and reshape given structures and create new locales for themselves. The longitudinal dimension also enabled a more systematic picture to be developed over time.

To this end, the concepts of *Institutional, Practice* and *Internal career scripts* overcame the rigidity of the initial fixed categories of *Mainstream, Portfolio* and *Niche* in understanding the fluid process of career-making that cuts across the formal requirements of institutional career templates. *Internal* and *Practice scripts* are in turn influenced by the diversification of the academic workforce, with individuals entering higher education from a range of practice environments, by professional practice itself, by new arenas of activity associated with academic work and by personal lifestyle considerations. Thus, a career is represented not only by public indicators such as promotion criteria, markers of esteem and impact, but also by individual constructions around these, whereby *Practice scripts* provide a supra-professional dimension, and *Internal scripts* promote individual accommodations and accomplishments, values and motivations.

It was also evident from the narratives that individuals were able to flex formal requirements in order to accommodate activity that was not necessarily recognized in *Institutional scripts*. This could occur when such activity was developmental, for example, in relation to graduate employability, particularly if an individual had a line manager who adopted a generous interpretation of progression criteria, and was able to argue that such activities played to university interests and goals such as widening participation. Even those in mid-career, who might appear to be on a relatively secure pathway, enshrined in an *Institutional script*, did not necessarily accept this script at face value. The dialogues created by both *Internal* and *Practice scripts*, therefore, influenced individuals as they expanded and contracted their activities in amoeba-like fashion. Chapter 5 will show the impact of this across both spatial and temporal dimensions, so that a career becomes a multifaceted process, involving unique patterns of movement as individuals adjust their positioning on an ongoing basis.

5

The Rise of the *Concertina Career*

Introduction

As shown in Chapter 4, the fluidity between career scripts demonstrates that, in practice, people may hold different scripts simultaneously or at different stages of their career, moving between activities for specific purposes and according to circumstances. In coming to an accommodation with *Institutional scripts*, it was evident that individuals may not necessarily be predisposed, or able, to follow a predetermined path. Examination of *Internal* and *Practice scripts* further revealed that individuals had rich hinterlands that influenced their career-making, incorporating both spatial and temporal dimensions. This provided an in-depth perspective that was not apparent from, for example, institutional progression processes and statistics, or Higher Education Statistics Agency (HESA) data. The cumulative effect of this is that a career is likely to accommodate detours and loops back and forth as individuals expand and contract their activity across both spatial and temporal dimensions in 'concertina-like' fashion, in the same way as the musical instrument expands and contracts in music-making (Whitchurch, Locke and Marini 2021). This chapter shows how, as a consequence, a career becomes a multifaceted process, involving unique patterns of movement as individuals adjust their positioning on an ongoing basis. This, in turn, challenges the concept of the one-dimensional, linear career path, with associated progression criteria.

From the Zig-Zag to the *Concertina Career*

Career paths tend to be represented formally by institutions as fixed, linear models that outline routes, markers of achievement and associated timescales. However, it was evident from the narratives that individuals had personal and professional hinterlands against which they contextualized and negotiated their careers, with different scripts dominating at different times and in response to different circumstances. Thus, one person, who had built their academic career from cumulative part-time appointments over time, against a background of other interests, plus caring responsibilities, described their trajectory as follows: 'There's a thing called a career and for some people it defines a sort of logical series of steps. In my case, it describes a sort of zigzagging way through the world' (senior lecturer, applied science, pre-1992 university, interview 1). Another person, who, in their fifties, was looking for promotion to a chair, had pursued an *Institutional script* insofar as they had been able, but reflected that their pathway had been tempered by a move between countries, a rebooting of their career and a late family:

> You start running out of energy, the thought of a complete career change, where, long hours …, I would rather be a dad …, I like to be home for bed times, I don't like to work on weekends and I realise that that's going to be a limiting step to career advancement. So, if I had my way, I'd be financially secure and living in the country … in terms of careers, this is the point of my life where I think I've taken it most seriously … I think previously …, opportunities come and you find yourself meandering through a career and finding yourself in a sweet spot and wondering how you got there, and that has worked for me thus far. (Reader, applied science, pre-1992 Russell Group university, interview 2).

In turn, another late career individual reflected that career-making is 'a lifestyle thing … does your career drive what you do, or does your enjoyment drive what you do, and I'm at the stage where I'd rather be enjoying what I'm doing … [career-making] becomes a lifestyle decision as much as anything else' (senior lecturer, applied science, pre-1992 Russell Group university, interview 2).

As a result of these types of considerations, and influenced by the three career scripts described in Chapter 4, career paths are likely to be characterized by an expansion and contraction of activity, as well as a stretching and compression of timescales, according to real-life circumstances and contexts. In practice, individuals flex activities, with a sense of testing out possibilities in relation to opportunities, setbacks and personal circumstances. This 'concertina' effect, whereby the process of career-making expands and contracts in relation to the different spaces that individuals find themselves in, over extended time periods, is driven by choices and micro-decisions that individuals make on an ongoing basis: 'You have these choices to make … you need to weigh up those choices' (professor, social sciences, post-1992 university, interview 2). The space-time nexus is exemplified in decisions such as whether to focus on achieving a balanced range of activity at the same time or to prioritize a specific activity such as a research initiative or setting up a new teaching programme. This was exemplified by one individual who said that they would have to 'let things go and create the space to allow [me] to do the things that will help [me] to progress' (educational developer, pre-1992 Russell Group university, interview 2). Space and time are therefore managed as resources that individuals seek to adjust as they endeavour to find an appropriate fit between the requirements of a career and their own unique circumstances, thus: 'You have to play a long game ..., where you choose which bits of the puzzle you can concentrate on at any one time' (reader, creative arts, post-1992 university, interview 2). The narratives therefore illustrate ways in which individuals 'build multiple, subjective positions' (Arvaja 2018) via *Internal* and *Practice scripts*, as well as calibrating progress against formal institutional criteria.

The following Pen Portrait illustrates the piecemeal fashion in which a career can develop, in ways that are not necessarily planned or anticipated from the start, using contacts and networks in different professional and disciplinary areas. It therefore demonstrates a nonlinear career that does not conform to institutional templates or broad assumptions about meeting certain progression criteria and targets within certain time periods. This person had built a career in higher education after roles in financial services, via part-time positions in different types of university, and around family commitments. They had also undertaken a part-time doctorate along the way:

Pen Portrait 4

I took a degree in [creative arts] and had an intention to teach ..., but that didn't work out due to moving location. I became self-employed for a couple of years and then I moved into a completely different field and ..., I went into [financial services] and I moved up ..., from being a temporary assistant, through to a person who was [more] senior ... and then I became a ... manager ... I paused to have two children and after that, came back into higher education ... as a staff member, so I had a sort of five year period of childcare break ... and it was quite fortunate in some ways, because I was also given the opportunity for some redundancy or a new post when the ... merger took place, so I thought, well, I'll take the redundancy for now and have a think about what I want to do. So ..., I took a really small part-time post at [post-2004 university] and this was as an administrator for a research unit ... and it was just four hours a week, but it fitted very well with really young children. They increased my hours to six ... and then I also took on, after a year or two, two more six-hour temporary contracts, which ended up with me doing eighteen hours in three different parts of the university; and so I did ten years in [post-2004 university] during that time, having done these smaller posts ... I ended up with a post [in online learning] and it was around the time when online learning was beginning to grow a little bit and so ..., I'd been working for six of my hours in an IT [information technology] services department and I applied for this small post ... and when I was successful in that, I started working with staff members, advising them on how they could introduce more technology into the way that they taught. At the same time, we started to look at having an e-learning strategy in that university, so I became involved in that. Alongside this, I had done another qualification as a staff member but as a part-time student and that was ... in IT [information technology] management ..., so I was working different contracts to be able to balance with home life. Then ... I'd applied for some temporary teaching, some sessional teaching, which was in the [management] school and at the same time, applied for a masters degree at [pre-1992 university] ..., which was in educational research ... they're a department that I'm still in contact with ... because ..., some really interesting relationships were ... started there ... So, I completed that ..., I ended up with a couple of modules of my own during that time and I also carried on doing some other work ... and I ran an externally funded project, so I managed that and that was related to teaching and research repositories ... Then, I decided to apply for a post over here at [pre-1992 university] ... and whilst the post was a sort of ... learning technologist type post, with a responsibility for one other employee, when I came to interview, they offered me a PhD at the same time, and that was a deciding factor for me to come. (Senior lecturer, teaching and learning, pre-1992 university, interview 1)

This person had built up their work in higher education hour by hour over several years and across more than one university, expanding the space in which they worked from administration to IT services, to educational research and latterly to educational technology. This became a bespoke trajectory that fitted in with raising a young family and accommodated a master's and doctoral degree, thereby developing this person's capabilities, intellectual development and skill set. It demonstrates a mobility and flexibility that is not tied specifically to the goals, timelines or chronological expectations of an established institutional career path. Alongside this was a cumulative building of confidence, which was reflected in a number of accounts, suggesting that individuals were testing out what was possible for them, in the light of their own circumstances, backgrounds and experience at any point in time. This was particularly the case when individuals came from a non-traditional route that did not involve a linear or chronological pathway of undergraduate degree, higher degree(s), and postdoctoral roles in their twenties or early thirties.

Negotiating Space

The expansion and blurring of disciplinary space within which academic faculty operate was evident in many of the narratives of the study, arising from factors such as:

- *The incorporation of practice disciplines*, ranging from health, social care and teaching to the police, probation work and the media, with the associated requirement to qualify students as professionals who are able to practice independently in community settings. Many such professionals, particularly in 'uniform' subjects, also worked for part of their time in practice settings and/or taught students on external placements. Even in those fields where registration by students with a professional body was not necessary for full qualification, experience in practice was regarded by faculty as essential to the enhancement of teaching: 'I think teaching without the professional experience in this field is ... doing an injustice to the students, because I think you need to keep up-to-date and current, particularly with media because the technology is changing ... Understanding the media landscape and how work is commissioned and the way that the commercial environment works, I think you have to be in it to understand it ... I don't think I could give the students as high a value if I wasn't working in the field alongside the teaching' (senior lecturer, humanities, post-2004 university, interview 1).
- *An increasing emphasis on a holistic approach to improving the student experience*, including, for example, community outreach, employability initiatives, equity and inclusion, academic writing and learning skills, mental health and pastoral care. Although specialist support may be available from, and delivered by, dedicated professionals, individual faculty are increasingly likely to have some everyday involvement in guiding students through specific difficulties and choices, even if they also refer them to dedicated units

for help and support. Thus, one individual demonstrated an *Internal script* that had led them to develop extended disciplinary space around community outreach and widening participation. They had entered higher education after spending time in a local schools service and were active in foundation programmes for students with non-traditional backgrounds: 'Because of my experience and my knowledge, I [am] involved in things like postgraduate open evenings and recruitment events … I'll also be involved in open days and things like that … I am happy to go out into schools and colleges if they need someone to speak about education, and I have a lot of contacts out in schools and colleges who will contact me directly and ask me to come and deliver something' (senior lecturer, social sciences, post-1992 university, interview 1).

- *The emergence of online learning and associated pedagogical techniques* was no longer a specialist activity, but required of all faculty in delivering teaching, even when the interviews took place, before the Covid-19 pandemic. Transferring lecture and interactive programmes to online platforms had involved individual faculty in developmental activity that could be time-consuming and challenging. Thus, one member of faculty had taken on responsibility for a distance learning programme, of which the associated issues were only just becoming apparent: 'There are a lot of things that happen with distance learning that …, I feel like don't happen for campus based learning; things like links break, a student will immediately email you, they're very "on it", they check things, it's not working, they email you and you have to really fix it straight away because they only have a short period of time that they can access it before they move on to the next topic … during that week they may only allot, you know, four hours on one day to do it, and if the link isn't working in those four hours, you've disadvantaged them, so …, you have to be quite responsive' (lecturer, social sciences, pre-1992 university, interview 1). Because there was a worldwide catchment of students, this person also had to take into account time zone differences, so that issues could not necessarily be dealt with on a nine-to-five basis, which literally extended their day. Online teaching and learning was an entirely new space for many faculty, who had experienced a gradual expansion into 'virtual' activity. This is unlikely to decrease post-Covid-19, especially with the trend towards blended programmes, combining face-to-face with online provision.

- *The requirement for impact*, as defined in the UK Research Excellence Framework (2014), in attracting research funding, particularly from the UK Research Councils, has resulted in an increased focus on the applications of research, including in the humanities and social sciences. This has led to individuals reaching out to colleagues, not only in other disciplines but also in the fields of policy and practice, thereby extending disciplinary spaces: 'Grant capture is really, really important, especially [as] [university] highly values interdisciplinarity now … public buzzword …, so if you manage to get some of these grants that are interdisciplinary, then definitely, [that] will help …, for … personal [advancement] … I have met really, really interesting people …, I'm working with medical scientists, environmental scientists, linguists, you name it and it's fascinating' (professor, humanities, pre-1992 Russell group university, interview 2). Furthermore, major policy agendas mean that, even in the humanities, 'that's how you have to think … big global challenges' (professor, humanities, pre-1992 Russell group university, interview 2).

Personal and Practice Drivers for Pushing Spatial Boundaries

It was evident that the spatial parameters of a career were being stretched by an extension of disciplinary, practice and personal spaces, often to accommodate what one person referred to as a 'patchwork' lifestyle. Individuals were not only interacting with existing structures but also creating new, lateral spaces. This expansion of academic hinterlands was often driven at an individual and personal level by professional practice, specific strengths and interests, and the desire to build a case for promotion. This was particularly evident in the humanities where pressure to attract funding and achieve impact had led to a focus on real-world problems, with conventional patterns of activity becoming distorted, so that academic careers were changing in shape:

> In many ways, I've seen my career has changed …, because I've become much more involved in … interdisciplinary networks and so on, then you're not your typical historian …, a lot of them are single scholars, they just apply for some time to just do a bit of writing, so …, it's a bit of that tension where …, if you're changing your research direction, do you still fit a model that's very much built around straightforward disciplines and departments. (Professor, humanities, pre-1992 Russell group university, interview 2)

In turn, another, mid-career, member of faculty was mixing language teaching with a range of activities, such as developing graduate employability and teaching enhancement, as a platform for moving on. To do this, they had accessed new networks:

A lot of my time ... is spent encouraging students to go on placement, working very closely with [careers service], to organize activities for a month for our students, working with employers and things like that ... it will be changing my career ... which is something I'm considering at the moment ..., it would be feasible for me to produce research in the area of learning and teaching ... you need the credibility of the research as well and because of [my] previous position [assistant dean] ... I've got access to the sort of conversations ... the sort of data. (Senior lecturer, humanities, pre-1992 university, interview 1)

Others had harnessed professional practice directly in support of a case for promotion. Thus, the following person, with a background in youth and undergraduate careers services, who had moved from a professional services to an academic contract, had initially followed the *Institutional script* with the aim of achieving a senior lectureship: '[for] senior lecturer, they are looking at course leadership, module development, and that is what I'm making sure I get involved in' (senior lecturer, social sciences, post-1992 university, interview 1). However, by the second interview, they had reinforced this by writing a successful bid for training funds that would play to the institution's impact agenda. This had been the critical factor in achieving promotion:

It was particularly the [postgraduate programme] that tipped the balance, because ... I wrote the bid, put the bid in ... We were successful, so I then developed the course and developed the relationships that meant we had students ... setting up the [postgraduate programme] was just a reaction to government policy ... that meant that there was an opportunity to develop some training ... I've been very lucky that there's been a lot of external influences that have allowed me to develop the courses that I run ... I think ... I've found my place ... I have a really good understanding of how the university works beyond an academic school ... I think I've got that overarching understanding of the sector ... I'm hoping that will stand me in good stead in terms of future career development ... I'd certainly be looking to go for a professorship. (Senior lecturer, social sciences, post-1992 university, interview 2)

They had therefore been able to stretch the space they occupied on initial appointment, utilizing their practice and community experience as credit towards their career advancement.

However, space was not only disciplinary, but also involved other commitments, internal and external to the university, as well as relationships with others. Thus, the following person demonstrated the way in which their career was nested within their immediate geographic locale, and relationships with colleagues, family and research associates: 'The question is in my case more about family and therefore location … the long-term plan is to stay here … I'll probably hope to be senior lecturer, [and in] ten years' time, reader … If things go very well, professor' (research fellow/lecturer, applied science, pre-1992 university, interview 1). Another individual felt that their teaching and research had been enriched by work with victims of conflict in an international setting, and that it could lead to work for a humanitarian organization:

> I really enjoy teaching, so I never would want to give it completely up, but I think it helps, especially on the [research] project, [that] I've been working in six other countries and doing workshops in two other countries beside that … having less teaching gives me flexibility, in order to do stuff … that's useful for victims of conflict …, so I guess [in future] maybe work for some sort of, NGO [non-governmental organisation] or a big organisation, like ICRC [International Committee of the Red Cross] … I'll keep on doing what I'm interested in, which is …, working on these victims issues around the world and try to, hopefully, actually get something passed in terms of legislation. (Senior lecturer, applied social sciences, pre-1992 Russell Group university, interview 2)

This illustrates the way in which both strong ties with family and colleagues, and weak ties externally (Granovetter 1973), i.e. spatial relationships, play their part in the development and direction of a career, with a fluid interaction between internal, institutional and external activity.

By contrast, another individual was deliberately cultivating and colonizing external, commercial space, through experience and contacts in businesses with which they were connected, in order to construct an exit plan for themselves:

> I … sit on the board of a [utilities] business, because I used to work in [utility] before I came into academia, and that is very profitable … I've been asked to do some voluntary work next year … in sustainable transport …, which [is an] interest of mine, and where I live we have a very active [social meeting] …, with a lot of …, very influential business people, and I join in that activity as well … I have close links with business and industry in the area … In five to ten years' time, I [may] have made my fortune because of the networking contact[s] …, there's a potential director role … in the private sector, and the steps that I'm taking is to keep in touch. So, if that comes off, I won't be in higher education. (Reader, social sciences, post-2004 university, interview 2)

Spatial stretch was therefore likely to arise from a combination of a drift in contemporary disciplinary and practice profiles, as well as initiatives stimulated by an individual's action to improve their prospects and achieve a desired lifestyle, incorporating other personal commitments. Such spaces, and the values attached to them, were more likely to emerge from *Internal* and *Practice scripts* than from *Institutional scripts*. However, they might in due course have an influence on the latter, for example, the incorporation of activity in areas such as online learning, employability and community engagement into promotion and progression criteria. This process is likely to be incremental and may not be perceived immediately by individuals as occurring in practice (Locke et al 2016). Nevertheless, all these factors have impacted the linearity of career paths assumed by formal systems and also put pressure on the timescales in which progression and preparations for promotion occur.

Negotiating Time

Although institutional pathways are likely to assume careers based on thirty- to forty-year timescales, with regular markers along progression routes, and each individual experiences the same amount of 'clock' time, such assumptions are disrupted by, for example, late entrants to the profession, individuals who work part-time and those with dual careers and caring responsibilities. They may also be affected by bottlenecks in higher education systems nationally and internationally, including a reduction of open-ended or 'tenure track' positions and increases in the numbers of short-term, casualized, and (in the UK) teaching-only contracts. These types of factors led to active approaches to time and its management and a stretching and compression of careers and timescales. These were recurring themes in *Internal scripts*:

- *Time as a resource.* Time itself was seen as a resource that could be invested or wasted. Thus, one person had calculated that some local roles carried more weight than others: 'I did the admissions tutor role for five years in the end. I didn't really want to do it for five years because it's not one that's particularly valued in terms of things like promotion or role, and it's very time-consuming. Both time-consuming and not valued is not a great combination' (reader, creative arts, post-1992 university, interview 1). However, although this person saw this role as consuming valuable time, others might well have seen this or similar roles as an investment in terms of the satisfaction or enjoyment they gained from it, reflecting different *Internal scripts*. There was also evidence of people undertaking an internal cost-benefit analysis in relation to one activity versus another, particularly early career faculty, in terms of the value that would accrue for the purposes of progression and/or promotion and the steps and time commitment needed: 'I would definitely be looking for a senior teaching fellow role and it would be one that actually has time for research … I do want to be successful in my career, so I think possibly having a more kind of actual think about where I want to go and be more strategic about the roles I'm taking on would be a good decision' (teaching fellow, science, pre-1992 Russell Group university, interview 1). This person took the view that decisions needed to be made about how best to allocate their time, by assessing the value of different activities and negotiating which they took on. Some people also spoke of time as being as valuable as money in terms of progressing a career, in particular being released from teaching, management or administrative roles to invest in research, or, as in the following case, to achieve a better work-life balance: 'I guess as I've taken on different managerial roles, my workload elsewhere hasn't always been reduced accordingly, until I've basically made a massive fuss …, when I made a fuss, I was first offered a pay rise, but I've now got [child] at home, so it's not about the money, it's about having time to do your job … I don't want any more money (professor, applied science, pre-1992 university, interview 2).

- *Time pressures.* Although pressure on time tended to be universal, reflecting factors such as increasing student numbers, reductions in faculty and the requirement to achieve research funding and impact, it became particularly acute when there was a cumulative effect arising from a range of demands on people's time. For example, this was evident in relation to interdisciplinary and applied research, with high impact value, as calls for bids were often in response to some immediate crisis (such as the Covid-19 pandemic) or policy issue: 'It's the time, isn't it … there's this one call around this one issue and you've got six weeks to do it' (professor, humanities, pre-1992 Russell group university, interview 2). Apart from the stress that could be caused to an individual or individuals because of the requirement for longer hours of work in terms of clock time, this could also disrupt ongoing activity. Such disruption often required a juggling of time by individuals, for example, by delegation in a team environment, which in turn took up time, so that the effect would be cumulative. This was likely to result in an expansion of 'hidden time', which was unlikely to appear in formal work plans, and was therefore out of view on a day-to-day basis.
- *'Hidden' time.* A recurrent theme was that the time spent by the individual on specific activities did not match the time formally allocated by the

Institutional script for that activity. This included less visible 'good-citizenship' roles: 'Most institutions for promotion routes require you to be fairly active as … what they would call somebody who is a good citizen ,… who is prepared to be on committees … to do external work as well as the work in your research and teaching … It's these kind of things that …aren't so visible' (professor, social sciences, post-1992 university, interview 2). However, for other activities representing 'hidden' time it was commonly felt that little credit accrued in *Institutional scripts*. The example most frequently given was pastoral care, particularly in relation to widening participation of students from underserved communities. Even for more senior faculty, the so-called buy out of time for research, or other responsibility such as head of department, did not necessarily bring equivalent relief from the time required for teaching and other activities, thus: 'I think … one of the things that I find quite difficult is that applying for research grants, or being involved in research grants that are led by others, where you've got nominal time …, like, two hours here … three hours there … effectively all of that money goes into my department, but I don't see any alleviation in my workload …, it's that tension where … I'm going to apply for these grants and it's important to bring the money in, but then … effectively …, on top of my normal workload, I do a lot more' (professor, humanities, pre-1992 Russell Group university, interview 2).

- *The juggling of time*. Efforts to manage time were particularly evident in relation to the balance between teaching, research and/or management roles. The cumulative effect of taking on additional work roles, for whatever reason, often led to a tipping point: 'It can be that … part-time [roles] add up to more than a full one …, people were giving me more and more managerial roles without cutting down on other things … probably part of the reason I took on this new role [assistant dean] was to stop all my other ones building up, so …, I get a lot of autonomy, I don't get micro-managed, I think that counts for a lot …, I just get given a project and then I can kind of run with it the way I want, so that's really good' (professor, applied science, pre-1992 university, interview 2). In the shorter term, a number of individuals spoke of trying to create dedicated blocks of time to allow for a specific research, teaching or writing task to take place, rather than trying to undertake a range of tasks simultaneously, as in the following case: 'I think that there's a lot of academics who feel that there's so much pressure …, that they aren't given the opportunity to really explore things and develop research, and I don't mean just being allowed to think blue skies all the time but even to, when you're writing papers and you're writing research grants – they're done to very tight timelines, and you're fitting it in around other things – that performance wise, if you didn't have the block of time to do it, it could make a difference [to your success]' (professor, applied science, pre-1992 Russell Group university, interview 1).

- *Control of time.* Where the individual had discretion over their use of time, this was regarded as a positive aspect of working in higher education. In the following case, for example, this allowed a focus on specific interests, and also flexibility in terms of family commitments: 'Importantly, you know, you can do what you want, largely …, you manoeuvre yourself into an area which you're interested in …, you can drive your own research agenda, what you want to do …, you've a lot of flexibility …. I'm going off tomorrow morning, I'm taking my daughter to the dentist, I don't have to ask anyone, I'm just going to do it' (senior lecturer, applied science, pre-1992 Russell Group university, interview 2). Nevertheless, there was also a sense that institutions were exerting increasing control over the time of individuals via mechanisms such as workload models that did not take account of extended academic activities such as pastoral care and the administration associated with research databases, and that this compounded 'hidden' time, for which no credit was given. Individual circumstances also meant that that time could disappear, and create strain, for example, if roles overlapped, as in the case of the following person, who had moved from a research fellow post to a lectureship at the same university in the two-year period between interviews: 'My main tension is my workload and it's really because I'm trying to do two jobs … I'm finishing off a backlog from a previous role and I'm sure that's not uncommon … [when] you've worked on something which is 80% done, you're not just going to stop … So, I've done it in the time that I can … the line manager of that project is kind of under the opinion that it's done when it's done and get on with it, but you know … I'm doing it my evenings and that's how it is' (lecturer, applied science, pre-1992 university, interview 2).
- *Future time* was seen in some cases as a reserve that could be drawn upon in order to explore options and alternatives that may help to overcome immediate setbacks. Thus, the following narrative reflects a willingness to overcome current blockages to a career by thinking forward with a view to testing alternative routes: 'My approach …. was … if it looks like this might be promising, let's have a go at that and …, see if we can then go further …, if that door closes …, we'll do it this way and … I had challenges in my immediate family …, but you can maybe find your way to … taking a

slightly longer route in. So, a lot of … furthering my own development has [been] to take a step forward and then maybe a bit of a gap, and then another …, it's not necessarily that you can even take the immediate opportunity in front of you … people are not necessarily equally placed at all to be able to take those routes, even when they [are presented] to them' (professor, social sciences, post-1992 university, interview 2). Such a juggling of time was therefore used to create opportunities and overcome present constraints. Thinking forward in this way helped in a psychological sense to overcome immediate constraints and perceived blocks to progress, albeit this was a retrospective account from someone who had achieved a chair. Such time calculations could also be influenced by the fact that, as noted by a number of respondents, in order to be promoted it was often the case that an individual had to demonstrate that they had already been working at a higher level, so in that sense it was a retrospective rather than an aspirational process: 'The academic promotion structure is very strange to a lot of people, because it's based on what you've done, not on what you're going to do in your new job' (professor, applied science, post-1992 university, interview 1). This could lead to a sense of trying to get ahead of oneself in terms of achievements over a certain timescale, in order to fulfil in advance the requirements for the next promotion.

The Impact of Time Adjustments on Careers

Therefore, if time was not available to gain the required markers of achievement within a designated period, this was likely to lead to adjustment of the timetable of a career, as exemplified by the following individual, who again focused on achieving credit in future time, rather than on current constraints and limitations. This person had made progress where they could, being proactive in seeking and accepting short-term deputizing roles to add to their portfolio of experience, with the ultimate goal of achieving a chair:

Pen Portrait 5

I think you've got to look forward, as well as looking back … I thought okay … I can't do a head of department role ,… I covered it for six months. I enjoyed it but they're not going to make me a head of department. If I want to do the sort of role that I can show leadership in, then the only ones left really are the kind of director of certain things … I had a period during which I was … subject leader. I also took 11 months off for parental leave, so you can imagine that having those sorts of things to juggle made it quite problematic or difficult at times to do research … I decided to focus primarily on publication during that time, rather than external grant income, because I didn't think I had time for both …, so again, it's hard to then see a route towards … promotion to professor, because I don't have a track record in big grant success …, so yeah, it's a longer road, I think, in trying to manage those things … So, for me, where there's something to do that might, in the longer term, lead to promotion, I'll do it, but I definitely haven't got time to do it with the same urgency as I might do if I didn't have … a family …, or a partner, or a life, or any kind of well-being at all … The admissions tutor that I did for five years, that was a thankless task to begin with, [although] you can make a difference and then after a while … they're just not very fun anymore and nobody cares … you just have to live [with] whichever path that you choose. I think, compared with two years ago, I feel more in charge of my path … I thought about where I would like to be and I've made this sort of … It's not really a plan, but a sort of acknowledgement that it's going to take me longer to get there. (Reader, creative arts, post-1992 university, interview 2)

On the one hand, this person had been opportunistic in accepting vacancies that had occurred for short-term and deputizing roles in order to gain credit for future promotion, but, on the other hand, acknowledged that because they had a limited publication and grant record, plus a young family, the route to professor would take longer than assumed in the formal institutional career pathway. Conversely, having seen that women with children who worked part-time tended not to be promoted, another interviewee had postponed having a family, in order to focus on developing their career at an earlier stage: 'Early on I thought, I need to get promoted before I have children, so I did lots and lots and lots … of uni[versity] things, research, that was probably when any publications I've got [were produced] …, and then … after I had [children] …, I came back part-time, and only worked three days [a week]' (senior lecturer, applied social sciences, post-1992 university, interview 1). These examples show the kind of disruptions to formal career timelines that characterize career-making, reflected in *Internal scripts*, as individuals focus on achieving what they can in the light of work contexts as well as personal drivers and commitments.

As a consequence of time adjustments, it was evident that people's careers differed not only in length but also in pace. Some individuals may enter higher education part way through their working lives. Others may move in and out. Some people make a positive decision to go for promotion early on, then focus on family life or a specific interest, or vice versa. Although everyone has the same amount of 'clock' time, the way they experience this is likely to differ, and the stages of an individual's career may be elongated or compressed in concertina-like fashion. This finding provides a further elaboration on perceptions of the acceleration of academic life and shortening of timescales (Gibbs et al. 2015; Henkel 2011; Locke 2017; Peters 2015; Vostal 2016) by focusing on ways in which individuals attempt to manage this in relation to the tempo of their careers. There was a sense of taking back control, for example, by segmenting a career, which could create disjuncture in relation to *Institutional scripts*. Although linear career models tend to assume that individuals will take action to meet certain milestones within certain timescales in order to progress, in practice they may also decide *not* to take action or to defer activity, for example, because of a specific interest or professional commitment, opportunities that arise at the wrong time or family circumstances. It was evident that individuals were effectively playing with time via the choices and micro-decisions displayed in their *Internal scripts*. Use of future time, particularly, created some elasticity in an approach to a career, beyond the confines of the *Institutional script*. The shape of a career may therefore stretch or compress over time, in the short and longer term, as individuals modulate *Institutional scripts* and extend the spaces and timescales available to them.

Conclusion

As shown in Chapter 4, individuals fashion *Internal*, subjective career scripts according to their own preferences, choices and opportunities, as well as being influenced by *Practice scripts* driven by professional commitments external to the university. This chapter shows how such scripts can lead to an extension of the spaces and timescales available to them. The stresses and strains arising from policy requirements at institutional and national levels, as well as the demands of personal and family commitments, were evident across the narratives. However, despite the sense of being overburdened by, for example, the volume of work in relation to teaching, the requirement to obtain funding and achieve impact in relation to research, and increased administrative burdens, the stretching of time and space represented a way of combating such immediate pressures. Implicit in this was the sense that the ability to adjust activity spaces and timescales gave individuals a feeling of discretion and indeed an element of control over the direction of their careers. At the very least, these processes enabled them to achieve a greater sense of equilibrium or balance, not only with respect to their work but also in their lives more generally. Taken collectively, the pressure exerted by individuals in the pursuit of *Practice* and *Internal scripts* contributes, in turn, to the development of the *informal economy* of institutions, as evidenced by, for example, more flexible working arrangements, increased recognition of extended academic activity, a stretching of criteria for promotion and the reshaping of careers across space and time.

The concept of the *concertina career* has been developed to illustrate how academic faculty, even when established in their careers, accommodate to local circumstances and develop workarounds by flexing the space and time available to them. Career-making, as experienced by the individual, is likely to be more dynamic and complex than suggested by fixed career models and linear career paths. The narratives demonstrate the way in which an individual may negotiate the terrain of a career in the light of opportunities that arise and their personal circumstances, reflecting their lived experience, which is likely to include stops and starts, in turn leading to both time compression and time extension over the individual life course. On the one hand, institutional (or system) career templates provide route maps, with promotion/progression criteria and timelines as place markers that assume a unitary direction and a uniform, or at least predictable, pace of travel. On the other hand, individual approaches to career-making are likely to involve an exploration, interpretation and stretching of spaces along the given route, as individuals not only interact with the structures they encounter but also discover and create new spaces that they may use for career credit. Timescales may also be adapted or extended in order to accommodate opportunities and personal circumstances. Moreover, this disruption of space and time has accelerated during the Covid-19 pandemic and is unlikely to decelerate post-pandemic (Aarnikoivu, Nokkala and Saarinen 2021). While acknowledging the strains of contemporary academic life, it was apparent that those who were aware of, and able to draw on, a broader hinterland of temporal and spatial perspectives appeared to be in a stronger position to cope with pressures and setbacks, and also to create building blocks that would further their careers. However, individuals were also aware that this could lead to dislocation between *Institutional*, *Internal* and *Practice scripts*, and Chapter 6 will show how individuals worked with the misalignments and disjunctures that could occur, drawing on *informal* as well as *formal economies*.

6

Negotiating Misalignments and Disjunctures

Introduction

As shown in Chapter 5, individual academic careers are likely to deviate from career paths defined in institutional templates, with fixed milestones, markers of achievement and timelines. This chapter considers the various disconnections and discontinuities that occur as individuals enact their given roles, ways in which they navigate these and, in this context, the influence of *Institutional*, *Practice* and *Internal scripts*. Despite attempts by university managers to expand the range of possibilities for career progression, for example, by broadening the range of pathways and promotion criteria to include a higher profile for teaching and associated academic activity, *Internal* and *Practice scripts* in the study pointed to misalignments between individuals' perceptions and aspirations, on the one hand, and formal expectations and requirements, on the other. In turn, this raised questions about the 'fit' of the individual in relation to, for example, disciplinary affiliation/departmental home, contractual arrangements and job profiles, progression pathways and promotion criteria, and workload models, all of which have the potential to be belied by day-to-day activity. The chapter goes on to demonstrate ways in which individuals navigate such misalignments and disjunctures in making their careers, drawing on *Internal* and *Practice scripts* as well as the advice and support of mentors and line managers. This process is framed theoretically by Engestrom's (2001) activity theory, showing how the three scripts relate to *formal* and *informal institutional economies*.

Types of Misalignment and Disjuncture

The following sections consider misalignments and disjunctures in relation to disciplinary affiliation, departmental location, contractual arrangements and job profiles, progression pathways and promotion criteria, and workload models.

Disciplinary Affiliation/Departmental Home

The diversification of the workforce in relation to, for example, an increasing range of practitioner and public service backgrounds, and mobility in and out of higher education with multiple entry and exit points, as well as a broadening of disciplinary applications, may mean that an individual's locale, for example, a department or faculty, does not clearly reflect their activities. This could have implications in relation to the colleagues they work with, the appropriateness of partners for research and teaching, and the availability of advice about career development. Thus, there were examples in the study of a linguist and a technologist working in creative arts, a historian in anthropology, a psychologist in engineering and a historian, a psychologist and an archaeologist in a law department. As a result, it could be difficult for individuals to find or fit into a departmental home: 'That kind of thing where, if you're changing your research direction, do you still fit a model that's very much built around straightforward disciplines and departments, making it much harder … with the one job I applied for in 2017, I would not have fitted in within [a mainstream humanities] department' (professor, humanities, pre-1992 Russell Group university, interview 2).

Although, as a result of diversification, academic faculty may have 'multiple identities' (head of educational development, pre-1992 Russell Group university, interview 1), that can be valuable in a team environment when collaboration is required, a 'merging of skills' (professor, applied science, pre-1992 Russell Group university, interview 2) could also lead to some people feeling displaced. The misalignment of disciplines could also be exacerbated by organizational restructuring, leading to alliances that did not seem to be the best fit for certain subjects, as in the following case of an applied science: 'There was institutional restructuring …, different skills were being merged in the institution, so we didn't end up being merged with anybody, … and there was some kind of question mark over what the future of [applied science] would be' (professor, applied science, pre-1992 Russell Group university, interview 2). This could put pressure on the direction of an individual's teaching or research and lead to individuals feeling that they were thrown back on their own resources in order to secure a position in the *formal institutional economy*, with associated *Institutional scripts*.

Contractual Arrangements and Job Profiles

Despite institutional efforts to formalize and document the requirements of individual roles, it was apparent that, although the standard teaching and research contract in the UK was likely to involve 40 per cent teaching, 40 per cent research and 20 per cent administration or knowledge exchange, a significant number of individuals were not aware of the precise balance of activity expected in their contract. Their understanding of this was likely to be modulated by discussions with their heads of department or colleagues in their department. In one case, two individuals in the same department gave different answers to a question about the proportions of time expected to be spent on teaching, research and administration. In other cases, job descriptions did not appear to reflect – or only to partially reflect – a role. Even those on 'standard' teaching and research contracts were not exempt from feeling a tension between the two activities, especially if they were running a module or programme and applying for research funding at the same time. As one individual said about a research grant they had applied for: 'I'll be so happy if I get it, [but] I'll be worried and stressed; if I don't get it, I'll be disappointed and relieved' (lecturer, social sciences, pre-1992 Russell Group university, interview 1). Workloads, and the balance between, in particular, teaching and research, represented an equation that individuals had to manage, often on an individual basis, and/or via negotiations with line managers about priorities at any point in time.

Furthermore, some individuals formally having teaching-only contracts found ways of undertaking research, and some having research-only contracts found ways of gaining experience in teaching, although this was not necessarily written into their job descriptions. Thus, one senior member of faculty recognized that someone on a teaching-only contract, particularly if early in their career, might wish to continue with disciplinary research, even if unfunded, for the sake of future opportunities:

> You might decide that you want to try and publish some of that research that you're doing anyway. I think people also see it as a way of keeping their options open, so they're on an education contract now but they might think that, well, if I don't keep my research ongoing, I'm going to be on an education contract forever. What if I wanted to move to another institution that might give me an education and research contract ..., I need to have kept my research going. Maybe [home institution] might even change my contract, if they can see that I can be a productive researcher and teach ... [but] I think people would prefer

to publish research, rather than publish this stuff about teaching. (Professor, applied science, pre-1992 Russell Group university, interview 2)

This also illustrates how there is a range of considerations for individuals in enacting their given role and in deciding the type of research that they might undertake, particularly between disciplinary research and pedagogic research/scholarship of teaching and learning (SoTL). Although enshrined formally in a fixed job description, a role, or the series of roles that make up a career, represent a dynamic process that can lead to some abrasion in relation to formal institutional expectations and requirements.

Others complained of a disconnect between different aspects of their roles. For example, one individual, who was employed as a lecturer, had responsibility for monitoring the progress of underserved student populations, and of designing appropriate interventions for those at risk of under-achieving. They described tensions arising because they had, by default, become involved in what was effectively a project management role. They also felt that, although synergy between the project and their teaching and research was likely to enhance the success of what was a flagship project, this work was invisible and therefore not recognized. It was, effectively,

> invisible legwork, you know, the kind of stuff where you're trying to cajole people into putting something on an agenda or you're trying to organise something … the … project is actually huge and is part of a university-wide project, so you have a lot of obligations to the central university and those are just never ending … and constant deadlines for things that are just not really achievable … It's not just about … legwork to convince people to run an intervention … It's also how to find information out that you need in order to do certain things … And that part of it could involve … several days of emailing round, waiting for someone to send something back to you, then it being in the wrong format. Really, it needs … it's always needed a project manager … but we don't have one …, for numerous reasons, we just have me and I'm actually a … lecturer, not a project manager. (Lecturer, social sciences, pre-1992 university, interview 2)

This situation led to feelings of dislocation, not only in relation to time management and the split of responsibilities between different line managers but also vis-a-vis criteria for progression, and credit for what was seen as 'boundary' work between the two sets of responsibilities.

There were also cases where those with academic qualifications, plus teaching and research experience, were, or had been, employed on professional contracts. Such individuals were likely to perform teaching- or research-orientated roles, for example, supporting student learning and applications for research funding, programme development, employability and outreach activity. Higher Education Statistics Agency (HESA) data suggests that the 2014 UK Research Excellence Framework (REF) exercise influenced this trend, in that some individuals who were deemed not 'research active' had been employed on professional contracts, so that they would not 'count' in the census and 'dilute' REF scores. This made gaining credit for research difficult, with consequences for the planning of a future career, as illustrated in the following Pen Portrait of someone who was appointed as a programme leader in the humanities, on a professional contract at senior lecturer level, and who was unable to make the *Institutional script* work effectively for them in relation to promotion:

Pen Portrait 6

> I think I probably am on the radar generally as somebody that the institution is not quite sure what to do with me … contractually …, so I think individuals are all very willing and supportive but the structures … the question nobody can seem to answer is what threshold of research I need to be able to show to move onto an academic contract, because when I first started asking, the dean was saying, oh, you know, it's not really about trying to prove yourself on the research side, you need to show your education, your leadership and that you're doing some research and …, you'll basically have a different profile …, but nobody's been able to say … what the threshold is to … qualify to move over and the latest I've heard is, oh well, we'd need world leading researchers on our academic contract … so at the moment, to be honest, I feel stuck in a bit of a Catch 22, that I can't do the research because there's just not the time, but I can't move over without that … I'm getting the message that the things that I do and that I'm being asked to do are then not being necessarily recognised or rewarded as valuable, even though it says in the [university] strategy …, there's that mismatch …, we don't fit into some of the more hidebound … structures of some departments … as soon as REF [Research Excellence Framework] comes back onto the radar, people need to be committing to things, their mind is on …, especially people who've got work to do …, need to be making sure they're in the position they need to be in for REF, so personally, if I wanted to be returned [in the Research Excellence Framework], I'd have to have some leave to get the book done in time to make the contract deadline. What I'm being told I need to do to progress, I'm just not in a position to do … I don't think there's a clear pathway and I don't think it's facilitated by the structures

that exist at the moment, so ideally, I'd like to be on the kind of contract where I have got time to develop a more balanced profile, so at the moment, I've got this asymmetric profile with, I'm doing actually lots of stuff that's probably higher than senior lecturer on the leadership and the education side but, as I say, the research is not considered to be commensurate with the [senior lecturer] profile ... I don't want to become the leading researcher in my field, that's not what drives me, but I do want personally to have made that progress ... so whether it's a programme director role or vice-dean role or something like that, I think that would be what I see myself doing in the next five or ten years ... Everybody who finds out about my contract is surprised, everyone expects me to be on an academic contract, people see me as an academic..., so it's something that people want to sort of help sort out, but we never get any further forwards because the institution doesn't know, I think, on a fundamental level, what to do with me ... I do trust the people involved to try and make things work, it's just I don't know if the structures are there to really help them figure it out. (Senior lecturer, humanities, pre-1992 Russell Group university, interview 1)

This illustrates how a mismatch between contractual arrangements, enshrined in an *Institutional script*, and the aspirations of the individual, evident in their *Internal script*, had become a stumbling block, despite a willingness of local managers to help in progressing matters, because underlying structures were not flexible enough to accommodate bespoke solutions.

Conversely, at more senior levels, it was pointed out that those promoted to management positions such as head of department may not have the necessary operational experience to undertake such roles, including managing people:

No industry outside academia puts people into management positions who don't have the skills to do that role and are dedicated to that role ... academic leaders have ... a world of experience in the research side of things, about what's expected for papers and REF [Research Excellence Framework] and how they manage REF and ... run conferences; they don't have any experience outside that for the operational side of the school. (Senior lecturer, applied science, pre-1992 Russell Group university, interview 2)

Thus, even if an individual gained such an appointment for credit, they might in practice be 'programmed to fail', or at least struggle, without the requisite training, experience and/or leadership skills. Therefore, the reality of these roles could be very different from what appeared on a job description. At the same time, there was often resistance to employing professional staff to support management roles by undertaking operational activity such as completing research databases, as such posts could be seen as taking resources away from funding to support the appointment of academic faculty.

Progression Pathways and Promotion Criteria

Although institutions had in many cases introduced an increased range of promotion criteria, most notably to include a teaching track leading to professor, innovation and leadership in teaching was not necessarily seen by individuals as being recognized in practice: 'The career path to a chair is extremely difficult …, there's a very small number of people who have progressed to a chair in education on the education route … It's not very well defined but it's also, it's very difficult …, if you're completely overloaded with routine, mundane tasks, you don't have time to build a research profile' (senior lecturer, science, pre-1992 Russell Group university, interview 1). Furthermore, promotion for those on teaching-only contracts often required evidence of pedagogical research. Several non-social scientists commented that they did not have expertise in the appropriate social science research methods (or interest) to pursue this route: 'It's very hard for [promotion committees] to know what criteria to use, so they often think you should do some pedagogy on teaching …, I'm not a social scientist, so why would I do that?' (senior lecturer, science, pre-1992 university, interview 2); and 'my biggest contention there is that I have a PhD in [application of technology], not a PhD in pedagogical science or education, so [although] I am interested in pedagogy, my training and my background and my research expertise and my knowledge of methodologies is not in social sciences, [or] pedagogical, educational research, it just isn't' (senior lecturer, creative arts, pre-1992 Russell Group university, interview 2).

Another individual tried to hedge their bets by progressing their work in their discipline, and also on the education side, but ended up without sufficient evidence to meet the promotion criteria in relation to either route, demonstrating the difficulty of matching institutional policy with the reality of preparing the next step in a career:

> A message went out that people are going to be evaluated holistically, so I've probably got as many education publications as I have disciplinary publications. I've … a significant amount of [research] money on both sides, so I don't necessarily reach the benchmark for either [set of] criteria, but I think, taken

collectively, it's reasonably successful. Just based on some of the other promotions that have happened, I was reasonably confident I would get it. [but] I didn't get it ... I think it was the lack of publications, but I would argue ..., I've generated significant other outputs and impacts, which ... were not taken into account ..., the number of chairs on the education track is absolutely dwarfed by the number handed out for disciplinary research'. (Senior lecturer, science, pre-1992 Russell Group university, interview 2)

Their failure to achieve promotion by spreading their efforts across disciplines was, in the view of this individual, further exacerbated by a lack of congruence between the perceived value of different types of output in *Institutional scripts*. This person therefore perceived themselves to be doubly disadvantaged by a misalignment between *Institutional scripts* and the reality of career-making across two fields of activity, demonstrating inflexibility in the implementation capability of promotion criteria to cases that did not precisely fit the template.

This experience was echoed in broad-brush terms elsewhere thus: 'There [are] definitely potential conflicts between the way in which the promotional system is seen to work on paper, and then how it seems to pan out within the process itself' (reader, creative arts, post-1992 university, interview 1). The following Pen Portrait corroborates these experiences, showing how another individual had tried to progress within the *formal economy* by undertaking pedagogical research, but had 'given up' because the resources were not available in practice to enable them to do this, and thereby meet the precise terms of institutional criteria for promotion. The complexity of the *Institutional script*, including a very tight definition of the term 'scholarship', meant that the provision of such resources was at the discretion of a number of gatekeepers. Achieving agreement to any variation meant going through several layers of bureaucracy, which took time and effort, particularly if the gatekeepers were not known personally to the individual.

Pen Portrait 7

Impact, going to conferences, publishing articles ... research is an external facing activity, teaching is an inward facing activity, so there's a bit of a paradox there. I think, to be fair to [university], they're trying to make it possible to be promoted to professor on a teaching track ... so those are the promotion criteria, so obviously you have to do excellent teaching, you might have a

Fellowship of the Higher Education Academy ... you might get invited to do, you know, be an external examiner, maybe do something a bit more on that ..., a bit more like a departmental review at another institution or something like that that's sort of teaching focused, but then there's this thing about ... writing scholarly publications and getting them published in journals ... In January, the pro-vice-chancellor of research at the time just drew the line and said no, if you're T[eaching] and S[cholarship], you're not allowed to be on any external funding application to do research, and went further than that, there was a list of ..., three bullet point things, it was, like, an understanding that ..., T[eaching] and S[cholarship] staff get scholarship time, so 15% of my contract is scholarship time, so this memo came round, it said, these are the things you should be doing with your scholarship time and it was, keeping up with your research area so that you can do research-informed teaching and writing scholarly publications ..., but you're not allowed to do 'research' research ..., so ..., I wouldn't be allowed to apply for external funding to do a research project, like a pedagogical research project ... Because it would say, you're T[eaching] and S[cholarship] staff, you're not allowed to do this, you have to have special permission from the pro-vice-chancellor for research and you have to have ..., head of department permission and they have to say that it aligns with their strategic departmental objectives, and then the pro-vice-chancellor for research [gives] special permission, so it's like, basically, don't even think about it ... 15% of my time is my scholarship time, [but] I'm not allowed to have a post-doc, I couldn't have somebody working with me ..., [so] how am I suddenly going to magic up publications that get published? ... I think I've given up. (Senior lecturer, creative arts, pre-1992 Russell Group university, interview 2)

Thus, despite the fact that across the eight case study institutions promotion criteria and career pathways were being broadened in *Institutional scripts* to include, for example, activity associated with learning support, scholarship, leadership and management, professional practice, community engagement, academic citizenship, knowledge exchange and contributions to diversity and inclusion, there were multiple examples of individuals being skeptical about the effectiveness of how such policies worked in practice, and believing that disciplinary (as opposed to pedagogical) research, and its impact, carried more weight than anything else. This suggests that efforts by institutions to adapt their policies to changes in workforce profiles were not yet mature enough to become embedded in practice, or at least in the consciousness of academic faculty and decision makers. Although the examples above reflect the specific circumstances of individuals, who may have been unfortunate in not having senior colleagues who could facilitate their progress, there was a general feeling that *Institutional scripts* tended not to be able to accommodate special cases and were not sufficiently open to interpretation.

Workload Models

The increased range of activity in higher education, and the fluidity experienced around the possibilities of a career, also led to a number of individuals saying that they felt disconnected from received organizational understandings in relation to work allocation models. In particular, those involved in innovative work could feel constrained because it was not yet fully recognized or integrated into organizational processes and systems, with career pathways significantly underdeveloped. Those involved in online teaching, for example, tended to experience disjuncture in relation to the form and content of employment models and the norms associated with them. Thus, 'I'm not part of any work allocation management … because it's set up with a standard model of … you deliver two lectures a week, you deliver three seminars a week, and I don't do that, I monitor online forums, I record lectures in advance … massively front loaded' (lecturer, social sciences, pre-1992 university, interview 1). The same individual pointed out that a lack of fit into a standard workload model could also lead to issues about being able to achieve visibility and therefore recognition: 'I never really had the opportunity to be a normal academic … a one-size-fits-all academic is sort of falling apart … I was really worried … that because of me being segregated doing this job [running a distance learning programme] … that the department … wouldn't know what I could offer' (lecturer, social sciences, pre-1992 university, interview 1). Similar issues arose for people when they were teaching on different sites, particularly in professional practice disciplines. An example that was given was the use of a more clinical style in relation to evidence-based practice on one campus, in comparison to another that was more theoretically based. There appeared, therefore, to be significant scope for workload models to be misaligned with the requirements of *Practice scripts*, especially when trying to achieve common currency between, for example, teaching in a classroom setting and teaching in a practice setting, which could be more intensive in terms of the one-to-one attention required by students learning hands-on skills. Thus, although workload models were designed to achieve equity, they could have the reverse effect, disadvantaging those whose work was not seen to fall inside them or to be within standard parameters.

Distortions could also occur in relation to day-to-day workloads as a result of practical considerations, such as pressure points during any given term or year, and/or dealing with discontinuities and breakdowns, particularly with regard to technology. Thus, in relation to research endeavour,

> If you looked at mine [work allocation model] over the last year, I'd probably say that's probably about rightish, but …, when you zoom in on any given week or month, it could be pretty out … the majority of the time it'll be things which are outside of [one's control], you know, resubmitting a paper, data delays, your computer breaks, there's all sorts of things where people just have these delays …, coding error, which means that you have to redo an analysis, that's very common, things like that. (Research fellow, social sciences, pre-1992 Russell Group university, interview 2)

Similarly, on the teaching side, popular courses, resulting in a bulge in student numbers, created additional pressure on those teachers who were most successful in attracting students:

> There are structural issues that are probably quite difficult to address in terms of … we count our teaching by the hour, so we're supposed to do eight hours, but of course, if you have 75 students and someone else has eight, there's obviously a massive discrepancy in the amount of marking you have to do, [and the] level of supervision. (Reader, humanities, pre-1992 university, interview 2)

Both these examples point to hidden components of activity that are not necessarily accounted for in standard workload models.

The lack of fit between the *formal economy* of rubrics, criteria and metrics, and day-to-day practice, was summed up by another individual as follows: 'I guess it's always the problem of having any sort of metric around something … it doesn't really capture the reality' (lecturer, social sciences, pre-1992 Russell Group university, interview 2). In turn, these types of concerns had contributed to an element of cynicism about workload models as being a blunt instrument that did not reflect reality: 'You don't really get to see anybody else's workload model and also there's this massaging of the figures, where things are dialled up or dialled down, just to make it all fit, so for me, it's a tick in the box, that we have it and we do it' (university teaching fellow, science, post-1992 university, interview 2). Thus, individuals ultimately bring their own perspective to the structures that they find themselves in, and although they may not be able to change them, they can endeavour to interpret them in ways that make them a more comfortable fit. In the case of workload models, this is likely to involve collaboration with a line manager in signing off individual work schedules. Without this interpretive element, workload models were seen as an imprecise and divisive tools.

Negotiating Misalignments and Disjunctures

Individuals were, therefore, obliged to negotiate misalignments and disjunctures, such as those outlined above, making decisions around their academic interests, career aspirations and other commitments on the basis of local situations. This was achieved by various means, the most common being the support of local managers and mentors in helping individuals to align their profiles and skill sets with formal requirements, by massaging, translating and legitimizing what might be bespoke activity, so as to achieve a fit with *Institutional scripts*. Thus,

> I think without him [head of department], I would have looked at the promotions criteria, even to senior lecturer and just gone, haven't got all of those, only got half of those, no way, whereas with somebody experienced like that, he could sit down and say, well, I think you are doing these things, aren't you and then explore it a little bit. (Senior lecturer, creative arts, pre-1992 Russell Group university, interview 2)

The interpretation of formal requirements in relation to the individual therefore appeared to be a vital process, at least from the individual's point of view. In some cases, such a discussion was built into professional development plans and processes. Thus:

> [the approach is] we'd expect you to be in this position, therefore, you know, we'll help you try to do that …, I think it's more …, I'm the one driving the car but they have the satnav, you know, I kind of roughly have an idea of where I'm going and I'm able to drive things forward, but I need a bit of kind of general overview about where I should be going and that's what I'd say the support here is really. (Research fellow, social sciences, pre-1992 university, interview 2)

The lack of such supportive relationships was seen as a significant disadvantage, particularly for individuals who, for whatever reason, did not have contacts who could facilitate their progress: 'I think it's not that easy, I think I'm just lucky or happen to have found out how to sort of be in the same room as these people, rather than there being … an obvious forum to speak to these people' (teaching fellow, science, pre-1992 Russell Group university, interview 1). This highlights the value of being proactive in fostering relationships with those who could influence one's career, although some individuals were more adept at, or in a better position for, doing this than others.

As part of this process, and in the light of experience, senior members of faculty tended to be more positive about the possibility of expanding activity beyond the purely disciplinary so as to create a wider range of applications and options, and thereby opportunities, inside or outside the university. Thus, in relation to promotion criteria, one senior manager took the view that emerging environments could provide opportunities, even if dislocation was experienced initially: 'We're introducing a new virtual learning environment here …, so here's something you could be leading out on instead [of mainstream disciplinary teaching or research], and that's the sort of thing …, that could actually lead to promotion' (professor, applied science, pre-1992 Russell Group university, interview 2). The same person had, on another occasion, made the case for an individual to be promoted on the basis of work that they had undertaken on internationalization, highlighting the value of being able to transfer and apply generic skills: 'I put a case through for them … saying that they had done a lot of work around internationalization and they'd increased their profile institutionally on that, so people sitting around the promotions table knew who they were and what they'd done, and it was successful' (professor, applied science, pre-1992 Russell Group university, interview 2). This also illustrates how individual cases can be furthered by one-to-one relationships with those who have a voice on decision-making bodies, thus harnessing the influence of the *informal* on the *formal economy*.

Advice and support, particularly from peers and mentors, could also be external to the discipline or institution, highlighting the value of networking on a more extended basis: 'I think I did very well in my interview as a result of talking to somebody from a completely different field … he basically drilled me for my interview … And I think I got to a place where I had a prepared answer to every question I could have expected' (lecturer, science, pre-1992 university, interview 2). Another individual who was waiting for the result of their application for a chair (which was subsequently successful), saw the momentum of their career as being stimulated from contacts and activity outside their institution: 'I received an enormous amount of help from outside my institution … from colleagues in other institutions …, often times your support can come from externally, as opposed to internally …, that's fine, as long as there's support somewhere' (reader, humanities, pre-1992 university, interview 2).

Although it was clear that misalignments between *formal* and *informal economies* could lead to setbacks and disappointments for some individuals, it was also evident that people adopted different approaches to dealing with disruptions to their plans or expectations. Some individuals took a pragmatic stance, accommodating new developments and requirements into a strategy for making their career, driven by both *Internal* and *Practice scripts*:

> I think what I've had to become is a chameleon …, I've had to blend in, fit into that environment as things change, as decisions are made, as the university environment changes … I've seen colleagues that don't change that I think now have a much harder time … I've done well I think because I have been very flexible and adaptable to the challenges that are put in front of me and receptive to them …, some things are very irritating …, but I think it's really important to know what things are worth pushing against and what things aren't … I think if you spend your whole career moaning about it … it's not constructive, so I try to maintain a positive philosophy and I think that has helped. (Lecturer, pre-1992 university, clinical science, interview 2)

This person, for example, was able to find satisfaction and fulfilment in the clinical application of their work, and this enabled them to deal with less rewarding aspects. Again, it was evident that the process of career-making involved micro-decisions about where pushback against local conditions might be possible and where adaptation might be appropriate. There was a sense of individuals weighing up what were the situations that they could do something about and, conversely, those that they would have to accept, at least for the time being, in the light of possibilities that were available across the *formal* and *informal economies* of their institution (although they would not articulate the options available to them using these terms).

However, being pragmatic could also include being open to serendipitous opportunities and collaborations, as in the case of the following person, who had primarily adopted an *Institutional script* in order to achieve a chair. However, their *Internal script* revealed that their approach had also included pursuing opportunities that arose via informal contacts, rather than necessarily following to the letter the requirements of a career pathway:

> The way I ended up becoming co-director of this … study centre is … somebody asked me to be involved in a grant [application], then somebody else got involved on that grant, three of us were pulled together and we decided to apply for funding to set this centre up. So …, my career has taken turns that I could not have predicted because of these opportunities … I haven't mapped out my career as much as other people might have done maybe … sometimes interesting opportunities that can arise … you can't predict …, whether it might

be just a one-off thing and you're just having a good time on that one-off thing, or it might actually lead to something bigger. (Professor, humanities, pre-1992 Russell Group university, interview 2)

This suggests that if a series of activities gain momentum and thereby develop synergy with other activities, whether or not they appear to 'count' precisely against promotion criteria, they can nevertheless have an influence on progress, particularly if they can be interpreted as showing innovation and leadership.

The narrative in the following Pen Portrait illustrates how an individual negotiated misalignments and disjunctures on an ongoing basis, demonstrating the ebb and flow of considerations of progressing a career at the same time as achieving an acceptable work-life balance. It also reflects a narrative of restriction around the value accorded to online learning and associated revenue streams at the same time as one of adaptation and possible recovery. This person had moved from a teaching and research role at an overseas university and had effectively 'rebooted' their career in the UK, with associated discontinuities. Despite careful choices being made to optimize progression opportunities, the strains of achieving the steps required for a linear career within the *formal economy* could be detected. During interview 1, their frustration leads to a sense that it might be better to move to a more teaching-orientated institution in order to gain promotion and/or make a sideways move to a less pressurized, more family-friendly environment so as to achieve a better work-life balance. By interview 2, they had been invited to undertake a central university role in online education and were also in the process of applying for chairs and senior management positions in other universities. In a sense, they were hedging their bets, and although they appeared to be on the cusp of progressing, they were also sanguine about what might and might not be possible. While they showed a strong awareness of *Institutional scripts* vis-a-vis promotion opportunities, their narrative also demonstrated the ebb and flow of personal and practical considerations, which provided an undercurrent. This narrative also illustrates an interweaving of considerations arising from *formal* and *informal economies*.

Pen Portrait 8

For a variety of reasons, I decided to migrate to [UK city] so gave up my position at [overseas university] …, did a one year senior research fellowship … And then was offered the senior lectureship… to head up a master's programme in [applied science] ... I've moved out of primary research and more into ... pedagogic research and education ... I was appointed as a standard research and education academic [but] ... the educational activities were successful and ... my career suffered because of it ... I wasn't pulling in the large grants ... I personally supervised fifteen MSc students' dissertations and provided thirty lectures, as well as running the distance education course, as well as redesigning the curriculum ... I put a lot of effort into ... education, such that I was barely able to spend one day a week on research, couldn't get the momentum going, but also suffered by being a single researcher ... Getting appointed to professor, I think, is going to be incredibly challenging, because the criteria is almost impossible to meet, even though the amount of revenue I've brought in, the status that I've brought in, that in a lesser university I would be a professor already. The responsibilities I have are professorial, but the promotion criteria ... [my role is] being an innovator and seen as an innovator, which is also a strength and a weakness ... basically since joining [university] ..., I've never felt secure in my job ... I'm aware that I'm not producing high impact research ..., I'm worried career-wise because I have a status, I think, in online education ..., but there are not too many jobs in being an online [expert] ..., I'm not interested in the technology, I'm interested in teaching and learning online, so I do worry about where the exit plan is ... I've brought in a lot of money for [institution], but still spend most nights tossing and turning, worrying about job security, frustrated that I haven't made it to a chair yet and can't see how I can in [institution] ... It's never clear to me who will fund us ... a teaching university I think [is] better placed to support those who teach ... there are times, especially because I've got a [child], that if I could get a nice position that I'm in now, at a lovely little university close to the sea, we'd be very happy (interview 1).

I've just applied for a Chair ... and we now have an education academic pathway which I've switched over to .., that in itself is a bit of a risk, I think, because it's a reasonably new initiative at [university] to have an academic pathway that's education focused, we'll see what happens in terms of future employability ... for the last 12 months, I've been the academic lead for digital education for [university] ... working directly for the deputy vice-chancellor. My task ... has been to develop a new digital education vision for [university], and that was endorsed by senior management ... and we're now into the implementation phase ... I feel like I've been working at a professorial level for a while and I would just like to feel like that's been acknowledged ... this interview's at an interesting time existentially – do I want to stay here and try and cement myself as the academic lead to the extent where [university] might consider making that a pro-vice-chancellor ... [or] do I take a director of distance learning role at [another] university, which is [a] professional services [role], and therefore not have to worry about grants ..., or do I go ... a different [route] ... I have been head hunted twice by private industry and both times I've pulled back at the last minute and I reflect on that a lot, and is it because I'm comfortable in the safety of academia, because this is all I've known really since graduating, or is it just because you reach the age that I'm at, I'm just over 50 ... The next move should be the last. (Reader, applied science, pre-1992 Russell Group university, interview 2)

This individual's *Internal script* had led them to relinquish disciplinary research in favour of pedagogical research into online learning. However, despite the fact that they felt that they were working at professorial level, their work did not align precisely with the *Institutional script*, and they were effectively departing from this script. They were therefore reshaping their career trajectory and potential pathway for the future, by considering, and in some cases rejecting, possible options, at the same time acknowledging that there were risks attached to this. Their work with commercial partners, reflected in a *Practice script*, had led to options to leave, which they had ultimately rejected on the basis that factors in their *Internal script*, such as security and work-life balance, were stronger. The *Internal script* shows how a career may be the result of multiple micro-decisions and influences, including balancing ambition with the need for an element of security, a sense of being valued (or not), concerns about work-life balance, and caring responsibilities. Even though this person had a readership and a senior role in a pre-1992 Russell Group institution, in an area that was likely to develop further (programmes were being run for overseas clients in an expanding field), they admitted to feeling insecure at times, and were therefore alert to possible alternatives which they monitored on an ongoing basis.

Framing Misalignments and Disjunctures in Activity Theory

Activity theory (Engestrom 2001) provides a frame for the relationship between *formal* and *informal institutional economies*, the associated *Institutional, Practice* and *Internal scripts*, and ways in which these interact to help individuals cope with the misalignments and disjunctures that they encounter. Within Engestrom's 'boundary zone', formal and informal systems come together to modify, and at times repurpose, activities and relationships, thereby allowing bespoke solutions

Table 6.1 Examples of Activity System Components in *Formal* and *Informal Institutional Economies*

Activity system component	*Formal economy*, expressed in *Institutional scripts* and *Practice scripts*, the latter via contractual arrangements with service providers such as the NHS	*Informal economy*, expressed in *Internal scripts* and *Practice scripts*, the latter via the professional commitments and relationships of individuals
Subject	Contracted employees Career structures Departments Disciplines Work allocation models Disciplinary and professional bodies Contractual arrangements with service (e.g. health care) providers	Academic faculty with individual aspirations, interests and strengths Colleague relationships, internal and external Professional and practice networks, internal and external Mentors and advisers
Object[ive]/outcome	Teaching programme delivery The student experience Research grant capture Research project delivery/outcomes Publications and dissemination Teaching in practice settings for university qualifications	Professional and social capital Collaborative working between faculty, between faculty and professional staff, and between faculty and external practitioners Exchange/development of innovative ideas
Mediating artefacts/tools and signs	Teaching or research project proposals Knowledge exchange protocols Written plans/critical paths Contracts with, for example, healthcare providers Conferences/seminars	Shared understanding via informal contacts between participants (faculty, external practitioners/partners), for example, coffee, lunch and sport Corridor meetings Social media
Rules	Employment contracts Promotion criteria Programme objectives Assessment rubrics Research contracts Service agreements with, for example, healthcare providers	Working relationships in practice Informal advice/mentoring Informal/bespoke arrangements Knowing 'what works' in specific contexts including practitioner settings
Community	Senior management team Research and teaching teams Academic departments Heads of department/line managers Joint working groups with service providers	Local colleagues, internal and external Mentors Extended and online networks One-to-one, bespoke advice

Table 6.1 (continued)

Division of labour	Disciplinary contributions in teaching and research Professional and institutional activity External practitioner contribution to teaching and research	Bottom-up combinations of disciplinary, professional and practitioner expertise Innovative local contributions Bespoke solutions

to be developed to meet individual needs. In some cases, informal solutions are reinterpreted and inserted into the formal system, although this is likely to be subject to negotiation. This is illustrated in Table 6.1.

The interaction between *formal* and *informal economies* provides a dynamic that can be useful to the individual in interpreting formal requirements and realizing *Internal* and *Practice scripts*, whether these be in relation to career progression, professional practice, personal satisfaction or work-life balance. The frame of activity theory illustrates ways in which individuals negotiate misalignments and disjunctures by establishing their own positioning amid a range of variables in the *formal* and *informal economies*. The interview narratives suggest that over time, by taking cognisance of the barriers and facilitators that they encounter, individuals construct their roles in the light of their personal aspirations, strengths, professional practice commitments and personal circumstances, demonstrating that 'multi-voicedness ... in networks of interacting activity systems ... is a source of trouble and a source of innovation, demanding actions of translation and negotiation' (Engstrom 2001:136). In this context, the diversification of the workforce and disciplines, and the extended academic activity associated with these, can be seen as providing 'multi-voicedness', and misalignments and disjunctures as limiting or liberating factors, depending on how they are perceived and managed by the individual.

Conclusion

This chapter demonstrates how, in dealing with misalignments and disjunctures arising from the *formal economy* of an institution, for example, disciplinary affiliations, job profiles, progression criteria and workload models, individuals are likely to draw on the *informal economy* as a way of shaping their career, at the same time as accommodating their activities within the formal parameters from which they might expect to accrue credit. They do this by drawing on their own *Internal* and *Practice scripts* to modulate requirements laid down in *Institutional scripts*. They are likely to call on line managers, mentors and colleagues in reinterpreting and repurposing activity, thereby moderating the components of established career pathways. The narratives also suggested that those who place total reliance on, and faith in, structural frameworks such as promotion criteria and career pathways may find it more difficult to accommodate misalignments and discontinuities that occur. By contrast, those who have confidence in *Internal* and *Practice scripts* may be more likely to find ways of accommodating to the spaces that they find themselves in, to adjust associated timescales, and to interpret structural requirements creatively.

Enablers such as mentors and professional networks can provide support in developing and promoting leading-edge and innovative work and, in particular, work that addresses emergent agendas, enabling this to be cashed for career credit as well as adding value to individual institutions. It was apparent that the more senior and experienced interviewees appreciated this process, enabling the expansion of the range of activity, at times via the *informal economy*, that can be seen to 'count' for the purposes of career progression. This suggests that it is important for individuals to receive advice and therefore gain confidence early in their careers that they might progress in this way, by seeking to push the boundaries of *Institutional scripts* in order to accommodate individual strengths and predilections. However, although it was evident that many middle managers, such as heads of department, listened to faculty for whom they were responsible, and understood the latter's articulation of individual strengths, needs and aspirations, there appeared to be a gap, or at least a time lag, between local understandings and formal recognition in reward and professional development policies. This is likely to become particularly pressing post-Covid-19, for example, in relation to extended activity arising from the shift to online learning, epitomized in Pen Portrait 8, whereby individuals had been appointed in order to develop such programmes but then found that they were not seen as a good fit with institutional career structures, promotion criteria, departmental profiles or administrative systems. Closing these types of gaps should be a priority, as outlined in Chapter 8. Furthermore, the narratives suggest that if innovative and pathfinding work is not recognized or integrated into reward systems, faith in formal institutional economies is likely to decline. The impact of such 'hidden' activities and processes, and their relevance in a broader international context, are explored further in Chapters 7 and 8, extending the themes developed in Chapters 4, 5 and 6 in relation to *Institutional, Practice* and *Internal scripts*, issues of space and time, the *concertina career* and ways in which individuals manage misalignments and disjunctures by using both *formal* and *informal economies*.

7

Whither the Academic Profession?

Introduction

Earlier chapters have demonstrated the dynamic that arises from the interaction between *Institutional*, *Practice* and *Internal scripts* in relation to individual approaches to roles and careers. They have shown how academic faculty navigate formal institutional frameworks such as career pathways and promotion criteria, taking account of personal predilections and circumstances, underpinned by individual commitments, strengths and practitioner allegiances. Individuals are likely to conduct a cost-benefit analysis in relation to the investment that they make in activities that are likely to meet the requirements of *Institutional scripts*, and those that are influenced by *Practice* and *Internal scripts*. This chapter considers these factors in relation to the profession as a whole and demonstrates how they have put pressure on the concept of a unified academic profession, identifying a collective momentum towards more open-ended approaches to roles and careers. It suggests that shifts in the relationship of individuals to disciplines, cross-disciplinary activity and professional practice, in the light of personal commitments and considerations, have influenced this trend. It goes on to offer some indicators for the future vis-a-vis a more holistic view of being an academic and possible directions of travel for a more loosely connected academic profession.

Disciplinary Stretch and an Expanding Hinterland

Although disciplines have traditionally been regarded as the core of academic identity, in terms of day-to-day working and the development of careers, they have, as shown in earlier chapters, been overlaid by approaches described as *Mainstream*, *Portfolio* and *Niche*, guided by *Institutional*, *Practice* and *Internal* scripts. The influence of practice subjects in higher education in the past twenty-five years or so, and activity around, for example, the student experience, equity and inclusion, public engagement and knowledge exchange, have therefore overlaid the disciplinary core. This has in turn created disciplinary stretch, reflecting the fact that policy developments, at government and institutional levels, have been internalized by individuals in terms of making a difference both to their students and to wider society, and that this in turn could benefit a career: 'I think people recognise what I do has direct translation, that it has impact, that it has a healthcare implementation and … it recognises the values that the university puts forward in terms of impacting locally and nationally and internationally, you know, with an end user in sight' (lecturer, clinical science, pre-1992 university, interview 2). Although there were obvious applications in health and social care, even those individuals who wanted to advance in what might be regarded as relatively boundaried disciplines, with less obvious practical applications, were encouraged to think about how they could scale up their activity in ways that were relevant to real world purposes. This was described by the following senior faculty member in relation to an early career researcher:

> One of my recently started colleagues [in the humanities] has a fascinating project about the UK digital economy, really, really interesting …, but [they] still operate[s] on a single scholar model, so you know, [their] project addresses quite important questions, but [they] can't conceive of it that …, [they] could speak to policy makers and to creative economy people …, that's the way things are at the moment … We recently had one of these UKRI [UK Research and Innovation] Fellows … [their] project is so interdisciplinary and it's addressing the big issues and [they've] got two research assistants …, but that big scale thinking, that ambitious thinking is not common to …, people who've been trained in a history PhD programme. (Professor, humanities, pre-1992 Russell Group university, interview 2)

This demonstrates a shift from in-depth specialization in relation to a specific area of interest, to the broader expansion and application of that knowledge, and illustrates how, even in the humanities, disciplinary spread is becoming influenced by societal needs.

By contrast, the following two examples of disciplinary extension demonstrate initiatives arising from individuals' own interests, but nevertheless influence university policy, and, in the second case, disciplinary practice. One individual, a scientist employed on a teaching and scholarship contract, had developed meditation programmes for students. They went so far as to say that this work had 'changed my world', by expanding their disciplinary worldview: 'If you can bring down people's stress levels they can do better in exams and coursework, and that's what I'm trying to do … so I will keep trying to balance those two aspects of teaching of [science and meditation] and not let one overtake the other too much' (senior lecturer, science, pre-1992 university, interview 2). Although this activity was not in their job description, and was undertaken outside a work allocation model, they had obtained a senior lectureship on the basis of this work. They saw this as being a partial substitution for the scholarship component of their contract (although this had not been formally articulated), and its value as supporting the university's employability and careers initiatives, helping students to realize their potential. It had also significantly changed their own career profile, as they were involved in rolling out similar initiatives to other institutions.

Another individual, an applied scientist, demonstrated a movement not only across disciplinary boundaries but also across methodological ones. They had developed an interest in teaching and learning and were establishing a new field, incorporating social science methods into their scientific discipline, thus demonstrating how disciplinary mutation can occur bottom-up:

> I spread myself too thinly in terms of the technical stuff, but the teaching and learning was something that I … really, really enjoyed and was really good at … in terms of sort of reading up on theory and reading the papers and starting to dig deeper into the theories that underpin the social science aspects, so I've started to read about critical realism … about social science research methods … It's really still starting to inform the way I think and … to become who I am. (Reader, applied science, post-1992 university, interview 1)

This person therefore became a pathfinder and disseminator in a new field, and was willing to push professional paradigms: 'So that's the critical awareness perspective … the difference between an open system and a closed system. In … hard science, you can isolate the mechanism, so you can control all the variables and then you can measure the rate of reaction for something … whereas with social sciences, we can't isolate the mechanisms' (reader, applied science, post-1992 university, interview 1). In parallel with this was a willingness to include staff on professional contracts, for example, data management, in the pedagogical endeavour: 'I think it's sort of a developing role and its a developing identity … We just have to … keep moving in that direction and perhaps create closer integration between academics and the support staff, academic skills support staff' (reader, applied science, post-1992 university, interview 1).

The following Pen Portrait illustrates how institutional agendas have expanded and led to disciplinary stretch, in the following example, via outreach activity to secondary schools in communities that were under-resourced for science teaching. Significantly, this example is from a pre-1992 Russell Group university, illustrating that this extension of activity is not confined to post-1992 universities with a regional mission:

Pen Portrait 9

We've got quite a large, WP [widening participation] and schools initiative, so I've been trying to work closely with them, to be a bit more strategic, because I know part of the REF [Research Excellence Framework] now is in community engagement and that's been brought to my attention by more senior people in the department, so I'm now running teacher training days, where I go to science subject leader events and have teachers come in, so there's a lot of ... PE [physical education] teachers teaching chemistry now, because they're so short staffed, so the younger years are being taught by non-chemists and the older people teaching chemistry often graduated a very long time ago, so the standard equipment is very different now and they're teaching them, like, spectroscopy theory and they're ..., they're referring to equipment that's extremely redundant basically. So, we're trying to show them what's kind of standard now in undergraduate labs and obviously ideally get their students in to come and have a go, especially the sort of non-selective underfunded schools tend to not have labs, they're just getting rid of them completely because they can cover most of their requirements in demos, so I'm now having A-Level practical days, so they'll come in and get the skills needed ... in a one day session, so we'll try and sort of target a practical that will cover things like re-crystallization or infrared and stuff like that, so I'm trying to kind of support ... work closely with teachers, to help them in that sense.

[However], it takes a lot of time ..., I did a double science lesson at a school in [suburb] and it was an hour each way, the journey, it was a double science, so that's like, that's a whole afternoon essentially, so it's an hour there, two hours double science and then an hour back, so things like that that ... will be time that I could have been doing other teaching ..., that's a lot more time than I wanted to be handing over for just one, like, one school group ... So, I'd like it to be a bit more strategic, but I think that's something that essentially, because there's just me doing it, I can facilitate, but I know that it's very difficult for schools to come out, so I want to be as kind of helpful and considerate of that as possible, but at the same time, for me to be time efficient ..., it would be great for them to come and I think there is a benefit to them being out of their normal environment and have an educational experience in that setting as well, so ... they didn't have any PPE [personal protective equipment] ..., so I had to bring all the lab specs and gloves and stuff myself ... and this was year nine, so 14-, 15-year-olds and they'd never worn a lab coat before, it was their first ever, so for me, it's just like how can I not do this, it's so important and so many of them have emailed me saying, they want to come and do work experience over summer and stuff, so you know, it is about inspiring young people. (Lecturer, science, pre-1992 Russell Group university, interview 1)

Although this person's activities were driven by the *Institutional script* relating to widening participation, in turn influenced by the requirement for impact, there was convergence with the individual's *Internal script*, evidenced by their enthusiasm for, and commitment to, outreach in the community, in particular widening take up of STEM (science, technology, engineering and mathematics) subjects, notwithstanding the time pressures that they experienced.

Furthermore, in support of wider societal agendas, many faculty were developing a focus on specific areas around teaching and learning, such as online learning, skills development, apprenticeships and vocational education, often with the aim of improving both student attainment and retention rates. Although at the heart of contemporary institutional missions, such areas were often seen as 'boundary' work, contiguous to disciplines, and as requiring significant innovation. More than one person referred to work in such areas as demanding project management skills, for example, in relation to evaluation and monitoring of student attainment, which could fall to academic faculty with these types of responsibilities. As a result, some individuals effectively had two reporting lines, one to their school for their disciplinary activity in teaching and research and one to the university, for example, in ensuring that their school met institutional goals in relation to access and widening participation. Responsibilities could become extended, with teaching and research being only one aspect of a role for some people: 'There are so many boxes to tick now as an academic ... you're responsible for the pastoral support of students ... for marketing the courses, for getting involved with recruitment' (professor, teaching and learning, post-1992 university, interview 1). In turn, such activities have become absorbed into formal requirements for progression: 'You have to prove yourself in so many different ways ... it used to be that you did your research and you had to do a bit of teaching as well but … There wasn't the sort of student engagement and student experience … You just have to balance everything …, especially coming into your career nowadays' (lecturer, social sciences, post-1992 university, interview 1). As a consequence, disciplinary factors were not necessarily seen as the sole indicators for career advancement, thus 'everyone must be doing some external engagement, otherwise they don't get promoted' (professor, social sciences, pre-1992 university, interview 1). Such activities also led to collaboration with professionals who were specialists in other fields, internal and external to the university.

The Influence of Practice

Disciplinary stretch has also arisen partly from the incorporation of a range of practitioner-orientated subjects into universities, partly from government and institutional responses to societal agendas such as widening participation, diversity and inclusion, and community outreach, and partly from the interests and commitments of individual faculty in both disciplinary and practitioner settings. Individuals influenced by *Practice scripts*, for example, are likely to have transitioned into an academic environment, often performing a bridging role in the classroom, contextualizing their professional knowledge in a conceptual frame for their students. In turn, their students would be likely to have come from a more practical, as distinct from an academic, background, with associated skills training, therefore their teachers were focused on 'encouraging [students] to be critical, using theoretical approaches, which they're not [necessarily] comfortable with' (lecturer, social sciences, pre-1992 university, interview 1). Such faculty were, therefore, effecting the development of their students' skill sets, roles and professional identities in their own practitioner settings. One interviewee, for example, had worked in a careers service, moved into schools liaison within a university and then became a lecturer in a programme for careers advisers. The curriculum included not only disciplinary elements drawn from the social sciences but also practical elements linking learning outcomes to the world of work in the field of careers advice. This also involved developing partnerships with local schools and colleges, 'building relations up so we can develop placement opportunities for students' (lecturer, professional studies, post-1992 university, interview 1). They were thereby contributing to the enrichment of their university's offerings in relation to employability and prosperity in the region and thus its local mission.

It was also apparent from the study that the practice of individuals, particularly across professional fields, could in turn influence *Institutional scripts*, as shown in the following Pen Portraits, although the *Practice scripts* reflect different drivers. In the first, the individual concerned had been entrepreneurial in fostering contacts in both commercial and public sectors, working on an employability project supported by a UK public funding agency and a programme on security funded by a bank, as well as promoting foundation level study for the purposes of widening participation, and developing a novel prescribing programme for health professionals. Their stories emphasize the practical applications that can arise from extended networking and collaborative working with external partners, in this case playing into employability and skills agendas, in turn furthering university agendas:

Pen Portrait 10

Together with our director of employability ..., we applied for some funding from [public funding agency] to try to look at [employability of underserved populations]. We did that across four different universities and we were successful in getting that funding, which was quite a big deal for the university, because I don't think we'd had much [public funding agency] funding before. So, that was quite a win ..., so that probably led to me having my contract extended, they thought, oh, that's useful, to have someone who can bring money in ..., maybe half a year or a year later, there was another [public funding agency] bid ... and it was about setting up new courses that are suitable for industry, closing the industrial skills gap and strangely, I'd met someone from [bank] ... a month or so earlier and they'd asked me, well, how come you don't do [digital security] at xxx ..., so I said to [line manager], what about asking for some money to set up a new degree on [digital security]. She said, I don't think we can do that, can we, we haven't got the expertise, and I was, like, well, no, but that's why you get the money, so you can build ..., so we applied for that and got that, so I got extended again ... I haven't got any evidence that [promotion to professor] was directly to do with that, but obviously if you bring in money and it helps pay a salary and gives you other opportunities ..., we did other things as well, set up a foundation year ... and that's grown quite a lot ..., at the moment we're writing ..., [a] strategic investment bid ... to employ a nurse to [develop health practitioner prescribing], and so it's a mixture of methods really, writing business cases sometimes to get the resource up front or try and do it with no resource. (Professorial teaching fellow, applied science, pre-1992 university, interview 2)

This person's extended activities, supporting practice agendas in the public and private sectors, had, in turn, developed their profile and furthered their case for promotion, demonstrating how a broad range of activities, as opposed to a narrowing down of disciplinary specialization, was valued by the institution as sufficient for the award of a chair. In the second case, in the following Pen Portrait, the *Internal script* was driven principally by an ideological commitment to community activism. This person nevertheless conformed for the time being to the *Institutional script* of their university by contributing to community-related teaching and research, while maintaining cognizance of the possibilities of the option to opt out:

Pen Portrait 11

Since I've had this role and the temporary roles leading up to it, I have continued to engage with community groups in different ways, so for example, outside of work, I do some voluntary work in the field that I research in and that I used to work in, that's clearly outside of work. Inside of work, I try to keep relationships with organisations in the community that are relevant to my research, and then there's a grey area of organisations that I'm part of, that I'd want to be part of even if I didn't have the academic job, so I don't feel like I'm kind of involved as a representative of my institution or something, and I don't feel like I'm involved simply because of my research interests, I'm involved because I believe in them as an activist, I'm committed and so on. Then, on the other hand, I have increasingly tried to incorporate most of that work into my paid work time, because I just felt like I could do more and more things that are related to my research, [that] will benefit my institution in terms of impact and in terms of me being likely to get research funding … it's quite blurry what counts as research or research-related or community engagement … and I think it's been good because it means that I'm not doing a huge amount of work that is related to work but isn't work and …, it just makes things a bit more achievable …, so it's one reason I really wanted to stay here … I actually don't know where my career will go and I feel quite fuzzy about that … for me, coming from a community based occupation, the pay is very good and that's not a kind of primary motivator for me. I just feel in a very privileged position, to work doing something I love, I love all the elements of my job … and doing research that I think does something useful and good in the world and getting paid well for it, I can't believe it, I sometimes just pinch myself …, I'm not very interested in moving around for kind of careerist reasons … So, my ten-year plan isn't, like, you know, get the next grant and go to the next level and be promoted, I see it like a two path thing, where, carry on and do good stuff and get better as a researcher and keep contributing here to the teaching and to my colleagues, or do it as far as I can, but I'm not going to stay if ... I can't do what I believe in ... there are parts of the impact agenda that are problematic, but it does give me an opportunity to be deeply engaged in the communities I want to be engaged in and that's really good. (Lecturer, social sciences, pre-1992 Russell Group university, interview 1)

This narrative also suggests that commitments to external community work undertaken on a semi-voluntary basis had the potential to become absorbed into institutional strategy and to contribute to impact. This was confirmed in the second interview, in which they described obtaining a research grant for community-based work, and is an example of policy being informed by practice, via a bottom-up initiative. The above two Pen Portraits therefore illustrate the cross-fertilization of activity that can occur between the university and other sectors via the *Practice scripts* of two individuals with very different backgrounds, the first having a business-orientated perspective and the second a community-oriented perspective.

Extended Communities Around Academic and Associated Activity

Because of the extension of the range of activity in an academic environment, a significant proportion of people felt that they did not fit into a single disciplinary grouping or predetermined location in the institutional structure, particularly in developmental areas such as activities associated with teaching and learning. In practice, they were likely to locate themselves across an academic and professional collective to share and develop practice, so that, for some, disciplinary activity became absorbed into broader clusters of activity. Such collectives could become quasi-academic communities in themselves, both within and across institutions. The following person, for example, with a teaching and learning portfolio, worked across a range of professional service operations such as careers, employability, academic practice and leadership, lifelong and online learning: 'There is a growing number of people like me, but we don't quite have a reference group ... I have several services portfolios and

I'm sitting beside people who have single portfolios, but nonetheless …, our community of practice helps to share … developments that are happening in their services that I can think about and bring back' (educational developer, pre-1992 Russell Group university, interview 1). This extension of disciplinary activity, also involving faculty not having academic contracts, and the creation of synergy with adjacent fields was in turn reflected in a development programme offered to academic faculty and professional staff by a teaching and learning professional at another university:

> I personally feel very proud of the fact that we've had two senior IT directors take a postgraduate certificate [in teaching and learning] … [and] library staff, careers [staff] … which helps a dialogue across the services and support staff and the many other professional staff that fall across that … We would go so far [as] … to call it a widening participation effort … amongst staff … It's quite clear to us … that there are some very clear benefits in the way that people then build further partnerships or work together on committees, you see it in different forms all the time … To help that flow of conversation, to see into each other's worlds. (Senior lecturer, teaching and learning, pre-1992 university, interview 1)

This demonstrates how novel, cross-disciplinary and cross-boundary approaches become absorbed into disciplinary practice, in this case, at the instigation of an individual seeking to be innovative in developing the collective, as well as the individual, potential of colleagues.

These examples suggest that the idea of the lone academic working on a specific issue or topic, even in the humanities, has become increasingly outmoded, and that a team approach adds synergy, in the broadest sense of creating added value to disciplinary activity for faculty, students and local communities. There also appeared to be a heightened level of consciousness among individuals of the public good likely to arise from their activity, for example, conferring benefits on students and underserved communities at home and overseas. As one individual said, 'I get to help the students in terms of developing themselves … I see my graduates as impact' (teaching fellow, applied science, post-1992 university, interview 1). Boundary work between disciplinary and the more service-oriented elements of the university's work was therefore seen as enriching the academic enterprise by achieving impact in the broader sense of conferring benefit on individual students and wider society, rather than being solely geared to achieving advantage from targeted government or UK Research Council funding, for which it was a requirement. This suggests not only a sense of vocation within the profession that goes beyond the purely disciplinary, but also a sense of contributing to the collective good, often expressed in team working across a mix of functions.

The Option to Opt Out

Having a broader hinterland also created options, including the option to opt out. Some saw higher education as one employment locale among a range of other public service or business environments. Those with professional, practitioner or business backgrounds, especially if they had worked outside higher education for a significant period, tended to be more sanguine about the possibility of moving to a different sector. Thus, one individual, who had worked in the private sector and had contacts in the charitable sector and the civil service, maintained this option, taking the view that 'if my contract didn't get renewed it wouldn't be a huge problem, because it might force me to do something otherwise, and I've given it a good go' (lecturer, social sciences, pre-1992 university, interview 2). Another mid-career individual saw academia as a bridge to discipline-informed practice in other contexts, rather than a permanent locale: 'I ... joined academia to become an expert in an area, so [to] help move certain debates on, particularly around victims issues, so I see academia as a sort of stepping stone to work in either a national or international organisation' (senior lecturer, applied social sciences, pre-1992 Russell Group university, interview 2). And another person who was moving towards the final stages of their career had taken the decision to move to a different sector, seeing this as a positive in opening up new possibilities: 'You are talking to a person that has always sought career progression over the decades and in the private sector achieved that progression, and to a certain extent, as a late entrant to academia ... So, in terms of positive aspects, I'm excited because it's going to be different' (reader, social sciences, post-2004 university, interview 2). Nevertheless, despite the pressures of academic life, less than half a dozen respondents in the study had firm exit plans. Two of these were retirements, although this did not preclude consultancy work in a university or elsewhere.

However, changing direction did not necessarily mean leaving an institution, and some individuals had taken on management and other responsibilities in order to progress their careers. Those with a disciplinary hinterland tended to be more comfortable about rebooting their careers after they had relinquished such a role. As an example, the following person was using external as well as internal networks to get back into research in an applied field:

> I … went to … a number of conferences, I met … a few people I knew in different universities in the UK, just to get a feel for what was happening in [applied science] education to say, is there anything we could do here. I … started to try and build up my knowledge and experience … build up a network again … and build up my knowledge, which had …, chronically declined over years of management … it's all moved on in terms of technology, because I'd been out of the game so long that I'm … trying to relearn the new software and various things …. I then got involved in a couple of very successful multimillion pound grants. (Senior lecturer, applied science, pre-1992 Russell Group university, interview 2)

This person, with strong links to business and industry in their field, was therefore relatively unfazed by the fact that practices had moved on, or the prospect of updating their knowledge and thereby moving forward to address the changing requirements of teaching and research. This reflected a mindset, apparent in those contemplating moving out of higher education into fields that might be relatively untested, that was comfortable about progressing to new activities, inside or outside the university. Thus, a career comes to represent an ongoing process of adaptation in building new knowledge and skills, as opposed to a process of solely meeting targets set by an institution.

Changing Components of Academic Activity

The extension of academic activity beyond disciplines and into other fields and sectors provides an additional dimension to the literature around the breakdown of assumptions in relation to linear career paths via open-ended contracts, against a background of less confidence in the ability of the higher education system to provide a secure career. What appears to be happening is a growing periphery around disciplines, in which there are three interlocking groups of individuals: one that is primarily focused on a discipline or disciplines and their direct applications, one that is strongly influenced by professional practice, and one that is geared towards extended academic activities such as those around teaching and learning and student support. This balance is likely to vary within and between institutions, faculties and departments, and individuals may shift their focus as circumstances change. This model therefore represents a fluid picture.

Thus, if disciplinary teaching and research is seen as the stable core of the university's endeavour, these activities would appear to be increasingly porous,

Figure 7.1 Adjunct activities around the academic core of disciplinary teaching and research

and, as a result, to inform, and be informed by, a range of adjunct activities, as shown in Figure 7.1.

Individuals may shift their focus over time and according to their positioning in their institutional locale, the responsibilities placed upon them, and their own preferences. However, the interview narratives suggested a collective drift from a disciplinary focus, including cross-disciplinary and disciplinary applications, towards a focus on teaching and research in practice settings, and to extended academic activities, particularly around the student experience, as shown in Figure 7.2. The examples are all taken from participants in the study. This was equally the case for those in 'hard' disciplines such as science and engineering as for those in 'soft' disciplines such as history or literature, or practice-oriented disciplines, such as health and law (as classified by Becher and Trowler 2001).

Although these three broad foci are likely to reflect the balance of contemporary institutional missions and agendas, the extent to which individuals engage with

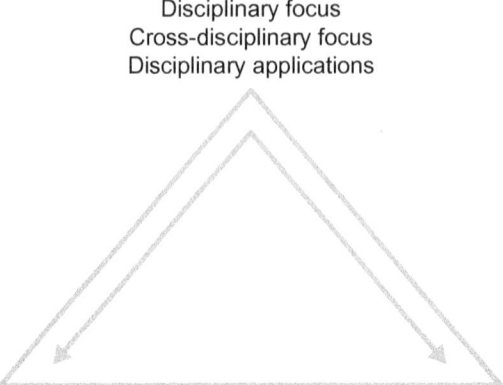

Figure 7.2 The collective drift from a disciplinary focus, including cross-disciplinary and disciplinary applications, towards a focus on teaching and research in practice settings, and to extended academic activities

each focus reflects the influence of their *Internal* and *Practice scripts* as the driving mechanism at any point in time. The interview narratives also suggested a shift towards more open-ended, even speculative, approaches, as encapsulated in Table 7.1, the second column of which suggests a sense of value added beyond the purely disciplinary.

At the same time, a greater fluidity of roles has contributed to the erosion of clear definition between, for example, teaching and research roles, and also of the boundaries between professional and academic roles, notwithstanding formal definitions used by institutions or the Higher Education Statistics Agency (HESA). Thus, it was evident from the study that not only do staff defined as 'research-only' undertake teaching, and 'teaching-only' staff undertake research, but some academics have management responsibilities at programme and department level. Moreover, senior management teams are likely to include academics with pro-vice-chancellor or similar titles; and staff formally classified as having professional contracts may be involved in academically-oriented activity such as teaching study skills, developing online learning and researching institutional data. Again, this fluidity demonstrates the interrelationship between *formal* and *informal institutional economies*, and also suggests that faculty, as well as professional staff,

Table 7.1 The Shift Towards More Open-Ended Approaches to Roles and Careers

Traditional elements of academic formation	Shifts in aspects of academic formation
Primacy of discipline as identifier	Discipline no longer a sole identifier; incorporation of other dimensions such as impact in its widest sense, public engagement, the student experience, equity and diversity
Disciplinary or interdisciplinary focus	Disciplinary stretch, including application in practice/co-creation of knowledge with colleagues, internal and external to the university
Dependence on institutional and disciplinary structures	Creation of alternative, bespoke options; capitalizing on opportunities; constructing a distinguishing self-profile
Good citizenship within own university	Increased emphasis on good citizenship within wider communities, regionally, nationally and internationally
Valuing of academic freedom/autonomy	Valuing of general working conditions: flexibility, colleagueship, equity, work-life balance, well-being, as well as availability of options
Formal arrangements and discourses	Informal understandings, networks and discourses

may work in a 'third space' (Whitchurch 2013) between academic and professional roles, either temporarily or permanently. The reduction in 'support staff' roles during the Covid-19 pandemic (HESA 2022) is likely to accelerate this process.

As shown in Chapter 5, contemporary academic career trajectories are unlikely to be based solely on established pathways, norms and expectations, so that meeting specific criteria for progression is likely to be only part of the equation for many faculty. The iteration between meeting formal requirements for promotion and progression, and the individual's own life and career 'journey', would appear to be critical, with consideration of personal and practitioner aspects increasingly evident. While this may have been the case to a greater or lesser extent in the past, it was clear from the study that contemporary academic faculty are willing to articulate their intentions in this respect with line managers, and did not feel obliged to claim that progression up the formal career ladder was their sole motivation at all times and in every circumstance, or try to disguise the fact that they might wish to deviate from an *Institutional script*. Thus, the instrumental and transactional process of career-making, reflected in the *formal institutional economy* and associated *Institutional scripts*, and involving the meeting of certain criteria and targets, is weighed against the transformational element of the role in terms of personal enrichment, working conditions, service to students and communities, and research that has the potential to change lives. The second column of Table 7.1 therefore represents impact in its widest sense as contributing to the public good. The narratives in the study appeared to demonstrate significant awareness of a distinction between what needs to be done to progress or even maintain one's position, and commitment to making a difference to one's own and others' lives. Although this was particularly the case with faculty in their thirties and forties, there was a growing sense of this phenomenon among the professoriate and those with management responsibilities, a number of whom reflected upon the positive aspects of this trend. Thus, 'I don't have a sense of [the academic career] as being a completely broken structure' (professor, humanities, pre-1992 Russell Group university, interview 1).

The Influence of the Informal Economy

As shown in Chapter 1, the dynamic between structure and agency in making academic careers has been recognized in the literature (Arthur and Rousseau 1996; Dowd and Kaplan 2005). The concept of a morphogenetic relationship is developed in Chapters 4 and 5 as individuals put their own interpretation on the structures that they find themselves in to create new arenas of activity, via *Internal* and *Practice scripts*, as well as extending the spaces and timescales available to them. What also became apparent in the study is the collective, as opposed to the individual, influence of academic faculty in modulating and adjusting the requirements of formal structures. This, in turn, is reflected in the development of an *informal economy* in institutions, which is less likely to be acknowledged explicitly. This is particularly evident in Chapter 5, in which movements across space and time are reflected in *concertina careers*, incorporating individual interpretations of academic activity across extended locales and timescales, whereby individuals draw on the *informal economy*. This tends to be implicit rather than explicit, although elements may in time be incorporated into the *formal economy*, for example, when criteria for promotion are expanded to incorporate areas such as student support, community outreach and innovation. The *informal economy*, therefore, is likely to be represented by a groundswell of local practices, that become more than the sum of individual initiatives. However, some of these practices are likely to be packaged and presented, by individuals and their line managers, in ways that are acceptable within the *formal economy*. They may also take time to become embedded. Thus, extended academic activities may need to be massaged, at least in the first instance, so that they do not appear to depart too far from institutional norms. This is likely to involve acts of interpretation on the part of both individuals and their line managers, such as heads of department and deans, and the narratives indicated that this was a skill that many interviewees had acquired. Nevertheless, the expansion of the *informal economy* has introduced an element of fluidity and discretion to career-making by the individual, in particular via the influence of *Internal-* and *Practice*-generated scripts.

Implications for Progressing a Career

The movements described above also reflect the fact that the idea of autonomy, traditionally considered a prerequisite of academic life, has tilted towards the idea of an extended professionalism, incorporating elements of individualism and self-reliance, so that 'being an academic … is a little bit …, like being self-employed, because it's only you that's going to drive that forward' (reader, applied science, post-1992 university, interview 1). Thus, alongside a modulation of the discipline as a prime location and identifier, individuals also position themselves within their communities, families and professional practice networks, and the relationships and colleagues that they encounter there. Such positionings are more likely to reflect the *informal* than the *formal economy*. The expansion of space within the professional envelope was exemplified by an individual with a strong teaching and research record, who had come into academia after a successful career in business:

> I find that working autonomously means that my reward comes from … things I do well, committee work outside the university … I have got this lovely network of people … mainly through [funding body] and so I get it all from outside … I get to do fun things with [funding body] that really … stretches me and develops me … on a personal level as well as an intellectual level, and an emotional level as well. (Reader (later professor), humanities, pre-1992 university, interviews 1 and 2)

Alongside personal and practice drivers, it was also apparent that individuals laid emphasis on the promotion of a unique profile that would distinguish them from others and help them to achieve recognition. This process, often via online media, was seen as vital, particularly by younger faculty, whose 'profile is sometimes more important than … their CVs' (lecturer, social sciences, pre-1992 university, interview 1). There was therefore a heightened awareness of the need to develop a 'brand':

> [It is now] more about your public profile …, it … has become an element that anyone who goes for promotion is asked to reflect upon and it can help people from …, one level to the next level and that can be …, doing a lot of media engagements, working with museums … my younger colleagues … are putting more emphasis on that …. I do think that is a shift. (Professor, humanities, pre-1992 Russell Group university, interview 2)

This effectively means building a 'unique selling proposition': 'I think …, for an academic [member of] staff to be very successful, there's an element where … their identity is what sells things out there' (educational developer, pre-1992 Russell Group university, interview 1). Rather than simply performing a specified role, therefore, individuals were geared towards making this more of a public performance, with a wider audience in mind, including those who could influence their careers. In effect, this was a process of self-promotion, using informal as well as formal channels.

Vertical networks were likely to be particularly helpful in building and promoting individual profiles, i.e. those networks that connected the individual with people of influence in the institutional and disciplinary hierarchy who can confer advantage (Angervall, Gustafsson and Silfyer 2018; Putnam 2000): 'It's a matter of finding out who are the specific people who you think actually can be beneficial to you and cultivating relationships with those people' (professor, science, pre-1992 Russell Group university, interview 1). This, in turn, could raise an individual's profile with those who might have an influence on their future: 'Getting a good and strong network … Talking to people, getting to show your work …, I think is the best way to open new doors in different places' (research fellow, social sciences, pre-1992 Russell Group university, interview 1). Such individuals were thereby likely to position themselves appropriately within the mechanisms of what Bourdieu (1993) terms 'cultural reproduction', for example, in the form of patronage from senior faculty. Thus, the following person acknowledged the support of their head of department as a critical factor: 'The head of [department] … has been a great mentor over the last five years … and has really helped me to develop my career and ... had a very nurturing influence, so we've co-published together and he's just been very supportive and very encouraging' (teaching fellow, applied science, post-1992 university, interview 2). However, this could also lead to vulnerability if a line manager changed, as in the case of the following individual: 'Whereas the previous ... dean thought that I was a great innovator, bringing lots of money ... while I wasn't returned [in the Research Excellence Framework], I was doing other things so [they were] happy to support me being promoted ... [but] you never know where you stand when you've got new [senior] staff coming through' (reader, applied science, pre-1992 Russell group university, interview 1).

Being able to recognize opportunities was also seen as a critical factor supporting the development of a unique profile: 'I am a believer that people aren't necessarily lucky, but luck comes ..., it's sometimes because an opportunity arose and you took a chance with it and I, way, way back, took that chance when I moved from [pre-1992 university] to [university in Europe] on a very short-term project, but it essentially framed ... the rest of my career' (educational developer, pre-1992 Russell Group university, interview 1). There was also a sense that, in order to be able to take advantage of opportunities that occurred, mapping out a career too closely in advance was neither feasible nor desirable. Thus, the expansion of the self within the professional envelope, supported by opportunism and the ability to network, gives an additional thrust to academic activity above and beyond purely disciplinary endeavours. Conversely there was also a sense that assumptions about the value accorded to service and 'good citizenship' within an institution were being eroded. Thus, one individual was discomforted by a perceived shift to a more competitive, individualized approach:

> I was at a meeting at one point, when ... [in relation to people who] don't know quite what to do or how to move their careers ... the senior leadership turned round and said, well, they should apply for jobs somewhere else and that will show us that, if they're any good, they'll get an offer and then they can negotiate. The three or four of us who'd spent our careers feeling we'd sort of earned something by being loyal ... have felt that actually it had been rather useful for [university] that we've accumulated historical memory of how the institution works and have committed ourselves to it long term. (Professor, humanities, pre-1992 Russell Group university, interview 1)

This was particularly unsettling to those in mid- or later career who had placed their confidence in giving service to an institution by undertaking roles such as student admissions, pastoral care or programme leadership, roles that might not be valued by younger faculty in terms of gaining credit in formal *Institutional scripts* in relation to promotion.

Implications for the Profession

The study also highlighted how less certain environments, likely to be exacerbated by the Covid-19 pandemic, have tended to reduce confidence in the higher education system as a whole and in *Institutional scripts*. Individuals therefore have less inclination to rely solely on the established structures of institutional career paths and timelines, and are to some extent thrown back on their own resources, including professional practice. They are likely to have a hinterland that takes them beyond the *formal economy* of their institutions, creates options for their immediate and longer term futures and facilitates adaptability as conditions change. As a result, although the core of the academic profession is likely to continue to centre around teaching and research, albeit across a widening range of disciplines and practice, the narratives suggest that it is becoming more porous and softer edged. It might be seen, therefore, as sitting alongside a suite of other contiguous professional groupings and associated activities, with interaction and synergy occurring between them. Furthermore, it was evident that those in both 'soft' and 'hard' disciplines might have such a hinterland beyond disciplinary and institutional boundaries.

The examples in this chapter show how disciplinary activity has become extended, in some cases as a result of institutional policies, for example, community outreach to students in underserved communities, but also through the interests and professional practice of individuals themselves. The study suggests that change can and does occur via the influence of *Internal* and *Practice scripts*, drawing on the informal institutional economy, although this may not be immediately apparent. Although the potentials of extended academic activity may in practice be realized, they are not necessarily recognized by institutions, despite the fact that, over time, they may become incorporated into policy. Arguments may be made by line managers in relation to individual cases, which in due course create a degree of momentum so that, for example, there may be a general broadening of criteria for promotion. The onus is therefore on institutions to recognize and incorporate an expanding range of contributions, in particular innovative work, and to reform their requirements so that these align with the lived reality of roles and careers in higher education in real, rather than deferred, time. This is likely to involve negotiating a new psychological and social contract with academic faculty to prevent faith in institutional structures declining. However, it is also up to individuals, supported by managers such as heads of department, to explore activities where they think that they can add value and to be persuasive about these. It is notable that the more senior faculty members, in the light of experience, tended to be more positive about repurposing activity so as to create a wider range of applications and options, and it was evident from the data that mentorship and sponsorship, formal or informal, were significant elements in the progression of younger faculty. Thus, confidence building among those earlier in their careers appeared to be an important element in enabling them to optimize their talents, pointing out directions and potentials that might not be immediately apparent, and thereby to progress.

The study therefore suggested that the professional formation of individuals in contemporary academic environments is an iterative process in which individuals not only take cues from the structural frameworks in which they find themselves, but also seek openings according to their own interests and opportunities that arise, or that they create for themselves. It showed how, through interactions with others, individual approaches to career-making, driven by *Internal and Practice scripts*, as well as *Institutional scripts*, may gather collective momentum, and ultimately result in the transformation of practice, described by Archer as 'morphogenesis'. Furthermore, the diversification of what might hitherto have been seen as a homogeneous academic profession would appear to have stimulated this shift away from academic faculty being what Archer terms 'primary agents', that is 'members of collectivities who share the same life chances' (Archer 2000: 11), to individuals who see themselves increasingly through their own interpretation of, and contribution to, their given role. In Archer's terms, the diversification of the academic workforce can be interpreted as expanding the number of people who offer 'unscripted performances' (Archer 2000: 7), creating new forms of activity, for example, around online learning and community engagement. Thus, in practice, performing academic roles involves individuals not only interacting with the structures in which they find themselves but also creating new fields of activity via the dialogues and relationships they create in relation to *Internal* and *Practice scripts*.

Conclusion

This chapter has shown how disciplinary stretch, an expanding hinterland, and professional practice have influenced the academic profession as a whole and the roles and activities of individuals. This has created greater fluidity within the profession, in particular across extended collectives that have formed around academic and associated activity, and led to more open-ended approaches to careers. At a macro level, this might be said to mirror the move to mass higher education over the past fifty years (Scott 2021). What has been less remarked, however, is the way in which the academic profession, as well as the student body, has become more inclusive. In progressing their careers, individuals have to some extent being thrown back on their own resources, for example, by developing unique profiles and seeking the support of those who can have influence on their futures. Nevertheless, there is also a sense that an academic career continues to have a vocational element for many, in that it enables a contribution to be made to the public good. While an expanding range of disciplines continue to represent the core of the profession, individuals within it may be propelled by a range of drivers. Thus, formal, contractual relationships with an institution are likely to be modulated by the development of 'soft' skills, and what might be seen as elements of 'soft' power, via relationships with colleagues, external networks and work in a variety of arenas. This applies to mid- and late career faculty, as well as those in the early stages of their careers. The final chapter that follows develops some concluding themes arising from the study and suggests how institutional policymakers might capitalize on its findings.

8

Rethinking Academic Careers in a Post-Pandemic World

This chapter reviews the key themes of the study in the light of the Covid-19 pandemic which began shortly after the empirical work was completed in January 2020, in particular building on evidence in Chapter 7 of a greater fluidity in academic and associated activities. It suggests that many of the trends identified by the study may have been accelerated and become more pronounced during the pandemic while new trends appear to have emerged. Academic faculty have developed strategies that will be useful to them in dealing with this changing environment, particularly in harnessing *informal institutional economies* in dealing with formal requirements. Nevertheless, the chapter suggests that faith in the *formal institutional economy* is likely to decline unless it begins to recognize and incorporate some of these changes and reward those who have taken essential initiatives in the face of major disruption. In particular, it needs to acknowledge innovative work, such as the development of online and hybrid forms of teaching and learning, the advancement of interdisciplinary education and research and the transformation of curricula to address global challenges. The book concludes by arguing that the elements of the *formal economy* – for example, contracts of employment, promotion and progression criteria, disciplinary and departmental affiliations, performance review and development processes and work allocation models – need to be reformed in order to realign with the lived reality of academic roles and careers in the mid-twenty-first century. It argues for attention to be paid to the building of resilience and trust among the workforce, as well as for new psychological contracts between universities and their employees, and a renewed social contract between higher education institutions and society.

Key Themes of the Study

The study on which this book is based was undertaken in eight UK institutions between 2017 and 2020 and comprised interviews with a range of academic faculty across disciplines and different types of institution. This was set in the context of international trends in the academic workforce, including the pressures of casualization, and a reducing proportion of faculty undertaking both teaching and research. The earlier chapters of the book explore the ways in which contemporary faculty, across an increasingly diverse workforce, are making their careers by negotiating institutional processes and structures in ways that move beyond the duality of boundaried (with an emphasis on structures) and boundaryless (with an emphasis on agency) careers. They explore approaches that individuals participating in the study took to their roles and careers simultaneously and over time. Chapter 3 describes and analyses *Mainstream*, *Portfolio* and *Niche* approaches to roles and careers, identifying the characteristics of these and showing how they are likely to affect individuals' interactions with four spatial domains: the disciplinary, the organizational, the external/community and the internal/motivational. It shows that the three approaches are not mutually exclusive and considers the fluidity that is apparent between them during the two-year period of field work of the study. It considers the variables affecting this categorization, including, discipline, institutional type, gender and career stage, and links the three approaches to *formal* and *informal institutional economies*, which are used as a metaphorical framework in relation to the production, exchange and consumption of academic or associated activity.

The study also included a survey, described in Chapter 2, which considered whether the previous employment experiences of academic faculty are indicators of current career trajectory and future career intentions, including whether they have an intention to leave employment in higher education and whether their preferred destination would be in the private, public or charitable sectors. It explored the options open to academics in a range of roles, including the aspiration to move from a teaching-only or research-only role to a combined teaching and research role, and/or a middle- or senior management role, in order to gain career advancement. It offered indicators of the increasing diversity of career trajectories in UK higher education and how these are constructed and managed in specific institutions.

Further chapters draw on the notion of career scripts to show how the career paths of individuals are informed by personal strengths, interests and commitments (represented by *Internal scripts*), and by activity associated with professional practice (represented by *Practice scripts*), as well as by formal career structures (represented by *Institutional scripts*). Hence, scripts are both internally and externally generated. The three scripts are framed so that the interplay between individual and institution becomes multifaceted during the process of career-making, as individuals not only interact with institutional structures but also incorporate new forms of activity, influenced by personal and professional interests and relationships outside the institution.

These chapters show how *Internal* and *Practice scripts* have in turn led to new forms of activity, within both *formal* and *informal institutional economies*. Whereas the *formal economy* is represented by, for example, promotion criteria and career pathways, the *informal economy* is represented by personal initiatives, together with professional relationships and networks that may be unique to the individual. It is shown how, by drawing on *Internal* and *Practice scripts*, individuals develop concertina-like careers, stretching the spaces and timescales available to them in order to accommodate, for example, new forms of work around disciplinary activity, professional allegiances, career moves in and out of higher education and personal responsibilities, thus reflecting the lived experiences of individuals. The concept of a *concertina career* is used in Chapter 5 to characterize the way in which an individual's activities may stretch and compress, both across spaces, represented by different commitments and relationships, and over time, thereby influencing the direction and tempo of a career. It demonstrates how, in the same way as the musical instrument expands and contracts, individuals shape their own careers, making constant adjustments at different stages and to suit the different circumstances of their lives. Thus, the interplay between individual and institution becomes multifaceted during the process of career-making, at the same time creating elasticity within formal career structures.

In Chapter 6, this conceptual framework is used to investigate how individuals address misalignments and disjunctures between their perceptions of their roles and formal institutional frameworks, including disciplinary affiliations, contractual arrangements, job profiles, progression criteria and workload models. It explores ways in which individuals negotiate such misalignments and disjunctures, making decisions about their career pathways on the basis of local situations. Some take a pragmatic stance in coping with disruptions to their plans, repurposing activity to create a wider range of options. Others find what they see as a safe space, focusing on a strength or interest in which they feel secure. Whatever approach is taken, a common factor in success is enlisting the support of local managers in helping individuals align their profiles and skill sets with formal requirements. A framework of activity theory (Engeström 2001) is used to demonstrate ways in which *formal* and *informal institutional economies* interact as individuals find ways of coping with misalignments and disjunctures.

Chapter 7 reviews pointers for the future of the academic profession, highlighting a collective momentum towards more fluid approaches to roles and careers. It suggests that, in future, the profession is likely to be influenced by a diversification and reshaping of disciplines, and an expanding hinterland for individuals, opening up academic activity to wider purposes, and at the same time expanding professional selfhood. The drift towards more fluid approaches to roles and careers is illustrated by a model demonstrating shifts in the professional formation of academic faculty. It is also noted that skills such as self-profiling, seeking and recognizing opportunities, and networking are increasingly evident in managing complex academic roles and career paths. While the onus is on institutions to recognize and incorporate a broadening range of contributions, it is also for individuals to explore spaces where they think they can add value and to be persuasive about these.

Emerging Developments Since the Start of the Covid-19 Pandemic

Given that the empirical work for this study was completed in January 2020, just before Covid-19 struck, it is pertinent to review how the characteristics of academic career-making explored in this book may have been impacted by the responses to the pandemic of governments, institutions and individual academic faculty. Chapter 2 places the study in the broader context of the key developments in the academic workforce prior to the pandemic, as indicated by national data sets. In this concluding chapter, some of the major discernible trends since the start of the pandemic, and how they might be impacting on academic career-making, will be explored. In particular, it asks how the formal employment processes in higher education institutions can better acknowledge innovative work and, specifically, how their reward and recognition frameworks can be realigned with the lived reality of academic roles and careers in the mid-twenty-first century. It is suggested that the shift, first to wholly online learning, and then to hybrid forms of in-person and online learning prompted by the pandemic, may be transforming conceptions of teaching and student engagement to the point where 'education-focused' roles could be viewed more positively and genuinely become an attractive and fulfilling career aspiration. The chapter also proposes the development of a better understanding of, and support for, the resilience of academics to adversity, individually and collectively, as they withstand, overcome and learn from crises such as the pandemic, and the rebuilding of trust as a critical dimension of the renewal of institutions, their re-engagement with external partners and the rediscovery of their social purposes. The chapter (and book) concludes with a proposal for new psychological and social contracts within academia that can create attractive academic career trajectories and more sustainable higher education communities with stronger relations with the broader society.

At the time of completing this book (early 2022), it is too early to judge what the long-term impact of Covid-19 – and the ways in which individuals, universities and the different parts of the UK higher education sector have responded to it – will be on approaches to academic career-making. One multination study (McGaughey et al. 2021; Shankar et al. 2021; Watermeyer, Crick et al. 2021; Watermeyer, Shankar et al. 2021), based on interviews with academics in the UK and several other countries, asked whether the pandemic was 'intensifying already established trends in higher education as a result of marketisation. These trends included work intensification, job insecurity, inadequate support from management, and lack of trust in institutional leadership'. It concluded, 'The global study findings … present universities in the grip of 'pandemia' with COVID-19 emboldening processes and protagonists of neoliberal governmentality and market-reform that undermine academic wellbeing' (McGaughey et al. 2021: 2). The survey of Australian academics within this study found 'a commonly shared perception that the future of the academic profession faces manifold risks to do with job security, access to research funds, and a general deterioration in quality of research and teaching over a period of time' (Shankar et al. 2021: 173–4).

There is a real danger of jumping to such conclusions so early into what is clearly going to be a long-term disruption, with reconfiguration and possible transformation of academic life and work, and of basing this solely on the opinions and feelings of academic faculty in the middle of lockdowns, largely separated from their colleagues and students, and experiencing significant uncertainty about the future. Longer term, more dispassionate studies of what faculty are actually doing are likely to reveal a more nuanced picture of the actual effects of the pandemic. This should also remind us of Watson's (2009) counsel that it is possible for low morale about the state of a university, or higher education in general, to coexist with optimism and enthusiasm about core academic activities of research and teaching undertaken at the local level: 'It is a matter of asking the right questions' (Watson 2009: 68) of a representative, non-self-selected sample, and of carefully interpreting the complex and differentiated nature of the answers.

Nevertheless, this and similar surveys of academics early in the pandemic (The Chronicle of Higher Education 2020; Sutherland et al. 2021; University and College Union [UCU] Scotland 2021; University of Tennessee Knoxville/CIBER Research [UTK/CIBER] 2021; Wray and Kinman 2021) revealed serious and common concerns about a range of issues, such as job security, the reduction of academic positions, growing role specialization, pay cuts, increased casualization, lack of career progression and damaged career prospects, in particular, for early-career academics and women. Some respondents reported that the pandemic conditions were hardly being taken into account in promotions processes, except perhaps for the extension of deadlines, and some annual procedures were cancelled altogether in 2020 (Sutherland et al. 2021). Many studies reported increased workloads and stress, and reduced well-being (UCU Scotland 2021; Watermeyer, Crick et al. 2021; Watermeyer, Shankar et al. 2021; Wray and Kinman 2021). Some respondents complained of not receiving clear and detailed information about restructures, mergers, redundancies or pay cuts. Latterly, some anxiety was expressed about returning to in-person, on-campus working after the lockdowns (UCU Scotland 2021). All of these issues and experiences are likely to have a bearing on academics' approaches to career-making in the short and longer term. One US survey found that more than a third of academic faculty had considered changing careers and leaving higher education or retiring altogether (The Chronicle of Higher Education 2020).

At the time of writing, there is no comprehensive and conclusive data about the extent of academic job losses across UK higher education institutions as a result of pandemic-related financial losses, although there are reports about developments at individual universities. According to an investigation by Edvoy (a platform for those wishing to study abroad), over 3,000 employees at UK universities – many of whom were on fixed-term contracts – were made redundant during the first wave of the pandemic, between 1 March and 20 September 2020. Universities with the highest number of redundancies included Manchester, Sheffield and Oxford (Wootton-Cane 2021). An Early Day Motion on 'University redundancies' was tabled in the House of Commons on 24 May 2021, expressing concern about compulsory and voluntary redundancies (Houses of Parliament 2021). At Southampton Solent University, some eighty faculty, or about 8 per cent of the workforce, were reported as having taken voluntary redundancy as part of a five-year strategy to expand areas such as health and nursing while cutting business courses (Staton 2021). Further redundancies among professional services staff were also reported as likely to increase the workload of academic faculty (McKie 2021).

The most recent Higher Education Statistics Agency (HESA) staff data (HESA 2022) provide the first official indication of the impact of the pandemic on the academic workforce, at least as of 1 December 2020. They show a significant slowing in the growth in the total number of academic faculty to 0.4 per cent in 2020–1, compared with around 2.5 per cent in previous years. A key factor in this was a fall in the number of research-only faculty for the first time in over a decade, confirming the vulnerability of those on fixed-term contracts and time-limited project funding. The number of atypical faculty also fell in 2020–1, compared with the previous year, by 10.7 per cent to 59,120.

Given pre-existing concerns about workloads and mental health in higher education (e.g. Erickson, Hanna and Walker 2021; Kinman and Wray 2020; Wellcome Trust 2020), it is not surprising that the rapid and sudden move to online teaching and remote working had a major impact on UK academics' working conditions, workloads and sense of well-being, and this was echoed in other anglophone countries undergoing similar shifts (The Chronicle of Higher Education 2020; Organisation for Economic Co-operation and Development (OECD) 2021; Ross 2021; Shankar et al. 2021; Sutherland et al. 2021). A national study of working life in UK higher education institutions after the start of the pandemic, by Wray and Kinman (2021), used a well-established risk assessment framework to investigate key psychosocial hazards at work after the first year of the pandemic. It repeated previous surveys of academic and academic-related employees which had found that well-being related to job demands, support from managers and colleagues, relationships, role and management of change were already considerably lower than recommended levels and for related professions (Kinman and Wray 2020). In their latest study, many respondents indicated that online teaching and remote working had significantly increased their workload and the stress that arose from this. The expectation from institutional management had been that they would continue to operate as usual and be available for students as and when required. This was considered by respondents to be unrealistic as it took little account of the additional time required to convert teaching to an online format, learn new technologies, develop fresh resources and provide more support to students and colleagues. In addition, line managers felt under considerable pressure to support a larger proportion of faculty who were having difficulties (Wray and Kinman 2021).

Interestingly, in this study, those on teaching and research contracts were less satisfied with these new job demands, and were more likely to feel they were being asked to undertake unnecessary tasks, than those on teaching-only and research-only contracts. This was partially echoed in a UCU survey among Scottish members, where those who described their roles as 'teaching and research' and 'teaching-only' reported increases in workload of greater than 20 per cent and at a much higher rate than members in research-only roles and in academic-related and professional support roles (UCU Scotland 2021). In a Joint Information Systems Committee (JISC) survey of higher education teachers, faculty who had taught in their organization the longest more often reported that online teaching had created technical challenges, changed their role as a teacher and added significant stress to their workload (JISC 2021a). Conversely, in the Wray and Kinman study, research-only academics were more satisfied than other types of academics with job demands, their levels of work autonomy, managerial support and workplace relationships, and they had a stronger overall sense of psychosocial safety. This type of academic also reported higher levels of mental health and lower levels of work-life conflict than those with teaching responsibilities (Wray and Kinman 2021).

However, respondents to other surveys also identified significant negative impacts of the pandemic on research, including the curtailment of field work and networking due to travel restrictions, limited laboratory time, the redirection of funds to pandemic-related research, less time for research due to increased teaching loads, cancelled study leave and reduced research outputs (Shankar et al. 2021; UTK/CIBER 2021). The effects on research funding and outputs, in particular, were felt likely to damage career prospects, especially for those early career researchers who were fixed-term and approaching the end of their contracts (UTK/CIBER 2021: 6):

> Most thought less travel and fewer significant face-to-face meetings in their fields would minimise networking and cause problems for them moving forwards. The fact that it was easier and cheaper to go to 'events' because you need only Zoom those bits you knew you wanted to see did not make up for the loss of face-to-face with its trust connotations.

UK surveys have not so far explicitly identified a gender dimension to these impacts of Covid-19, but those from other English-speaking countries have reported reduced productivity among female academics due to taking on the bulk of home schooling and additional caring responsibilities during lockdowns (The Chronicle of Higher Education 2020; Shankar et al. 2021; Sutherland et al. 2021). A survey of principal investigators in the United States indicated that female scientists, those in laboratory-based sciences and, especially, those with young children experienced a substantial decline in the time they were able to devote to research (Myers et al. 2020). This was backed up by analysis of journal submissions during the first wave of the pandemic, which have highlighted reductions in submissions of articles to journals by women and in the proportion of female first and corresponding authors (Kibbe 2020; Squazzoni et al. 2021). There are also reports of fewer 'rapid response' pandemic-related research grants being awarded to female researchers than men, and more to the physical sciences than the social sciences which are likely to impact women more (Shankar et al. 2021). One analysis of Australian universities' information and guidance on remote working and care for faculty found it to be 'gender blind', in effect, evading responsibility for ensuring women's full participation in the academic labour force (Nash and Churchill 2020). 'Six universities provided information to staff about forthcoming academic promotions. New information pertaining to COVID-19 was administrative, largely relating to changes to deadlines, submission processes or the cancellation of promotions for 2020. None acknowledged the possibility that COVID-19 may pose additional barriers to women seeking promotion' (Sutherland et al. 2021: 9).

It is important, however, to acknowledge where there was a mixed reaction to these developments. 'Whilst some report serious disruptions for their research activities, others much more see this as relatively un-impacted' (Goedegebuure and Meek 2021: 3). Indeed, some respondents to these surveys have reported potentially positive impacts of the pandemic on academic work and careers: 'Many expressed hope that more traditional working hours and expectations of presenteeism would change for good with more flexibility for how, where and when (including across time zones) academic staff would work. As such, there were strong threads of reported increased autonomy and the potential for this on an ongoing basis if supported by universities' (McGaughey et al. 2021: 2240). Such flexible working had helped some families cope with the disruptions (Shankar et al. 2021). The rapid shift to online teaching had also developed new digital skills among teachers (JISC 2021a; McGaughey et al. 2021). One commentator even suggested that the Covid-19 lockdowns could lead to a 'kinder' research culture which, in addition to flexible working and relaxed deadlines, might encourage greater support and empathy among researchers, more foresight and an increasingly open and accessible approach to collecting evidence and reporting findings (Derrick 2020).

Further longitudinal research on academic work and careers, in the UK and other countries, would be of value, and the material in this book could provide a framework for such a comparative study. In particular, there is a need for further research which investigates career-making during the post-pandemic recovery phase, beyond the short-term individual reactions noted early on in the crisis. This would provide a longer term and deeper understanding of what may be complex, variable and evolving outcomes. It is suggested that the following questions could be explored in such a programme of investigation:

- What has been the longer term impact of the Covid-19 pandemic – and the responses to it – on academic work and careers in the UK and elsewhere? These could include potentially positive, as well as negative, impacts (e.g. flexible working and greater inclusivity through online communications), and even countervailing and paradoxical tendencies.
- Has (and, if so, how has) this accelerated or decelerated existing trends, such as casualization, role specialization, work intensity, well-being, salaries and employment conditions, promotion processes and institutional support for faculty?
- Has (and, if so, how has) this changed the nature of teaching, research, 'service' and other aspects of academic (and professional) roles?
- What have been the specific impacts in terms of gender, career stage, age, ethnic diversity, international faculty, disability and other characteristics?
- What are the implications of these impacts on managing people in higher education, leadership, the governance of institutions and policies at institutional, national and international levels?
- What are the implications of these outcomes for approaches to academic career-making, again differentiated by role, characteristics and career stage, for example?

And in relation to individuals,

- In what ways has this changed the balance between *formal* and *informal economies* and the extent to which individuals rely on either?
- To what extent and in what ways do individuals continue to be influenced by *Institutional*, *Practice* and *Internal scripts*?

The following section explores how individuals, institutions and higher education generally, might respond to some of the challenges analysed throughout this book and arising from the pandemic. It focuses on three propositions:

1   a reconceptualization of the educational role of academics in higher education that would reestablish this at the core of academic work and careers

2   developing a better understanding of, and support for, the resilience of academics to adversity, individually and collectively, as they withstand, overcome and learn from crises such as the pandemic; and
3   the rebuilding of trust as a critical dimension of the renewal of institutions, their re-engagement with external partners and the rediscovery of their social purposes.

Responding to the Challenges

Reconceptualizing the Educational Role

A survey of higher education teaching faculty in 2021 by the JISC echoed many of the negative impacts of the pandemic and responses to it already referred to in this chapter. However, it also found that 84 per cent of respondents rated the quality of online and digital learning as above average, with many reporting positive experiences of teaching online, including improved productivity and increased engagement and interaction with less confident learners (JISC 2021a): 'High numbers of teaching staff felt that the move to online teaching … had changed their role as a teacher. Redesigning curricula and assessment practices takes time to do well' (JISC 2021a: 6). Also on the positive side, 'The move to a new way of teaching and assessing learning was exciting and presented opportunities to reflect on, and reassess curriculum design, learn new skills, develop pedagogic practices and master new technologies' (JISC 2021a: 17). According to one respondent, 'It has allowed us to challenge the pedagogy underpinning our previous approaches and adapt both for digital delivery, and also when physically present' (JISC 2021a: 17).

It is clear there are differences between remote teaching in an emergency and carefully designed and planned online learning (Commonwealth of Learning 2020). Most universities have now moved beyond emergency remote teaching to something more sophisticated, which is adding in the basics that would be expected in face-to-face learning and teaching. This includes course navigation, confirming that all students have access and ensuring the integrity of assessment, but it might also include addressing issues around course design, copyright and amending academic regulations. These are fundamental elements that have long been features of face-to-face education. However, as Hodges and colleagues in the United States have noted, effective online learning aims to create a learning community and support for learners, not just instructionally but with co-curricular engagement and other social supports (Hodges et al. 2020). The infrastructure that exists around face-to-face education in order to support student success includes, for example, library resources, study spaces, help with language learning, study support, student housing, career services, health and counselling services. Hodges and colleagues went on: 'Face-to-face education isn't successful because lecturing is good. Lectures are one instructional aspect of an overall ecosystem specifically designed to support learners with formal, informal, and social resources.' 'Ultimately', they argued, 'effective online education requires an investment in an ecosystem of learner supports, which take time to identify and build. Relative to other options, simple online content delivery can be quick and inexpensive, but confusing that with robust online education is akin to confusing lectures with the totality of residential education' (Hodges et al. 2020: paragraph 11). This suggests that educators should be fashioning this 'overall ecosystem' providing online educational, social and personal support for students that goes far beyond 'simple online content delivery' and matches what is already provided on campus, even with the online enhancements already available. However, this will require considerable resources.

This reasoning suggests that the scale and pace of the shift to online learning, which involved almost all teachers and students in UK higher education in a very short timescale, could be the impetus for the design of new forms of 'blended learning' (Hazelkorn and Locke 2021). These new forms would need to accommodate a return to campus where online learning is no longer merely a supplement to in-person learning but also an integral part of the educational environment for students and educators. They could increasingly embrace hybrid forms of teaching and learning, where teachers bring together students in person with those studying remotely in one cohort. In hybrid education, all students interact and engage with each other, in real time sometimes, but more often than not asynchronously. They bring individuals and groups of students with their devices on campus, in classrooms and in new learning spaces, together with individuals and groups of students online, at home or at work and in remote study centres. University educators might think about ways of facilitating these distributed learning communities, encouraging engagement, building in interaction, constructing and curating open educational resources and access to expertise, that is unbounded by time and space. Internal and external quality assurance processes would need to ensure quality regardless of format. Universities could also be looking for ways in which learning technologies offer a superior, rather than a substitute, way of interacting, compared with face-to-face teaching and learning. Indeed, they could be taking a careful, considered, evidence-based look at the range of pedagogies available, technology-enhanced as well as in person, and finding the optimum mix for a specific subject or topic, for a particular group or cohort of students and at a precise stage in their development (Locke 2021).

As a recent report by the OECD (2021: 4) put it,

> In principle, the use of digital technology in universities holds great promise, including transforming teaching and learning practices; widening access to non-traditional learners; reducing instructional costs; improving opportunities for student and teacher collaboration; and expanding individualised and adaptive instruction. But it will require higher education institutions to commit to the development of a next-generation learning environment, including large-scale investments in hardware and software, sufficient time and training for teaching staff, and adapting pedagogical and assessment approaches to the new digital environment.

This could in turn lead to more distinctive and varied career paths for faculty, depending on the discipline and the interests and talents of individual teachers, and may increase the influence of *Practice* and *Internal scripts* on prescribed ways of working enshrined in *Institutional scripts*, as described in Chapter 4.

This holistic approach to understanding and redesigning the overall education ecosystem would require significant support from higher education institutions for their educators. Indeed, the JISC report called for a greater engagement from universities with teaching faculty, with a focus on more training, guidance and personal support for well-being as well as for the digital capabilities to teach, assess and counsel students online. It went further to recommend collaboration between the further and higher education sectors with both JISC and the government, to develop the digital infrastructure that enables teachers to access the right technology and equipment to modernize learning (JISC 2021b). This level of investment, at a time of economic recovery from the pandemic, would warrant a reconceptualization of the activity of higher education teaching as a broader educational purpose which incorporates a range of contributions to students' learning and overall educational experience, including from counsellors, librarians and specialists in technology enhanced learning, study support, language learning and careers education, for example. In turn, this could help break down the boundaries between academic faculty and professional services staff, and the disparities in career opportunities and trajectories within, and between, these groups. Again, this could impact approaches to careers, with an acceptance of more fluid, concertina-like trajectories, as described in

Chapter 5. This would require a reconsideration of the systems for reward and recognition across the higher education workforce, including recruitment and promotion policies and processes for performance review and development, as part of *formal institutional economies*. A broader conception of the educational purpose of institutions could also include students as proactive learners, capable of contributing to the creation and exchange of knowledge, including through lifelong education. In short, it could open up a wider range of possibilities for education-focused academics that would sustain a career to the highest levels of achievement.

Understanding the Nature of Academic Resilience

The notion of resilience has been gaining currency in higher education for a number of years (Karlsen and Pritchard 2013; Whitchurch and Gordon 2013b). It is likely to be even more relevant after the ruptures created by the pandemic in relation to, for example, pressure from institutions to regenerate academic programmes in blended formats, student expectations of contact hours and the challenge of meeting career goals and criteria for advancement. This has been recognized more recently:

> Given the importance of universities to economies … it is critical that we have a better understanding of responses of academics to the change which has occurred and will be a feature of higher education for the foreseeable future. A better understanding of the responses of academics to stress, will enable strategies and tools to be developed to allow academics to respond to the adversity more positively, especially for those Early Career Academics (ECAs) who are just starting out. The concept of resilience may allow academics to better reach their potential and deliver on expectations of high-quality contributions in research and education. Given the further uncertainty and change looming for higher education, resilience is critical for academics and higher education if they are to persist and create solutions to the challenges which the planet faces such as COVID-19 and realise the educational sustainability development goals. (Ross et al. 2023 [forthcoming])

In the study that is the subject of this book, resilient responses are reflected in ways in which individuals developed 'concertina-like' careers (described in Chapter 5) and negotiated misalignments and disjunctures such as non-alignment with disciplinary affiliation or departmental location, contractual arrangements, job profiles, progression pathways, promotion criteria and workload models (described in Chapter 6).

Academic faculty in higher education experience stress from a number of sources, including those already referred to, such as increasing workloads and employment insecurity, but also from a hyper-competitive environment in which rejection and criticism are endemic, whether from peer reviewers or student feedback surveys. As we have seen from a number of recent studies, the pandemic and responses to it appear to have amplified these stresses. In order to survive, let alone succeed, academics must be resilient against various forms of adversity in higher education. However, most manage to do more than merely cope and survive; they are able to learn from dealing with adversity, adapt to stress and develop the capacity to 'bounce back'. The interviews reported in the study on which this book is based provided many examples of this, including how academic faculty shape their careers and working lives, via *Practice* and *Internal*, as well as *Institutional*, *scripts*.

Nevertheless, *how* academics respond to adversity and develop resilience – and how institutions can support them in this – has remained largely invisible in the research literature (de los Reyes et al. 2021). It is assumed that academics and other higher education staff are – or will be – resilient, but the means by which they are remains unobserved and unacknowledged for the most part. Academic resilience represents a dynamic interaction of academics with their institutional and personal environments (Masten and Wright 2010; de los Reyes et al. 2021), and can be nurtured or weakened in the dialogue between the *informal* and *formal economies* within institutions. The collective dimension of resilience, including support provided by academic colleagues, mentors, line managers, heads of department and professional and technical staff within the university, is critical. So, too, are their disciplinary and professional communities and networks which extend beyond the confines of the institution and individuals' geographical locations. Families and friends are, of course, significant as well. So, it is important to recognize that academic resilience is not just an individual characteristic but also a feature of collective co-operation and a characteristic of a scholarly community. It is likely to be particularly important in dealing with the misalignments and disjunctures described in Chapter 6.

Because resilience is partly a learning process, it evolves over time, as individuals and communities gain experience of responding to adversity. They make changes, acquire resources – or make up for the lack of these – seek training, find creative solutions and access professional and support networks, as reflected in the concept of the *concertina career*, described in Chapter 5. This means that resilience reduces the magnitude of the impact of adversity and the time it takes to recover from increased stress and anxiety (Ross et al. 2022). This temporal dimension has been important in the shift to online teaching, with a rapid, emergency phase followed by a period of consolidation, a subsequent reconsideration of curriculum design and pedagogical practices and, potentially, a move towards hybrid education, incorporating the best of online and in-person modes. Each of these phases has its own stresses and challenges, but the experiences and expertise gained from one phase will inform individuals and institutions about how to approach the next. They will seek to do better by their students, make the most of the resources available and achieve successful outcomes.

As well as recognizing the nature of academic resilience as a collective, dynamic, learning process, higher education institutions need to understand how to support individuals and groups to build resilience. As noted by the following commentators, the surveys of academic faculty during the early stages of the pandemic began to appreciate the necessity for longer term, more sustainable changes: 'Higher education policies must be re-calibrated to mitigate their negative impact on the academic community as much as possible. In the short term, universities need to prioritise a "human-centric" model of productivity and academic labour that accounts for the ongoing toll the pandemic has been taking on staff, students, and all citizens' (Shankar et al. 2021: 174), and 'there is a need for university leaders to address the wellbeing needs of academic staff; not only through Employee Assistance Programs and other supports but through reasonable and sustainable expectations beyond a crisis modus operandi' (McGaughey et al. 2021: 12). This is an institutional responsibility as well as an individual's professional obligation to look after themselves and manage their working lives and careers. While the focus here has been on academics and their educational role, the importance of resilience in research and engagement activities should also be recognized and better understood. Resilient faculty, professional services staff and the institutions they work in will strengthen the quality of both research and education, as well as the resilience of students. The study that is the subject of this book has shown that academic faculty can be resilient and adaptable in relation to career-making, but it will be important to maintain conditions that facilitate this for the broadening range of faculty and professional staff.

The Critical Importance of Trust

As shown in the study, formal, structural relationships, such as those with heads of department, deans and members of senior management teams, likely to be represented by *Institutional scripts*, can be subject to strain, and, in such cases, a possible erosion of trust. Conversely, where they are positive, with robust levels of trust, they can have a disproportionate effect on the individual's career within an institution (see also Whitchurch and Gordon 2017). Furthermore, the high profile given by many respondents in the study to relationships outwith formal structures, likely to be represented by *Informal*, and to some extent *Practice scripts*, were regarded as particularly valuable, providing what one interviewee described as 'succour'. Such relationships were more likely to be based on an individual having a certain amount of discretion in developing a relationship, allowing trust to be built step by step, over time.

However, rather like resilience, trust has not been a major focus in the study of universities as institutions, either internally, in relation to their students and faculty, or externally, in relation to the communities in which they are located. Similarly, it is assumed by universities themselves that they are trustworthy simply because they are public institutions serving society. However, as UK higher education has become more market oriented as a result of government policies, and universities have responded by pursuing strategies that are geared to market success, trust is increasingly an issue, whether it is expressed as concerns about vice-chancellors' salaries, the level of student debt, freedom of speech or controversial research findings, for example. Although trust and trustworthiness are not new concepts in higher education (Engwall and Scott 2013; Gibbs 2004), the fact that trust has been both conceptually and methodologically downplayed in the field of higher education studies is striking. It may be that 'trust' is perceived as a 'soft' and somewhat subjective subject. Yet, many profit-making corporations have overtaken universities in taking their social and environmental responsibilities seriously, albeit to market themselves better to their customers. So, even in a market environment, trust can be critical. Moreover, as some 'global' research universities have become disengaged from their local communities – and a few have even alienated some of their own faculty as a result of casualization of employment and the reduction of posts – trust is an issue for universities and those who work in them, and it is not something that can be taken for granted.

The pandemic has amplified the question of trust, as global surveys such as the Edelman Trust Barometer indicate a declining public trust in academic faculty as credible spokespeople (Edelman 2021). Nevertheless, the role of scientists such as the chief medical officer, deputy chief medical officer and directors of public health, as spokespersons in the UK during the Covid-19 pandemic, contributing to regular Downing Street press conferences, as well as virologists, statisticians and psychologists contributing to news programmes, have in some cases been more trusted than the government. However, universities have in the past had a tendency to depend on an 'expert' model that prizes academic knowledge above other forms of knowledge and learning, particularly those in practice subjects, which are often de-legitimized. Research predominates in the reward structure of universities, in particular, research funding, peer-reviewed publications and patents. This can hamper constructive collaborations between universities and communities, government, businesses and non-profit organizations (Firth and Nyland 2020). In the higher education market, knowledge exchange and engagement – the 'third mission' of universities after teaching and research – has been redefined as the creation of assets that can be capitalized, commercialized and traded (Hughes and Kitson 2012).

Therefore thinking about this third mission from the perspective of developing trust could help universities value again a broader range of purposeful and ethical engagement policies and activities. It could help them re-engage with their local regions as stewards of place, and to act again as effective civic institutions. It could provide new perspectives on the civic role of universities, moving beyond the confines of existing knowledge exchange and engagement activities to more permeable relationships with society (University of Lincoln 2019). Rather than knowledge transmission or exchange, research translation and commercialization, this perspective highlights the importance of place and universities being embedded in their surrounding communities, as well as in their national and global networks. 'Knowledge circulation' might be a better way of understanding the 'permeable' university's relationship with society. This means universities listening to, and learning from, their communities rather than talking to, or at, them. The emergence of *Practice scripts* in the study demonstrates the bottom-up potential for the circulation of knowledge. It is for universities to recognize and promote this potential in building trust both with their communities and with their faculty.

Furthermore, several of those interviewed for the study on which this book is based were involved in such knowledge exchange and engagement activities, and sought to incorporate these into their career plans, including promotion and job applications. However, besides the odd appearance in universities' mission statements, the structures and systems for reward and recognition, such as selection, promotion and performance review criteria enshrined in *formal institutional economies*, have yet to develop so as to transform and encourage academic exchange that contributes to the broader public good. A lack of shared understanding, strategic direction, consistent guidance and high-quality professional development opportunities has often led to fragmented and *ad hoc* arrangements for individuals (Law, Cattlin and Locke 2021). Nevertheless, the

Covid-19 pandemic has provided an opportunity to reflect on what engagement means and how to best facilitate it, highlighting the importance of building genuine and trusting relationships with external organizations. Fostering the right university culture, systems and structures, supported by clearer strategic direction, prioritizing and investment within universities could strengthen and promote more purpose-driven and reciprocal engagements. External stakeholders offer important insights that university communities could learn, and benefit from, in achieving their strategic priorities and goals. Hence, the importance of two-way knowledge exchange and knowledge co-creation to promote mutuality and reciprocal, accountable and impactful partnerships between universities and society, reflected in many of the *Practice scripts* in the study.

Trust *within* universities is also important, and several of the surveys undertaken in the early part of the pandemic indicated a perception that this may have been eroded by senior management teams. Some respondents to these surveys even felt the crisis was being used as an excuse for cost-cutting exercises, rationalizing courses, creating redundancies and increasing faculty workloads (McGaughey et al. 2021; Watermeyer, Shankar et al. 2021). Whether or not this was the case, the impression is important for the morale of faculty, and to perceptions of the leadership and governance of universities. Concerns about reopening campuses after lockdowns have been voiced across the world (UCU Scotland 2021; Wray and Kinman 2021; Yamey and Walensky 2020), and the quality and timeliness of information about decision-making has been questioned. As a report by *The Chronicle of Higher Education* in the United States put it, 'It is a moment that calls for empathy and support for faculty well-being from college leaders, as well as tangible actions to confront the challenges and obstacles that faculty members are facing' (The Chronicle of Higher Education 2020: 5). Therefore, 'not only do institutions need to tackle the immediate concerns of faculty members, but also broader areas that the pandemic's impact has underscored, such as the tenure-promotion process. In the end, how institutions grapple with the fallout of this year in both the short term and long term will define them' (The Chronicle of Higher Education 2020: 22).

Creating a Sustainable Academic Workforce

The developments reviewed in this chapter suggest the lack of coherent strategies for the development of the academic workforce, at national, institutional and departmental levels. This has led to cases of *ad hoc* decision-making, without taking an overview of, for example, the overall balance in numbers of part-time and fixed-term faculty, teaching-only and research-only faculty, and early career and female faculty. In some cases, the interplay between institutions' internal recruitment and resourcing arrangements and external drivers such as the Research Excellence Framework (REF) may have created dynamics that have rendered universities' policies and efforts ineffective in influencing trends (Wolf and Jenkins 2021). This can be seen as a consequence of a *laissez faire*, market approach to higher education, which has tended to treat at least some academic faculty and professional services staff as a flexible 'human resource' to recruit when needed and release when not. Most higher education institutions were certainly not well prepared for the Covid-19 pandemic and the responses to it of national governments, being reliant on face-to-face education, high proportions of international students, tuition fee income and competitive research funding. On top of this, their responses to the pandemic have created a sense of uncertainty about projected cuts in income, restructures, potential reductions in the faculty available on campus and the overall size of the workforce, and increased teaching workloads arising from new forms of pedagogy, with the consequent impact on the time available for research (Baré, Beard and Tjai 2021).

For some academic commentators, the human cost of the pandemic in higher education has intensified a perception among higher education faculty of a lack of considered decision-making by some senior university executives, which is damaging faculty morale:

> "Academics, regardless of their employment status, gift considerable unpaid labour to keep their job and to sustain the sector because they are passionate about their research and teaching. While there is significant staff goodwill to try and save jobs …. They wish to see some reciprocity from executive management and the government by codeveloping more collegial and socially just approaches to re-imagining university futures post-pandemic, with a focus on the relationship between a sustainable and fair university sector and a strong democracy. (Blackmore 2020: 1335–6)

New Psychological and Social Contracts in the Academy

These pleas to emphasize the human side of the employment relationship and higher education's role in society lend strong support for the idea of new psychological and social contracts in higher education institutions. The notion of a 'psychological contract' has been developed and investigated for a number of decades and describes the expectations and assumptions of employers of their workers and vice versa, which are not necessarily inscribed in legal contracts of employment (Conway and Briner 2005; Guest and Clinton 2017). The concept has mainly been developed from the perspective of the employee, in order to understand the positive and negative impacts of organizational policies and practices on individuals' commitment, loyalty, trust, motivation, engagement and identity, for example. It has been developed from an original static notion to a more dynamic concept of a process which recognizes the evolving nature of the 'deal' between employers and employees. Like resilience and trust, it has not often – to date – been applied in the context of higher education (although, see Whitchurch and Gordon 2017), but as universities become larger and more corporatized, the similarities with private companies are growing. In particular, the shift from relational psychological contracts, based on trust, to transactional arrangements, based on fixed-term monetary rewards (Rousseau 1996), has become observable in higher education institutions (Dean 2017; Sewpersad et al. 2019). A third component, the 'ideological' commitment to a 'higher cause', has also been added (Herriot, Manning and Kidd 1997).

The psychological contract is both a concept that has been operationalized by human resources professionals for some time (Guest and Conway 2002) and a phenomenon to be investigated in higher education. Ideally, the latter process would inform the former. It may be particularly complex in universities, given their multiple purposes, and it will not be the same in every institution. Nor will it be the same for every role or employee profile in an institution, although it is likely there would be considerable overlap. The key differences might be between professional services staff and academic faculty, and, among academics, between those who undertake both teaching and research, those who only teach and researchers employed on fixed-term contracts. There might be more nuanced distinctions according to age, career stage, length of time in the profession and whether individuals have worked in other professions, including the private sector. In a higher education context, it is worth noting the importance in other sectors of psychological contracts for temporary employees (Guest, Isaksson and De Witte 2010). There is a particular interest in the literature on psychological contracts in whether or not employees feel the contract has been broken or breached and, given the 'seismic shift' in higher education institutions since the start of the Covid-19 pandemic (Wooldridge 2021), this would be a question for further investigation. It has been observed more generally that, while the pandemic has brought many changes, 'one thing that won't vanish is the importance of organisations really valuing their people, and treating them accordingly ... there's an urgent need for work to become more human, not less. How we act in these times could strengthen the psychological contract – or sever it' (Jacobs 2020). Those who have applied the concept to higher education have explored whether recent changes have undermined academics' autonomy and sense of self as professionals (Dean 2017), increased their self-monitoring through performance management systems and changed the educational relationship with students when they are increasingly treated as consumers (Sewpersad et al. 2019). Although it is beyond the scope of this book, the concept of a psychological contract could be widened to include students (see, e.g. Yale 2020).

Moreover, it could also be linked to a broader concept of the *social* contract that public universities have with external stakeholders, such as their local communities, government, alumni, employers and the public at large. Grant (2021) has offered a compelling argument for universities to refresh and strengthen their critical role in society in the age of social movements and networked technologies. By embracing social responsibility as part of their academic mission, he argues, they could discover a wider public purpose, be shaped by the societies they were founded to serve and renew their legitimacy as social institutions. In his provocation, he also proposes a restructuring of the academic workforce to introduce greater security for early career academics, more flexibility for established academics and a dissolution of the divide between academic faculty and professional services staff. Such a conception is worth exploring further, if it helps address the questions of trust and resilience, the efficacy of the *formal economies* of higher education institutions, an enhanced role for *informal economies* and the needs of a more fluid workforce outlined in Chapter 7.

The responses to the survey, outlined in Chapter 2, and the interviews indicated the importance of middle management roles, such as head of department, director of a research centre and leader of a taught programme, and academic-related professional roles, in the career progression of early- and mid-career faculty. Other recent research confirms this. For example, in the United States, Bäker and Goodall (2020) found that academic faculty who rated their department chairs as being distinguished researchers reported higher job satisfaction overall, and with their job characteristics, and less desire to leave their current positions. However, current research also suggests that strategic changes at the institutional level can constrain the autonomy of these mid-level figures as they become encumbered with operational demands (Creaton and Heard-Laureote 2021). It is possible that such positions could be made to be more attractive if they can be combined with active research, rather than the delayed gratification of study leave or a sabbatical following a fixed-term position, say, as a head of department. These developments can be seen as part of the psychological contract, which affects those with management responsibilities as well as those with teaching and research responsibilities, and would be worthy of further investigation post-pandemic.

Understanding and Supporting Academic Career-Making

Clearly, universities are complex institutions, and it is likely that individual academics' career aspirations will not always align with an organization's strategic aims and objectives. As knowledge-based operations, it is important that institutional leaders and managers understand the different reasons that individuals will have for moving to another position within the same institution, for leaving to go to a position in another university or to exit higher education altogether (Ryan, Healy and Sullivan 2012). Their career aspirations will also differ according to their previous employment experiences, current circumstances and career stage, and be modified by the reality and perceptions of what opportunities might actually be available to them, in their discipline and within their mobility range. As shown in Chapters 4 to 6, such factors are reflected in the way that *Internal*, and to an extent, *Practice scripts*, drive decisions. Personal characteristics, such as age, sex and caring responsibilities will also be material in their decision-making.

At the same time as individuals make their own decisions, given the specialist and 'cutting-edge' nature of much of the knowledge held by individual faculty, it is crucial for managers to monitor, evaluate and make strategic interventions where necessary. As Gandy, Harrison and Gold (2018) comment, 'Given the increasing complexity of managing talent in universities, with their predominantly knowledge-type employees … high localized staff turnover can adversely impact on a university's research capacity, which in turn presents risks to the achievement of its strategic aims and objectives. Therefore, detailed scrutiny of staff turnover dynamics can pinpoint where recruitment and retention policies and practice require focus' (Gandy, Harrison and Gold 2018: 597).

Likewise, higher education researchers need to construct and validate conceptual models that can distinguish between different types of institution and different subgroups of academics in order to develop a more nuanced and inclusive understanding of the factors that influence career trajectories and aspirations (Daly and Dee 2006; Zhou and Volkwein 2004). In particular, it will be important to investigate the role of supportive organizational cultures in improving job satisfaction, organizational commitment and intention to stay among academics (Daly and Dee 2006; Mashile, Munyeka and Ndlovu 2021; Trung et al. 2021). This will include appropriate professional development and career support (Heffernan and Heffernan 2019). As Medina (2012) noted,

> Job satisfaction is inversely associated with turnover intention and … organizational culture moderates the magnitude of this relationship. Sub-group analyses reveal that job satisfaction is more predictive of turnover intention for younger workers. These findings have significant implications for the changing composition of workforce due to the ageing population. These factors and how they interact with each other can help us to understand better the nature of academics' resilience in the face of adversity and how they can best be supported in contributing to a university's mission and succeeding in achieving their career aspirations. (Medina 2012: 3)

In turn, institutions may wish consider ways in which their *informal economies* are likely to be instrumental in helping to build resilience and trust.

Conclusion

This book has aimed to bring together a review of broad trends in the careers of academic faculty, drawn from an international literature and national statistics, with an understanding of how individuals manage and develop their careers in the light of their specific locales, interests, relationships and aspirations. It shows how UK institutions have been influenced by government policies such as the Research Excellence Framework (REF), more market-oriented environments and the emergence of a broader spread of disciplines, particularly around practice subjects. The empirical study, in the form of a survey and one-to-one interviews, provided detailed evidence of how individuals are managing their day-to-day roles and careers in the light of these developments, offering insights into the increasing diversity of faculty trajectories in UK higher education and how these are constructed by different individuals. In turn, these findings enabled the development of a conceptual framework of *formal* and *informal institutional economies* to understand ways in which these may be used by individuals, as well as examining the influence of *Institutional*, *Practice* and

Internal scripts in driving 'concertina'-like careers, in which individuals manage the time and space available to them. Finally, consideration has been given to how universities might respond to issues arising during the Covid-19 pandemic in relation to faculty career-making, in particular the re-conceptualization of educational roles, the development of resilience and trust, and greater attention to the different dimensions of the psychological contract.

Appendix 1

Survey Questionnaire

Q1. Current employer
Q2. Current job title
Q3. Length of time working in higher education (in total):
Less than 1 year
1–5 years
6–10 years
11–15 years
Over 15 years
Q4. Have you worked in sectors or industries other than higher education?
Yes/No
Note: If you have answered No, skip the following question.
Q5. For how long (in total)?
Less than 1 year
1–5 years
6–10 years
11–15 years
Over 15 years
Note: If you have answered No to Q4, skip the following question.
Q6. In which sectors or industries?
Other education sector
Central or local government
Not-for-profit sector
Business and private sector other than education
Other public sector (e.g. NHS, NGOs)
Professional body
Other (please specify)
Q7. With which broad disciplinary or professional field do you identify?
Academic services
Administrative, business and social studies
Agriculture, forestry and veterinary science

Architecture and planning
Biological, mathematical and physical sciences
Design, creative and performing arts
Education
Engineering and technology
Humanities and language-based studies and archaeology
Medicine, dentistry and health
Central administration and services, staff and student facilities

Q8. Formal contract hours (expressed as a fraction of full-time)
1.0 (full-time)
0.9
0.8
0.7
0.6
0.5
0.4
0.3
0.2

Note: If you have answered full-time to Q8, skip the following question.

Q9. Do you also undertake other employment?
No/Yes

Note: If you have answered No to Q9, skip the following question.
Note: If you have answered 1.0 (full-time) to Q8, skip the following question.

Q10. On average, how many hours do you work per week in other employment?
0–10
11–20
21–30
31+
Prefer not to say

Note: If you have answered No to Q9, skip the following question.
Note: If you have answered 1.0 (full-time) to Q8, skip the following question.

Q11. In which sectors or industries?
Other education sector
Central or local government
Not-for-profit sector

Business and private sector other than education
Other public sector (e.g. NHS, NGOs)
Professional body
Other (please specify)
Note: If you have answered Yes to Q9, skip the following question.
Note: If you have answered 1.0 (full-time) to Q8, skip the following question.

Q12. What are the reasons for your not having a full-time academic job? (Tick all that apply)
I couldn't find one
I am studying or planning to study
I don't wish to have full-time employment
Family e.g. childcare or elder care commitments
Prefer not to say

Q13. Terms of employment contract
Open ended
Fixed term
Sessional (please describe)
Other (please specify)

Q14. What percentage of your time on average do you usually spend on each of the following activities? (Please note that the total of the percentages in each row should add up to 100)
Research
Teaching
Management and administration
Knowledge exchange
Engagement
Pastoral care
Other (please specify)

Q15. Do you have an informal understanding or agreement (e.g. with a head of department or line manager) about the proportion of time you actually spend on each function mentioned in the previous question?
Yes/No

Q16. Function of employment (by contract)
Teaching and research
Teaching-only
Research-only
Neither teaching nor research

Q17. Does your institution, school or department, have a workload allocation system as a framework for reviewing time allocated to different types of activity?
Yes/No
I don't know
Note: If you have answered I don't know to Q17, skip the following question.
Q18. If so, to what extent does the workload allocation system reflect different activities?
It reflects the balance of my activity 100 per cent
It reflects the balance of my activity 75 per cent or more
It reflects the balance of my activity 50 per cent or more
It reflects the balance of my activity less than 50 per cent
Q19. Please state how many hours you work for your primary employer in a typical week
0–10
11–20
21–25
26–30
31–35
36–40
41–45
46–50
51+
Q20. Are there aspects of your work that have increased, or decreased, in the past two years? (please specify)
Q21. Are there any activities that you undertake that are not formally part of your contract?
No/Yes (please list examples)
Q22. What are your key relationships, internal and external to the university?
Senior managers (e.g. vice-chancellor, pro-vice-chancellors, director of human resources, chief operating officer/registrar)
Dean of faculty/head of school
Head of department
Research team
Principal investigator
Teaching team

Programme leader
Departmental colleagues
Disciplinary colleagues
Business and industry partners
Community partners
Other (please specify)

Q23. What, if any, support networks do you draw upon?
Departmental colleagues
Disciplinary colleagues in own institution or elsewhere
Peer group community e.g. early career
Online communities (please specify)

Q24. What career tracks are you aware of at your institution in relation to promotion to professorial level? If you have chosen 'other', please specify:
Teaching and research
Teaching
Research
Knowledge exchange/enterprise/public engagement
Don't know
Other (please specify)

Q25. What are your career aspirations during the next five years? (Please select all those that apply)
Continue on same academic career pathway
Continue on different academic career pathway: research and teaching
Continue on different academic career pathway: research only
Continue on different academic career pathway: teaching only
Take on professional role and/or contract, e.g., in relation to teaching and learning, online learning, widening participation, engagement
Take on management responsibilities such as principal investigator, head of department, pro-vice-chancellor
Work outside the higher education sector: private sector
Work outside the higher education sector: public sector
Work outside the higher education sector: charitable sector
Don't know
Withdraw from labour market
Continue to work in the UK
Work outside the UK

Q26. How likely do you think it is that you will be in the higher education sector in five years' time?
1 (very unlikely) 2 3 4 5 (very likely)
Don't know

Q27. Highest qualification
BA
MA
PhD
Professional doctorate
Professional qualification
Other (please specify)

Q28. Nationality
British
Other EU
Non-EU
Prefer not to say

Q29. Gender
Female
Male
Intermediate
Prefer not to say

Q30. Age
25 years and younger
26–30
31–35
36–40
41–45
46–50
51–55
56–60
61–65
66 years and over
Prefer not to say

Q31. Are you currently studying for a qualification? Yes/No
Note: If you have answered No to Q31, skip the following question.

Q32. Which qualification are you studying for?
BA
MA

PhD
Professional doctorate
Professional body membership
Postgraduate teaching certificate
Other
If you have chosen 'other', please specify.

Appendix 2

Topic Guide for First Round of Interviews, Autumn 2017 to Spring 2018

1. How would you describe your current role at the university?
   1.2 What is the balance of your activities (e.g. between teaching, research, other academic activities and professional/management/administrative activities)?
   1.3 How has your role and the balance of your activities changed over time?
   1.4 To what extent do you see yourself as an academic, a manager, a member of professional services staff or a hybrid of these?
2. How would you describe your relationship with the university and the way in which you engage with it?
   2.1 How is this informed by, for example, your discipline, the department or faculty you belong to, the type of institution, your line manager?
   2.2 What are the most positive aspects of this relationship, and the most negative, from your point of view?
   2.3 How do you engage with communities outside the university (in other words, at a local, regional or national level)?
   2.4 How do you engage internationally (e.g. with collaborators or partners from other countries, with organizations from outside the UK, and so on)?
   2.5 Have you personally experienced or noticed any changes as a result of the Brexit vote and developments since?
3. What tensions and/or synergies arise from the diversification of roles in universities, for instance:
   3.1 Between individual aspirations and institutional missions
   3.2 Between different types of staff (traditional teaching and research, teaching-only, research-only, professional staff and those with mixed

roles involving both academic and professional activity; also between part-time and full-time staff)
- 3.3 Between your role as specified in your contract and your job description and other activities you undertake for various reasons. What are the reasons for undertaking these other activities?
4. If you undertake activities that are not formally part of your contract:
    - 4.1 Could you give some examples and quantify these in terms of time commitment?
    - 4.2 In what ways do such additional activities enhance (or detract from) your career. In what ways do they relate to your formal role (or not); in other words, is there synergy with your formal role?
    - 4.3 Do you feel that you have a clear career pathway? How far is this facilitated by
        - a) formal structures and
        - b) informal networks and relationships, for example, with colleagues and/or your line manager?
    - 4.4 Have there been tensions between your own aspirations and the university's formal requirements and opportunities, and how have these been managed and resolved?
    - 4.5 Can you give examples of cases when tensions arose but have not yet been acknowledged or resolved? How might you go about addressing these?
    - 5.1 Where do you see yourself career-wise in five and ten years' time?
    - 5.2 Is there anything else you would like to say that might be relevant to our study?

Appendix 3

Topic Guide for Second Round of Interviews, Autumn 2019 to Spring 2020

1. Has your role changed since you were last interviewed in 2017 and, if so, in what ways? (e.g. balance between teaching, research, other academic activities, professional/management/administrative activities, online work in virtual environments).
    1.2 Have you agreed any such changes, formally or informally, with your line manager? Are they included in a work allocation model?
    1.3 Have there been any critical factors, critical events or turning points in your career progress in the past two years?
2. In what ways, if any, has your relationship with the university, and the way in which you engage with it, changed in the past two years? (e.g. key relationships with line manager, head of department, programme or project leader)
    2.1 How is this informed by, for example, your discipline, the department or faculty you belong to and/or the type of institution?
    2.2 What are currently the most positive aspects of this relationship, and the most negative, from your point of view?
    2.3 Has your engagement with communities and networks outside the university, including internationally, increased or decreased in the past two years – for example, disciplinary, professional body, business and/or industry?
3. Have any tensions and/or synergies between yourself and your institution intensified in the past two years, for example, between your role as specified in your contract, your job description and the day-to-day activities you undertake?
    3.1 Have you taken on additional activities in the past two years that are not formally part of your contract? Can you quantify these?

3.2 Can you give examples of cases when tensions arose but have not been acknowledged or resolved? How did you go about addressing these?
4. What would you like your next role to be? Where do you see yourself career-wise in five and ten years' time?
    4.1 What steps are you taking to progress your career?
    4.2 Would you consider leaving higher education if you had the opportunity?
    4.3 Are there any general trends or developments you have noticed in the past two years that you have not mentioned and that you think might be relevant to our study?

References

Aarnikoivu, M., Nokkala, T., and Saarinen, T. (2021), 'This Could Be the Turning Point': Rethinking Times and Spaces of Academic Work as a Result of Covid-19, Centre for Global Higher Education (CGHE) Webinar 222, 1 July. https://www.researchcghe.org/events/cghe-seminar/this-could-be-the-turning-point-rethinking-times-and-spaces-of-academic-work-as-a-result-of-covid-19/. Accessed 3 November 2022.

AHEIA, FBS, and UCEA (2015), *Contingent Academic Employment in Australia, Canada and the UK*, A Joint Comparative Research Project of the Australian Higher Education Industrial Association, Faculty Bargaining Services (Canada) and the (UK) Universities and Colleges Employers Association, London: UCEA.

Altbach, P. G. (ed.) (1996), *The International Academic Profession: Portraits of Fourteen Countries*, San Francisco: Jossey-Bass/The Carnegie Foundation for the Advancement of Teaching.

Angervall, P., Gustafsson, J., and Silfver, E. (2018), 'Academic Career: On Institutions, Social Capital and Gender', *Higher Education Research and Development*, 37(6): 1095–108.

Archer, L. (2008), 'Younger Academics' Constructions of "Authenticity", "Success" and "Professional Identity"', *Studies in Higher Education*, 33(4): 385–403. doi: 10.1080/03075070802211729.

Archer, M. (2000), *Being Human: The Problem of Agency*, Cambridge: Cambridge University Press.

Arthur, M. B., and Rousseau, D. M. (eds) (1996), *The Boundaryless Career*, New York: Oxford University Press.

Arvaja, M. (2018), 'Tensions and Striving for Coherence in an Academic's Professional Identity Work', *Teaching in Higher Education*, 23(3): 291–306.

Baik, C., Naylor, R., and Corrin, L. (2018), 'Developing a Framework for University-Wide Improvement in the Training and Support of "Casual Academics"', *Journal of Higher Education Policy and Management*, 40(4): 375–89. doi: 10.1080/1360080X.2018.1479948.

Bäker, A., and Goodall, A. (2020), 'Feline Followers and "Umbrella Carriers": Department Chairs' Influence on Faculty Job Satisfaction and Quit Intentions', *Research Policy*, 49(4). https://doi.org/10.1016/j.respol.2020.103955.

Balbachevsky, E. (2017), 'Values and Beliefs in Higher Education', in J. C. Shin and P. Teixeira (eds), *Encyclopedia of International Higher Education Systems and Institutions*, Dordrecht: Springer: 2737–43.

Baré, E., Beard, J., and Tjia, T. (2021), *Alleviating the Human Cost of COVID-19 in Australian Universities*, Melbourne Centre for the Study of Higher Education, University of Melbourne. https://melbourne-cshe.unimelb.edu.au/lh-martin-institute/fellow-voices/human-cost-of-covid-19-in-aus-unis. Accessed 3 November 2022.

Barnes, L. L. B., Agago, M. O., and Coombs, W. T. (1998), 'Effects of Job-Related Stress on Faculty Intention to leave academia', *Research in Higher Education*, 39(4): 457–69. https://link.springer.com/article/10.1023/A:1018741404199. Accessed 3 November 2022.

Barnett, R., and di Napoli, R. (eds) (2008), *Changing Identities in Higher Education: Voicing Perspectives*, Abingdon: Routledge.

Baruch, Y. (2004), 'Transforming Careers – From Linear to Multidirectional Career Paths: Organizational and Individual Perspective', *Career Development International*, 9: 58–73.

Baruch, Y. (2013), 'Careers in Academe: The Academic Labour Market as an Eco-System', *Career Development International*, 18: 196–210.

Becher, T., and Trowler, P. R. (2001), *Academic Tribes and Territories: Intellectual Enquiry and the Cultures of Disciplines*, Buckingham: Open University Press/Society for Research into Higher Education.

Behari-Leak, K., and Le Roux, M. N. (2018), 'Between a Rock and a Hard Place, Third Space Practitioners Exercise Agency'. *Perspectives in Education*, 36(1): 30–43.

Belfield, C., Britton, J., Buscha, F., Dearden, L., Dickson, M., van der Erve, L., Sibieta, L., Vignoles, A., Walker, I., and Zhu, Y. (2018), *The Relative Labour Market Returns to Different Degrees*, London: Institute for Fiscal Studies. https://www.ifs.org.uk/publications/13036. Accessed 3 November 2022.

Bhabha, H. K. (1994), *The Location of Culture*, London: Routledge.

Blackmore, J. (2020), 'The Carelessness of Entrepreneurial Universities in a World Risk Society: A Feminist Reflection on the Impact of Covid-19 in Australia', *Higher Education Research and Development*, 39(7): 1332–6. doi: 10.1080/07294360.2020.1825348.

Blackmore, P. (2016), *Prestige in Academic Life: Excellence and Exclusion*, New York: Routledge.

Bossu, C., and Brown, N. (2018), *Professional and Support Staff in Higher Education*, Dordrecht: Springer.

Bourdieu, P. (1993), *The Field of Cultural Production*, Cambridge: Polity Press.

Boyer, E. L., Altbach, P. G., and Whitelaw, M. J. (1994), *The Academic Profession: An International Perspective*, Princeton: Carnegie Foundation for the Advancement of Teaching.

Braun, V., and Clarke, V. (2013), *Successful Qualitative Research: A Practical Guide for Beginners*, London: Sage.

Brew, A. (2015), 'Academic Time and the Time of Academics', in P. Gibbs, O.-H. Ylijoki, C. Guzman-Valenzuela and R. Barnett (eds), *Universities in the Flux of Time: An Exploration of Time and Temporality in University Life*, London: Routledge: 182–96.

Brew, A., Boud, D., Lucas, L., and Crawford, K. (2018), 'Academic Artisans in the Research University', *Higher Education*, 76: 115–27.

Broadbent, K., Brown, T., and Goodman, J. (2018), 'Scholarly Teaching Fellows: Drivers and (Early) Outcomes', *Research and Development in Higher Education: (Re)Valuing Higher Education*, 41(1): 14–24.

Bryson, C. (2013), 'Supporting Sessional Teaching Staff in the UK: To What Extent Is There Real Progress?', *Journal of University Teaching and Learning Practice*, 10(3). https://doi.org/10.14453/jutlp.v10i3.2.

Callender, C., Locke, W., and Marginson, S. (2022), *Changing Higher Education for a Changing World*, London: Bloomsbury.

Carli, G., and Tagliaventi, M. R. (2022), 'Can You Do All in One Professional Label? Complementarity, Substitution, and Independence Effects in Academic Life', *Higher Education*. https://doi.org/10.1007/s10734-022-00868-y.

Carvalho T., Marini, G., and Videira, P. (2016), 'Is New Public Management Redefining Professional Boundaries and Changing Power Relations Within Higher Education Institutions?', *Journal of the European Higher Education Area*, 3: 1–16.

Cashmore, A., Cane, C., and Cane, R. (2013), *Rebalancing Promotion in the HE Sector: Is Teaching Excellence Being Rewarded?*, York: Higher Education Academy. https://www.advance-he.ac.uk/knowledge-hub/rebalancing-promotion-he-sector-teaching-excellence-being-rewarded. Accessed 3 November 2022.

Chattopadhyay, S., Marginson, S., and Varghese, S. (2023), *Changing Higher Education in India*, London: Bloomsbury.

The Chronicle of Higher Education (2020), *On the Verge of Burnout: Covid-19's Impact on Faculty Well-Being and Career Plans*. https://connect.chronicle.com/rs/931-EKA-218/images/Covid%26FacultyCareerPaths_Fidelity_ResearchBrief_v3%20%281%29.pdf. Accessed 3 November 2022.

Claeys-Kulik, A.-L., Jorgensen, T. E., and Stöber, H. (2019), *Diversity, Equity and Inclusion in European Higher Education Institutions: Results from the INVITED Project*, Brussels: European Universities Continuing Education Network, European Students' Union, European University Association.

Clarke, C. A., and Knights, D. (2015), 'Careering through Academia: Securing Identities or Engaging Ethical Subjectivities?', *Human Relations*, 68(12): 1865–88.

Clarke, C. A., Knights, D., and Jarvis, C. (2012), 'A Labour of Love? Academics in UK Business Schools', *Scandinavian Journal of Management*, 28(1): 5–15.

Clegg, S. (2010), 'The Possibilities of Sustaining Critical Intellectual Work Under Regimes of Evidence, Audit, and Ethical Governance', *Journal of Curriculum Theorizing*, 26(3): 221–35.

Coates, H., and Goedegebuure, L. (2010), *The Real Academic Revolution*, Melbourne: L. H. Martin Institute.

Collett, T., Capey, S., Edwards, J., Evans, D. J., McLachlan, J. C., Watson, H., and Bristow, D. (2021), 'Teaching, Research or Balanced? An Exploration of the

Experiences of Biomedical Scientists Working in UK Medical Schools', FEBS Open Bio. https://doi.org/10.1002/2211-5463.13304.

Commonwealth of Learning (2020), *Guidelines on Distance Education during COVID-19*. http://oasis.col.org/bitstream/handle/11599/3576/2020_COL_Guidelines_Distance_Ed_COVID19.pdf?sequence=4&isAllowed=y. Accessed 5 January 2021.

Conway, N., and Briner, R. (2005), *Understanding Psychological Contracts at Work: A Critical Evaluation of Theory and Research*, Oxford: Oxford University Press.

Copeland, R. (2014), *Beyond the Consumerist Agenda: Teaching Quality and the 'Student Experience' in Higher Education*, London: University and College Union.

Corbin, M., Campbell, K., and O'Meara, A. (2014), 'Faculty Agency: Departmental Contexts that Matter in Faculty Careers', *Research in Higher Education*, 55: 49–74.

Crawford, C., Gregg, P., Macmillan, L., Vignoles, A., and Wyness, G. (2016), 'Higher Education, Career Opportunities, and Intergenerational Inequality', *Oxford Review of Economic Policy*, 32(4): 553–75. https://doi.org/10.1093/oxrep/grw030.

Creaton, J., and Heard-Laureote, K. (2021), 'Rhetoric and Reality in Middle Management: The Role of Heads of Academic Departments in UK Universities', *Higher Education Policy*, 34: 195–217. https://doi.org/10.1057/s41307-018-00128-8.

Creswell, J. (1998), *Qualitative Inquiry and Research Design: Choosing Among Five Traditions*, Thousand Oaks, CA: Sage

Crimmins, G. (2017), 'Feedback from the Coal-Face: How the Lived Experience of Women Casual Academics Can Inform Human Resources and Academic Development Policy and Practice', *International Journal for Academic Development*, 22(1): 7–18. doi: 10.1080/1360144X.2016.1261353.

Crozier, D. (2017), *Modernisation of Higher Education in Europe: Academic Staff. Eurydice Brief*, Brussels: European Commission.

Curtin, N., Malley, J., and Stewart, A. J. (2016), 'Mentoring the Next Generation of Faculty: Supporting Academic Career Aspirations Among Doctoral Students', *Research in Higher Education*, 57: 714–38.

Daly, C. J., and Dee, J. R. (2006), 'Greener Pastures: Faculty Turnover Intent in Urban Public Universities', *Journal of Higher Education*, 77(5): 776–803. doi: 10.1080/00221546.2006.11778944.

Dany, F., Louvel, S., and Valette, A. (2011), 'Academic Careers: The Limits of the "Boundaryless Approach" and the Power of Promotion Scripts', *Human Relations*, 64(7): 971–96.

de los Reyes, E. J., Blannin, J., Cohrssen, C., and Mahat, M. (2021), 'Resilience of Higher Education Academics in the Time of 21st Century Pandemics: A Narrative Review', *Journal of Higher Education Policy and Management*, 44(1): 39–56. doi: 10.1080/1360080X.2021.1989736.

Dean, L. (2017), 'The Psychological Contract in Higher Education: Its Benefits for Investigating Academics' Experiences', Conference Paper: 10th Annual International Conference of Education, Research and Innovation, November. https://www.researchgate.net/publicat

ion/321762309_THE_PSYCHOLOGICAL_CONTRACT_IN_HIGHER_ EDUCATION_ITS_BENEFITS_FOR_INVESTIGATING_ACADEMICS%27_ EXPERIENCES. Accessed 3 November 2022.

Degn, L. (2018), 'Academic Sensemaking and Behavioural Responses Exploring How Academics Perceive and Respond to Identity Threats in Times of Turmoil', *Studies in Higher Education*, 43(2): 305–21.

Delanty, G. (2008), 'Academic Identities and Institutional Change', in R. Barnett and R. di Napoli (eds), *Changing Identities in Higher Education: Voicing Perspectives*, Abingdon: Routledge: 124–33.

Department for Business, Energy and Industrial Strategy (DBEIS) (2016), *Building on Success and Learning from Experience: An Independent Review of the Research Excellence Framework*, London: Department for Bu:siness, Energy and Industrial Strategy, July. https://assets.publishing.service.gov.uk/government/uploads/system/uploads/attachment_data/file/541338/ind-16-9-ref-stern-review.pdf. Accessed 3 November 2022.

Derrick, G. (2020), 'How COVID-19 Lockdowns Could Lead to a Kinder Research Culture', Nature Career Column, *Nature*, 581: 107–8. https://doi.org/10.1038/d41586-020-01144-8.

Djerasimovic, S. (2021), 'Exploring the Ways of Studying Academic Identity as a Dynamic Discursive Performance: The Use of Diary as a Method', *European Journal of Higher Education*, 11 Sup 1: 506–21. https://doi.org/10.1080/21568235.2021.2001349.

Dowd, K. O., and Kaplan, D. M. (2005), 'The Career Life of Academics: Boundaried or Boundaryless?', *Human Relations*, 58(6): 699–721.

Duberley, J., Mallon, M., and Cohen, L. (2006), 'Exploring Career Transitions: Accounting for Structure and Agency', *Personnel Review*, 35(3): 281–96.

Edelman (2021), *Edelman Trust Barometer 2021*, Global Report. https://www.edelman.com/trust/2020-trust-barometer. Accessed 3 November 2022.

Enders, J., and de Weert, E. (eds) (2009), *The Changing Face of Academic Life: Analytical and Comparative Perspectives*, London: Palgrave Macmillan.

Engeström, Y. (2001), 'Expansive Learning at Work: Toward an Activity Theoretical Reconceptualization', *Journal of Education and Work*, 14: 133–56.

Engwall, L., and Scott, P. (eds) (2013), *Trust in Universities*, London: Portland Press, ISBN: 978-185578-194-8.

Erickson, M., Hanna, P., and Walker, C. (2021), 'The UK Higher Education Senior Management Survey: A Statactivist Response to Managerial Governance', *Studies in Higher Education*, 46(11): 2134–51. doi: 10.1080/03075079.2020.1712693.

Fanghanel, J., McGowan, S., Parker, P., McConnell, C., Potter, J., Locke, W., and Healey, M. (2016), *Defining and Supporting the Scholarship of Teaching and Learning (SoTL): A Sector-Wide Study*, Literature Review, York: Higher Education Academy. https://www.advance-he.ac.uk/knowledge-hub/defining-and-supporting-scholarship-teaching-and-learning-sotl-sector-wide-study. Accessed 3 November 2022.

Finkelstein, M. J., Conley, V. M., and Schuster, J. H. (2016), *The Faculty Factor: Reassessing the American Academy in a Turbulent Era*, Baltimore, MD: Johns Hopkins University Press.

Finkelstein, M. J., Iglesias, K. W., Panova, A., and Yudkevich, M. (2015), 'Future Prospects for Young Faculty Across the Academic World', in M. Yudkevitch, P. Altbach and L. Rumbley (eds), *Young Faculty in the Twenty-first Century: International Perspectives.* Albany: State University of New York: 321–50.

Fink-Hafner, D., and Dagen, T. (2022), 'Debating the Relationship between Academics and Practitioners in the Higher Education field', *Teorija in Praksa* let. 59, 1/2022. UDK (Universal Decimal Classification)[378:001-051]:378-051-027.22. doi: 10.51936/tip.59.1.5-24.

Firth, V., and Nyland, J. (2020), *After Coronavirus, Universities Must Collaborate with Communities to Support Social Transition*, National Centre for Student Equity in Higher Education. https://www.ncsehe.edu.au/coronavirus-universities-collaborate-communities-social-transition/. Accessed 3 November 2022.

Franco-Santos, M., Rivera, P., and Bourne, M. (2014), *Performance Management in UK Higher Education Institutions: The Need for a Hybrid Approach*, London: Leadership Foundation for Higher Education.

Freidson, E. (1994), *Professionalism Reborn: Theory, Prophecy and Policy*, Chicago, IL: University of Chicago Press.

Fritsch, N. S. (2016), 'Patterns of Career Development and Their Role in the Advancement of Female Faculty at Austrian Universities: New Roads to Success?', *Higher Education*, 72(5): 619–35.

Frølich, N., Wendt, K., Reymert, I., Tellmann, S., Elken, M., Kyvik, S., Vabø, A., and Larsen, E. (2018), *Academic Career Structures in Europe: Perspectives from Norway, Denmark, Sweden, Finland, the Netherlands, Austria and the UK*, Oslo: Nordic Institute for Studies in Innovation, Research and Education (NIFU).

Fumasoli, T., Goastellec, G., and Kehm, B. (eds) (2015), *Academic Work and Careers in Europe: Trends, Challenges, Perspectives*, Switzerland: Springer.

Fumasoli, T., and Marini, G. (2022), 'The Irresistible Rise of Managerial Control? The Case of Workload Allocation Models in British Universities', in C. S. Sarrico, M. J. Rosa and T. Carvalho (eds), *Research Handbook on Academic Careers and Managing Academics*, Cheltenham: Edward Elgar: 298–309.

Galaz-Fontes, J. F., Arimoto, A., Teichler, U., and Brennan, J. (eds) (2016), *Biographies and Careers throughout Academic Life*, Switzerland: Springer International.

Galaz-Fontes, J. F., and Scott Metcalfe, A. (2015), 'Changing Biographies and Careers of Academics', in U. Teichler and W. Cummings (eds), *Forming, Recruiting and Managing the Academic Profession*, Dordrecht: Springer: 23–50.

Gandy, R., Harrison, P., and Gold, J. (2018), 'Talent Management in Higher Education: Is Turnover Relevant?', *European Journal of Training and Development*, 42(9): 597–610. https://www.emerald.com/insight/content/doi/10.1108/

EJTD-11-2017-0099/full/pdf?title=talent-management-in-higher-education-is-turnover-relevant. Accessed 3 November 2022.

Garbe, E., and Duberley, J. (2019), 'How Careers Change: Understanding the Role of Structure and Agency in Career Change. The case of the Humanitarian Sector', *The International Journal of Human Resource Management*, 32(11): 2468–92.

Gibbs, P. T. (2004), *Trusting in the University: The Contribution of Temporality and Trust to a Praxis of Higher Learning*, Dordrecht: Springer. ISBN 978-1-4020-2344-6.

Gibbs, P., Ylijoki, O.-H., Guzman-Valenzuela, C., and Barnett, R. (eds) (2015), *Universities in the Flux of Time: An Exploration of Time and Temporality in University Life*, London: Routledge.

Giddens, A. (1990), *The Consequences of Modernity*, Cambridge: Polity Press.

Giddens, A. (1991), *Modernity and Self-Identity: Self and Society in the Late Modern Age*, Cambridge: Polity Press.

Glaser, J., and Laudel, G. (2015), *The Three Careers of an Academic*, Discussion Paper Nr. 35/2015, Technishe Universitat Berlin.

Goedegebuure, L., and Meek, L. (2021), 'Crisis: What Crisis?', *Studies in Higher Education*, 46(1): 1–4. https://doi.org/10.1080/03075079.2020.1859680

González Ramos, A. M., Fernández Palacín, F., and Muñoz Márquez, M. (2015), 'Do Men and Women Perform Academic Work Differently?', *Tertiary Education and Management*, 21(4): 263–76.

Goodman, J., Broadbent, K., Brown, T., Dados, N., Junor, A., Strachan, G., and Yasukawa, K. (2020), *Scholarly Teaching Fellows as a New Category of Employment in Australian Universities: Impacts and Prospects for Teaching and Learning*, Canberra, Australia: Australian Government Department of Education, Skills and Employment.

Gordon, G., and Whitchurch, C. (eds) (2010), *Academic and Professional Identities in Higher Education: The Challenges of a Diversifying Workforce*, International Studies in Higher Education, New York: Routledge.

Gormley, D. K., and Kennerly, S. (2011), 'Predictors of Turnover Intention in Nurse Faculty', *Journal of Nursing Education*, 50(4): 190–6.

Gornall, L., Cook, C., Daunton, L., Salisbury, J., and Thomas, B. (2014), *Academic Working Lives: Experience, Practice and Change*, London: Bloomsbury.

Graham, A. T. (2015), 'Academic Staff Performance and Workload in Higher Education in the UK: The Conceptual Dichotomy', *Journal of Further and Higher Education*, 39(5): 665–79.

Granovetter, M. (1973), 'The Strength of Weak Ties', *American Journal of Sociology*, 78(6): 1360–80.

Grant, J. (2021), *The New Power University: The Social Purpose of Higher Education in the 21st Century*, London: Pearson. ISBN-10 1292349425.

Green, D. A., and Little, D. (2017), On the Other Side of the Wall: The Miscategorization of Educational Developers in the United States? *To Improve the Academy*, 36(2): 77–88.

Groark, C. J., and McCall, R. B. (2018), 'Lessons Learned from 30 Years of a University-Community Engagement Center'. *Journal of Higher Education Outreach and Engagement*, 22(2): 7–30.

Guest, D. E., and Clinton, M. (2017), 'Contracting in the UK: Current Research Evidence on the Impact of Flexible Employment and the Nature of Psychological Contracts', in N. de Kuyper, K. Isaksson and H. de Witt (eds), *Employment Contracts and Well-Being among European Workers*, London: Routledge: 201–24.

Guest, D. E., and Conway, N. (2002), 'Pressure at Work and the Psychological Contract: An Employer Perspective', *Human Resource Management Journal*, 12: 22–39.

Guest, D. E., Isaksson, K., and De Witte, H. (eds) (2010), *Employment Contracts, Psychological Contracts, and Employee Well-Being: An International Study*, Oxford: Oxford University Press.

Gupta, S., Habjan, J., and Tutek, H. (2016), 'Introduction: Academia and the Production of Unemployment', in S. Gupta, J. Habjan and H. Tutek (eds), *Academic Labour, Unemployment and Global Higher Education*, London: Palgrave Macmillan: 1–20.

Harland, T., McLean, A., Wass, R., Miller, E., and Sim, K. (2015), 'An Assessment Arms Race and Its Fallout: High-Stakes Grading and the Case for Slow Scholarship', *Assessment and Evaluation in Higher Education*, 40(4): 528–41. doi: 10.1080/02602938.2014.931927.

Hartman, Y., and Darab, S. (2012), 'A Call for Slow Scholarship: A Case Study on the Intensification of Academic Life and Its Implications for Pedagogy', *Review of Education, Pedagogy, and Cultural Studies*, 34(1–2): 49–60. doi: 10.1080/10714413.2012.643740.

Hazelkorn, E., and Locke, W. (2021), Editorial: 'Blended Learning Is Dead, Long Live Blended Learning', *Policy Reviews in Higher Education*, 5(1): 1–3.

Heffernan, T. A., and Heffernan, A. (2019), 'The Academic Exodus: The Role of Institutional Support in Academics Leaving Universities and the Academy', *Professional Development in Education*, 45(1): 102–13. doi: 10.1080/19415257.2018.1474491.

Henkel, M. (2000), *Academic Identities and Policy Change in Higher Education*, London: Jessica Kingsley.

Henkel, M. (2011), 'New Public Management, Academic Time and Gender Inequality', in R. M. O. Pritchard (ed.), *Neoliberal Developments in Higher Education*, Bern: Peter Lang: 231–53.

Herriot, P., Manning, W. E. G., and Kidd, J. (1997), 'The Content of the Psychological Contract', *British Journal of Management*, 8(2): 151–62.

Higher Education Statistics Agency (HESA) (2012–22), *Higher Education Staff Statistics: UK* (annual series), Cheltenham: Higher Education Statistics Agency.

Hodges, C., Moore, S., Lockee, B., Trust, T., and Bond, A. (2020), 'The Difference Between Emergency Remote Teaching and Online Learning', *Educause Review*,

March. https://er.educause.edu/articles/2020/3/the-difference-between-emergency-remote-teaching-and-online-learning. Accessed 3 November 2022.

Holcombe, E., and Kezar, A. (2018), 'Mental Models and Implementing New Faculty Roles', *Innovation in Higher Education*, 43: 91–106.

Houses of Parliament (2021), 'Early Day Motion: 'University Redundancies', 24 May. https://edm.parliament.uk/early-day-motion/58532/university-redundancies. Accessed 3 November 2022.

Hughes, A., and Kitson, M. (2012), 'Pathways to Impact and the Strategic Role of Universities: New Evidence on the Breadth and Depth of University Knowledge Exchange in the UK and the Factors Constraining its Development', *Cambridge Journal of Economics*, 36(3): 723–50.

Jacobs, K. (2020), 'Has Coronavirus Brought a New Normal?', *People Management* (online) 23 April. https://www.peoplemanagement.co.uk/long-reads/articles/has-coronavirus-brought-new-normal#_ga=2.126931149.1191443477.1642901903-99049235.1636962558. Accessed 3 November 2022.

Janke, E. M. (2019), 'Scholar-Administrators as Change Agents', *Metropolitan Universities*, 30(2): 109–22.

Joint Information Systems Committee (JISC) (2021a), *Teaching Staff Digital Experience Insights Survey 2020/21: UK Higher Education (HE) Survey Findings*, November, Bristol: JISC. https://repository.jisc.ac.uk/8568/1/DEI-HE-teaching-report-2021.pdf. Accessed 3 November 2022.

Joint Information Systems Committee (JISC) (2021b), 'Pandemic Has Fundamentally Changed Role of Teachers, New Surveys Show', 29 November. https://www.jisc.ac.uk/news/pandemic-has-fundamentally-changed-role-of-teachers-new-surveys-show-29-nov-2021. Accessed 3 November 2022.

Jones, D., Visser, M., Stokes, P., Ortenblad, A., Deem, R., Rodgers, P., and Tarba, S. (2020), 'The Performative University: "Targets", "Terror" and "Taking Back Freedom" in Academia', *Management Learning*, 51(4): 1–15.

Kallio, K.-M., Kallio, T. J., Tienari, J., and Hyvönen, T. (2016), 'Ethos at Stake: Performance Management and Academic Work in Universities', *Human Relations*, 69(3): 685–709.

Karlsen, J.-E., and Pritchard, R. (eds) (2013), *The Resilient University*, Bern: Peter Lang.

Kaulisch, M., and Enders, J. (2005), 'Careers in Overlapping Institutional Contexts: The Case of Academe', *Career Development International*, 10(2): 130–44.

Kehm, B., Freeman, R. P. J., and Locke, W. (2018), 'Growth and Diversification of Doctoral Education in the United Kingdom', in J. C. Shin, B. M. Kehm and G. A. Jones (eds), *Doctoral Education for the Knowledge Society: Convergence or Divergence in National Approaches?*, The Netherlands: Springer: 105–21. ISBN 978-3-319-89713-4.

Kenny, J. (2017), 'Academic Work and Performativity', *Higher Education*, 74(5): 897–913.

Keohane, N., and Petrie, K. (2017), *On Course for Success? Student Retention at University*, London: Social Market Foundation. www.smf.co.uk/publications/course-success-student-retention-university/. Accessed 3 November 2022.

Kibbe, M. J. (2020), 'Consequences of the COVID-19 Pandemic on Manuscript Submissions by Women', *JAMA Surgery*, 155(9): 803–4. doi: 10.1001/jamasurg.2020.3917.

Kinman, G., and Wray, S. (2020), 'Well-Being in Academic Employees: A Benchmarking Approach', in R. Burke and S. Pignata (eds), *Handbook of Research on Stress and Well-being in the Public Sector*, Cheltenham: Edward Elgar: 152–66.

Knights, D., and Clarke, C. (2014), 'It's a Bittersweet Symphony, This Life: Fragile Academic Selves and Insecure Identities at Work', *Organization Studies*, 35(3): 335–57.

Kolsaker, A. (2014), 'Relocating Professionalism in an English University', *Journal of Higher Education Policy and Management*, 36(2): 129–42.

Kwiek, M. (2019), *Changing European Academics: A Comparative Study of Social Stratification, Work Patterns and Research Productivity*, London: Routledge.

Kwiek, M., and Antonowicz, D. (2015), 'The Changing Paths in Academic Careers in European Universities: Minor Steps and Major Milestones', in T. Fumasoli, G. Goastellec and B. Kehm (eds), *Academic Work and Careers in Europe: Trends, Challenges, Perspectives*, Dordrecht: Springer: 41–68.

Law, S. F., Cattlin, J., and Locke, W. (2021), *Understanding University Engagement: The Impact of COVID-19 on Collaborations and Partnerships*, Melbourne Centre for the Study of Higher Education: Melbourne. https://minerva-access.unimelb.edu.au/bitstream/handle/11343/279434/Engaged%20University%20Research_final.pdf?sequence=2&isAllowed=y. Accessed 3 November 2022.

League of European Research Universities (LERU) (2014), *Tenure and Tenure Track at LERU Universities: Models for Attractive Research Careers in Europe*. https://www.leru.org/files/Tenure-and-Tenure-Track-at-LERU-Universities-Full-paper.pdf. Accessed 3 November 2022.

Leisyte, L. (2016), 'New Public Management and Research Productivity: A Precarious State of Affairs of Academic Work in the Netherlands', *Studies in Higher Education*, 41(5): 828–46.

Leisyte, L., and Hosch-Dayican, B. (2016), 'Boundary Crossing and Maintenance Among UK and Dutch by Scientists: Towards Hybrid Identities of Academic Entrepreneurs', in L. Leisyte and U. Wilkesmann (eds), *Organising Academic Working Higher Education: Teaching, Learning and Identities*, New York: Routledge: 223–42.

Locke, W. (2011). 'The International Study of the Changing Academic Profession: A Unique Source for Examining the Academy's Perception of Governance and Management in Comparative Perspective', in W. Locke, W. K. Cummings and D.

Fisher (eds), *Changing Governance and Management in Higher Education: The Perspectives of the Academy*, Dordrecht: Springer: 381–3.

Locke, W. (2012), 'The Dislocation of Teaching and Research and the Reconfiguring of Academic Work', *London Review of Education* (Special issue on Managing Higher Education in the Post-2012 Era), 10(3): 261–74.

Locke, W. (2014), *Shifting Academic Careers and Their Implications for Enhancing Professionalism in Teaching and Supporting Learning*, York: Higher Education Academy. https://www.heacademy.ac.uk/node/10079. Accessed 3 November 2022.

Locke, W. (2017), *The Changing Dynamics of UK Higher Education Institutions in an Increasingly Marketised Environment: Academic Work and Rankings*, PhD Thesis, University College London. https://discovery.ucl.ac.uk/id/eprint/10038660/. Accessed 3 November 2022.

Locke, W. (2021), 'A Provocation: Blended learning Is Dead, Long Live Blended Learning!', *Pacific Journal of Technology Enhanced Learning*, 3(1). https://ojs.aut.ac.nz/pjtel/article/view/105/53. Accessed 3 November 2022.

Locke, W., and Bennion, A. (2011), 'The United Kingdom: Academic Retreat or Professional Renewal?', in W. Locke, W. K. Cummings and D. Fisher (eds), *Changing Governance and Management in Higher Education: The Perspectives of the Academy*, Dordrecht: Springer: 175–97.

Locke, W., Freeman, R., and Rose, A. (2018), *Early Career Social Science Researchers: Experiences and Support Needs, Special Report*, London: Centre for Global Higher Education. http://www.researchcghe.org/publications/early-career-social-science-researchers-experiences-and-support-needs/. Accessed 3 November 2022.

Locke, W., and Marini, G. (2021), 'The Rapid Increase in Faculty from the European Union in UK Higher Education Institutions and the Possible Impact of Brexit', in F. Huang and A. R. Welch (eds), *International Faculty in Asia in comparative global perspective*, Singapore: Springer Nature: 185–202.

Locke, W., Whitchurch, C., Smith, H., and Mazenod, A. (2016), *Shifting Landscapes: Meeting the Staff Development Needs of the Changing Academic Workforce*, York: Higher Education Academy. https://www.heacademy.ac.uk/sites/default/files/shifting_landscapes_1.pdf. Accessed 3 November 2022.

Lopes, A., and Dewan, I. (2014), 'Precarious Pedagogies? The Impact of Casual and Zero-Hour Contracts in Higher Education', *Journal of Feminist Scholarship*, 7–8 (Fall 2014/Spring 2015): 28–42. https://www.researchgate.net/publication/281586174. Accessed 3 November 2022.

Loveday, V. (2018), 'The Neurotic Academic: Anxiety, Casualisation, and Governance in the Neoliberalising University', *Journal of Cultural Economy*, 11(2): 154–66. https://doi.org/10.1080/17530350.2018.1426032.

Machado-Taylor, M., Soares, V. M., and Teichler, U. (eds) (2017), *Challenges and Options: The Academic Profession in Europe*, Dordrecht: Springer.

Mainiero, L. A., and Sullivan, S. E. (2006), *The Opt-Out Revolt: Why People Are Leaving Companies to Create Kaleidoscope Careers*, Palo Alto, CA: Davis-Black.

Marginson, S., and Xu, X. (2022). *Changing Higher Education in East Asia*, London: Bloomsbury.

Marini, G. (2017), 'New Promotion Patterns in Italian universities: Less Seniority and More Productivity? Data from ASN', *Higher Education*, 73: 189–205. https://doi.org/10.1007/s10734-016-0008-x.

Marini, G. (2019), 'A PhD in Social Sciences and Humanities: Impacts and Mobility to Get Better Salaries in an International Comparison', *Studies in Higher Education*, 44(8): 1332–43. doi: 10.1080/03075079.2018.1436537.

Marini G. (2023 [forthcoming]), 'The Unequal Strife for Representation in Professional Organizations: The University and College Union in English research-intensive universities', *Higher Education Forum*.

Mashile, D. A., Munyeka, W., and Ndlovu, W. (2021), 'Organisational Culture and Turnover Intentions among Academics: A Case of a Rural-Based University', *Studies in Higher Education*, 46(2): 385–93. https://doi.org/10.1080/03075079.2019.1637844.

Masten, A., and Wright, M. O. (2010), 'Resilience Over the Lifespan: Developmental Perspectives on Resistance, Recovery, and Transformation', in J. Reich, A. J. Zautra and J. Hall (eds), *Handbook of Adult Resilience*, New York: Guilford Press: 213–37.

McAlpine, L. (2010), 'Meaning and Purpose in Academic Work: Implications for Early Career Academics', Paper to the Society for Research into Higher Education Annual Research Conference, 14–16 December, Newport.

McAlpine L., and Amundsen, C. (2016), *Post-PhD Career Trajectories: Intentions, Decision-Making and Life Aspirations*, London: Palgrave Macmillan.

McAlpine, L., Amundsen, C., and Turner, G. (2014), 'Identity-Trajectory: Reframing Early Career Academic Experience', *British Educational Research Journal*, 40(6): 952–69.

McComb, V., Eather, N., and Imig, S. (2021), 'Casual Academic Staff Experiences in Higher Education: Insights for Academic Development', *International Journal for Academic Development*, 26(1): 95–105. doi: 10.1080/1360144X.2020.1827259.

McGaughey, F., Watermeyer, R., Shankar, K., Ratnadeep Suri, V., Knight, C., Crick, T., Hardman, J., Phelan, D., and Chung, R. (2021), 'This Can't Be the New Norm. Academics' Perspectives on the COVID 19 Crisis for the Australian University Sector', *Higher Education Research and Development*. https://doi.org/10.1080/07294360.2021.1973384.

McIntosh, E., and Nutt, D. (2022), *The Impact of the Integrated Practitioner in Higher Education: Studies in Third Space Professionalism*, London: Routledge.

McKie, A. (2021), 'Purge of Administrators Leaves UK Universities Exposed', *Times Higher Education*, 4 October. https://www.timeshighereducation.com/news/purge-administrators-leaves-uk-universities-exposed. Accessed 3 November 2022.

Medina, E. (2012), 'Job Satisfaction and Employee Turnover Intention: What Does Organizational Culture Have to Do With It?', Masters of Arts Thesis, Columbia

University, Fall. https://academiccommons.columbia.edu/doi/10.7916/D8DV1S08. Accessed 3 November 2022.

Miles, M., and Huberman, M. (1994), *Qualitative Data Analysis*, London: Sage.

Mingers, J., and Willmott, H. (2013), 'Taylorizing Business School Research: On the 'One Best Way' Performative Effects of Journal Ranking Lists', *Human Relations*, 66(8): 1051–73.

Morrish, L. (2019), *Pressure Vessels: The Epidemic of Poor Mental Health among Higher Education Staff*, London: HEPI Occasional Paper 20. https://www.hepi.ac.uk/wp-content/uploads/2019/05/HEPI-Pressure-Vessels-Occasional-Paper-20.pdf. Accessed 3 November 2022.

Musselin, C. (2005), 'European Academic Labor Markets in Transition', *Higher Education*, 49: 135–54.

Musselin, C. (2009), *The Markets for Academics*, New York: Routledge (first published in French: *Le marché des universitaires. France, Allemagne, Etats-Unis*. Paris: Presses de Sciences Po, 2005).

Musselin, C. (2013), 'Redefinition of the Relationships Between Academics and Their University', *Higher Education*, 65: 25–37.

Musselin, C. (2018), 'New Forms of Competition in Higher Education', *Socio-Economic Review*, 16(3): 657–83.

Myers, K. R., Tham, W. Y., Yin, Y., Cohodes, N., Thursby, J. G., Thursby, M. C., Schiffer, P., Walsh, J. T., Lakhani, K. R., and Wang, D. (2020), 'Unequal Effects of the COVID-19 Pandemic on Scientists', *Nature Human Behaviour*, 4: 880–3. https://doi.org/10.1038/s41562-020-0921-y.

Nash, M., and Churchill, B. (2020), 'Caring During COVID-19: A Gendered Analysis of Australian University Responses to Managing Remote Working and Caring Responsibilities', *Feminist Frontiers*, 27(5): 833–46. https://doi.org/10.1111/gwao.12484.

Noor, K. M. (2011), 'Work-Life Balance and Intention to Leave among Academics in Malaysian Public Higher Education Institutions', *International Journal of Business and Social Science*, 2: 240–8.

Noordegraaf, M. (2016), 'Reconfiguring Professional Work: Changing Forms of Professionalism in Public Services', *Administration and Society*, 48(7): 783–810.

Organisation for Economic Co-operation and Development (OECD) (2021), *The State of Higher Education: One Year into the COVID-19 Pandemic*, Organisation for Economic Co-operation and Development. https://www.oecd-ilibrary.org/docserver/83c41957-en.pdf?expires=1642737704&id=id&accname=guest&checksum=9E1AAD7CA824CF16A0B75277E37EE8BF. Accessed 3 November 2022.

Ortlieb, R., and Weiss, S. (2018), 'What Makes Academic Careers Less Insecure? The Role of Individual-Level Antecedents', *Higher Education*, 76(4): 571–87.

Peters, M. A. (2015), 'The University in the Epoch of Digital Reason: Fast Knowledge in the Circuits of Cybernetic Capitalism', in P. Gibbs, O.-H. Ylijoki,

C. Guzman-Valenzuela and R. Barnett (eds), *Universities in the Flux of Time: An Exploration of Time and Temporality in University Life*, London: Routledge: 9–31.

Pietilä, M. (2017), 'Incentivising Academics' Experiences and Expectations of the Tenure Track in Finland', *Studies in Higher Education*, 44(6): 932–45.

Pietilä, M., and Pinheiro, R. (2020), 'Reaching for Different Ends Through Tenure Track: Institutional Logics in University Career Systems', *Higher Education*. https://doi.org/10.1007/s10734-020-00606-2.

Pifer, M. J., and Baker, V. L. (2016), 'Professional, Personal, and Relational: Exploring the Salience of Identity in Academic Careers', *Identity: An International Journal of Theory and Research*, 16(3): 190–205.

Putnam, R. D. (2000), *Bowling Alone: The Collapse and Revival of American Community*, New York: Simon and Schuster.

Reale E., and Marini G. (2017), 'The Transformative Power of Evaluation on University Governance', in I. Bleiklie, B. Lepori and J. Enders (eds), *Managing Universities*, London: Palgrave: 107–37.

Renfrew, K., and Green, H. (2014), *Support for Arts and Humanities Researchers Post-PhD*, London British Academy and Arts and Humanities Research Council. https://silo.tips/queue/support-for-arts-and-humanities-researchers-post-phd?&queue_id=-1&v=1667473239&u=ODEuMTAzLjE4OC4xNTc=. Accessed 3 November 2022.

Research Excellence Framework (REF) (2014), Assessment Framework and Guidance on Submissions: Contents. https://www.ref.ac.uk/2014/pubs/2011-02/#contents. Accessed 3 November 2022.

Robinson, S. (2016), 'Forging Academic Identities from Within', in J. Smith, J. Rattray, T. Peseta and D. Loads (eds), *Identity Work in the Contemporary University: Exploring an Uneasy Profession*, Rotterdam: Sense: 17–32.

Rosewell, K., and Ashwin, P. (2019), 'Academics' Perceptions of What it Means to Be an Academic', *Studies in Higher Education*, 44(12): 2374–84.

Ross, J. (2021), 'University Stress Levels Worse than Ever, says New Zealand Union', *Times Higher Education,* 2 October. https://www.timeshighereducation.com/news/university-stress-levels-worse-ever-says-new-zealand-union?mc_cid=dcbe3765a5&mc_eid=8a221e2e95. Accessed 3 November 2022.

Ross, P. M. R., Scanes, E., and Locke, W. (2023 [forthcoming]), 'Stress Adaptation and Resilience of Academics in Higher Education', *Asia Pacific Education Review*.

Ross, P. M. R., Scanes, E., Poronnik, P., Coates, H., and Locke, W. (2022), 'Understanding STEM Academics Responses and Resilience to Educational Reform in Higher Education', *International Journal of STEM Education*, 9(1):11. doi: 10.1186/s40594-022-00327-1.

Rosser, V. J. (2004), 'Faculty Intention to Leave: A National Study on Their Worklife and Satisfaction', *Research in Higher Education*, 45(3): 285–309.

Rothwell, A., and Rothwell, F. (2014), 'Sustaining Academic Professional Careers', in L. Gornall, C. Cook, L. Daunton, J. Salisbury and B. Thomas (eds), *Academic Working Lives: Experience, Practice and Change*, London: Bloomsbury: 129–37.

Rousseau, D. M. (1996), 'Changing the Deal While Keeping the People', *Academy of Management Perspectives*, 10: 50–9. https://journals.aom.org/doi/abs/10.5465/ame.1996.9603293198. Accessed 3 November 2022.

Ryan, J. F., Healy, R., and Sullivan, J. (2012), 'Oh, Won't You Stay? Predictors of Faculty Intent to Leave a Public Research University', *Higher Education*, 63(4): 421–37. https://link.springer.com/article/10.1007/s10734-011-9448-5. Accessed 3 November 2022.

Sang, K., Powell, A., Finkel, R., and Richards, J. (2015), 'Being an Academic Is Not a 9–5 Job': Long Working Hours and the 'Ideal Worker' in UK Academia', *Labour and Industry: A Journal of the Social and Economic Relations of Work*, 25(3): 235–49. https://doi.org/10.1080/10301763.2015.1081723.

Santoalha, A., Biscaia, R., and Teixeira, P. (2018), 'Higher Education and Its Contribution to a Diverse Regional Supply of Human Capital: Does the Binary/Unitary Divide Matter?', *Higher Education*, 75(2): 209–30.

Schuck, S., Kearney, B., and Burden, K. (2017), 'Exploring Mobile Learning in the Third Space', *Technology, Pedagogy and Education*, 26(2): 121–37.

Scott, P. (2014), 'The Death of "the Don" ', in B. Cunningham (ed.), *Professional Life in Modern British Higher Education*, London: Institute of Education: 17–22.

Scott, P. (2021), *Retreat or Resolution? Tackling the Crisis of Mass Higher Education*, Bristol: Policy Press.

Seeber M., Lepori, B., Montauti M., Enders, J., de Boer, H., Weyer, E., Bleiklie, I., Hope, K., Michelsen, S., Mathisen, G. N., Frolich, N., Scordato, L., Stensaker, B., Waagene, E., Dragsic, Z., Kretek, P., Kruecken, G., Magalhaes, A., Ribeiro, F. M., Sousa, S., Veiga, A., Santiago, R., Marini, G., and Reale, E. (2015), 'European Universities as Complete Organizations? Understanding Identity, Hierarchy and Rationality in Public Organizations', *Public Management Review*, 17(10): 1444–74.

Sewpersad, R., Ruggunan, S., Adam, J. K., and Krishna, S. B. N. (2019), 'The Impact of the Psychological Contract on Academics' *SAGE Open* 9(2), April–June 1–10. https://journals.sagepub.com/doi/full/10.1177/2158244019840122.

Shams, F. (2018), 'Managing Academic Identity Tensions in a Canadian Public University: The Role of Identity Work in Coping with Managerialism', *Higher Education Policy and Management*, 41(6): 619–32.

Shankar, K., Phelan, D., Suri, V. R., Watermeyer, R., Knight, C., and Crick, T. (2021), '"The COVID-19 Crisis Is not the Core Problem": Experiences, Challenges, and Concerns of Irish Academia during the Pandemic', *Irish Educational Studies*, 40(2): 169–75. https://doi.org/10.1080/03323315.2021.1932550.

Shattock, M., Horvath, A., and Enders, J. (2021), *The Governance of European Higher Education Convergence or Divergence*? London: Bloomsbury.

Shattock, M., and Horvath, A. (2021), *The Governance of British Higher Education: The Impact of Governmental, Financial and Market Pressures*, London: Bloomsbury.

Siekkinen, T., Pekkola, E., and Carvalho, T. (2019), 'Change and Continuity in the Academic Profession: Finnish Universities as Living Labs', *Higher Education*, 79(3): 533–51.

Siekkkinen, T., and Ylijoki, O.-H. (2021), 'Visibilities and Invisibilities in Academic Work and Career Building', *European Journal of Higher Education*, 12(4): 351–5. doi: 10.1080/21568235.2021.2000460.

Sousa, C. A., de Nijs, W. F., and Hendriks, P. H. (2010), 'Secrets of the Beehive: Performance Management in University Research Organizations', *Human Relations*, 63(9): 1439–60.

Squazzoni, F., Bravo, G., Grimaldo, F., García-Costa, D., Farjam, M., and Mehmani, B. (2021), 'Gender Gap in Journal Submissions and Peer Review during the First Wave of the COVID-19 Pandemic. A study on 2329 Elsevier Journals', *PLOS ONE*, 16(10), e0257919. https://doi.org/10.1371/journal.pone.0257919. Accessed 3 November 2022.

Staton, B. (2021), 'English Universities Face Upheaval as Financial Strains Hit Jobs', *Financial Times*, 24 May. https://www.ft.com/content/6a30e430-95cf-4eec-a435-b7b98077ce23. Accessed 3 November 2022.

Stevenson J., O'Mahony, J., Khan, O., Ghaffar, F., and Stiell, B. (2019), *Understanding and Overcoming the Challenges of Targeting Students from Under-Represented and Disadvantaged Ethnic Backgrounds*, Bristol: Office for Students.

Stoltenkamp, J., van de Heyde, V., and Siebrits, A. (2017), 'The Third-Space Professional: A Reflective Case Study on Maintaining Relationships within a Complex Higher Education Institution', *Reflective Practice*, 18(1):14–22.

Strike, A., and Taylor, J. (2009), 'The Career Perceptions of Academic Staff and Human Resource Discourses in English Higher Education', *Higher Education Quarterly*, 63(2): 177–95.

Sullivan, S. E., and Baruch, Y. (2009), 'Advances in Career Theory and Research: A Critical Review and Agenda for Future Exploration', *Journal of Management*, 35: 1542–71.

Super, D. E. (1992), 'Toward a Comprehensive Theory of Career Development', in D. H. Montross and C. J. Shinkman (eds), *Career Development: Theory and Practice*, Springfield: Charles C Thomas: 35–64.

Sutherland, G., Vazquez Corona, M., Bohren, M., King, T., Moosad, L., Maheen, H., Scovelle, A., and Vaughan, C. (2021), 'A Rapid Gender Impact Assessment of Australian University Responses to COVID-19', *Higher Education Research and Development*, 41(6): 2079–93. https://doi.org/10.1080/07294360.2021.1971163.

Sutherland, K. A. (2017), 'Constructions of Success in Academia: an Early Career Perspective', *Studies in Higher Education*, 42(4): 743–59.

Teichler, U. (2017), 'Academic Profession, Higher Education', in J. C. Shin and P. Teixeira (eds), *Encyclopedia of International Higher Education Systems and Institutions*, Dordrecht: Springer: 50–5.

Teichler, U., Arimoto, A., and Cummings, W. K. (2013), *The Changing Academic Profession: Major Findings of a Comparative Survey*, Dordrecht: Springer.

Teichler, U., and Cummings, W. K. (2015), 'Forming, Recruiting and Managing the Academic Profession', in U. Teichler and W. K. Cummings (eds), *Forming, Recruiting and Managing the Academic Profession*, Dordrecht: Springer: 1–10.

Trung, T. V, Thien, N. H., Thai, D. D., Trung, V. M., and Chuong, H. L. A. (2021), 'Investigating Academic Staff Turnover Intention among Vietnamese Education Environments', *Journal of Legal, Ethical and Regulatory Issues*, 24 (Special Issue 5). https://www.abacademies.org/articles/investigating-academic-staff-turnover-intention-among-vietnamese-educational-environments-12766.html. Accessed 3 November 2022.

UK Research and Innovation (UKRI)/Research England (2021), *Knowledge Exchange Framework*, Swindon: UK Research and Innovation. https://www.ukri.org/our-work/supporting-collaboration-in-the-uk/supporting-collaboration-research-england/knowledge-exchange-framework/. Accessed 3 November 2022.

Universities and Colleges Employers Association (UCEA) (2019), *Higher Education Workforce Report 2019*, London: Universities and Colleges Employers Association. https://www.ucea.ac.uk/library/publications/he-workforce-report-2019/. Accessed 3 November 2022.

UniversitiesUK (UUK) (2019), *Widening Opportunity in Higher Education. The Third Phase: Beyond Graduation*, London: UniversitiesUK.

University and College Union (UCU) (unpublished), Results of a Survey on Teaching in Higher Education. (Other results are reported in Copeland 2014 above).

University and College Union (UCU) Scotland (2021), *Report of COVID-19 Survey of Members* (August). https://www.ucu.org.uk/media/11732/UCU-Scotland-report-of-Covid-19-survey-of-members/pdf/UCUS-Covid-survey-report_Aug21.pdf. Accessed 3 November 2022.

University College London (UCL) (2020), *Improving Our Offering for Teaching Fellows at UCL*, University College London, 30 September. https://www.ucl.ac.uk/human-resources/news/2020/sep/improving-our-offering-teaching-fellows-ucl. Accessed 3 November 2022.

University of Lincoln (2019), *The Permeable University: The Purpose of Universities in the 21st Century: A Manifesto*, 21st Century Lab. https://cpb-eu-w2.wpmucdn.com/blogs.lincoln.ac.uk/dist/9/8300/files/2019/11/J22424_UNIL_21st-Century-Lab_Publication_Web-Version.pdf. Accessed 3 November 2022.

University of Tennessee Knoxville/CIBER Research (UTK/CIBER) (2021), *Harbingers-2: Taking the Pulse One Year on* (Early Career Researchers: Scholarly Communication Trends, Work Life and Impact of Pandemic), University of Tennessee Knoxville/CIBER Research, November. http://ciber-research.com/download/20211204-Harbingers2_Taking%20the%20pulse%20one%20year%20on.pdf. Accessed 3 November 2022.

Veles, N. (2022), *Optimising the Third Space in Higher Education: Case Studies of Intercultural and Cross-Boundary Collaboration*, New York: Taylor and Francis.

Veles, N., and Danaher, P. A. (2022), 'Transformative Research Collaboration as Thirdspace and Creative Understanding: Learnings from Higher Education Research and Doctoral Supervision'. *Research Papers in Education*. doi: 10.1080/02671522.2022.2089212.

Vostal, F. (2016), *Accelerating Academia: The Changing Structure of Academic Time*, Basingstoke, Hampshire: Palgrave Macmillan.

Waaijer C. J. F. (2015), 'The Coming of Age of the Academic Career: Differentiation and Professionalization of German Academic Positions from the 19th Century to the Present', *Minerva*, 53: 43–67.

Watermeyer, R., Crick, T., Knight, C., and Goodall, J. (2021), 'COVID-19 and Digital Disruption in UK Universities: Afflictions and Affordances of emergency online migration', *Higher Education*, 81(3): 623–41. https://doi.org/10.1007/s10734-020-00561-y.

Watermeyer, R., Shankar, K., Crick, T., Knight, C., McGaughey, F., Hardman, J., Suri, V. R., Chung, R., and Phelan, D. (2021), '"Pandemia": A Reckoning of UK Universities' Corporate Response to COVID-19 and Its Academic Fallout', *British Journal of Sociology of Education*, 42(5–6): 1–16. https://doi.org/10.1080/01425692.2021.193705.

Watermeyer, R., and Tomlinson, M. (2021), 'Competitive Accountability and the Dispossession of Academic Identity: Haunted by an Impact Phantom', *Educational Philosophy and Theory*, 54(1): 92–103. doi: 10.1080/00131857.2021.1880388.

Watson, D. (2009), *The Question of Morale: Managing Happiness and Unhappiness in University Life*, Maidenhead, UK: Open University Press/McGraw Hill. ISBN-13 978-033523560-5

Webber, K. (2018), 'The Working Environment Matters: Faculty Member Job Satisfaction by Institution Type', *Research Dialogue*, 142, TIAA Institute, March.

Wellcome Trust (2020), *What Researchers Think about the Culture They Work in*. London: Wellcome Trust. https://wellcome.org/reports/what-researchers-think-about-research-culture. Accessed 3 November 2022.

Whitchurch, C. (2013), *Reconstructing Identities in Higher Education: The Rise of Third Space Professionals*, New York: Routledge.

Whitchurch, C. (2018), 'From a Diversifying Workforce to the Rise of the Itinerant Academic', *Higher Education*, 77(4): 679–94.

Whitchurch, C., and Gordon, G. (2013a), *Staffing Models and Institutional Flexibility*, London: Leadership Foundation for Higher Education.

Whitchurch, C. and Gordon, G. (2013b). "Universities Adapting to Change – Implications for Roles and Staffing Practices". In The Resilient University (Eds). R. Pritchard and J. Karlsen. Bern: Peter Lang: 213–37.

Whitchurch, C., and Gordon, G. (2017), *Reconstructing Relationships in Higher Education: Challenging Agendas*, New York: Routledge.

Whitchurch, C., Locke, W., and Marini, G. (2019), *A Delicate Balance: Optimising Individual Aspirations and Institutional Missions in Higher Education*, London: Centre for Global Higher Education (CGHE) Project 3.2, Working Paper 45.

Whitchurch, C., Locke, W., and Marini, G. (2021), 'Challenging Career Models in Higher Education: The Influence of Internal Career Scripts and the Rise of the "Concertina Career"', *Higher Education*, 82(3): 635–50. doi: 10.1007/s10734-021-00724-5.

Whitchurch, C. (2023a [forthcoming]), 'Academic and Professional Identities in Higher Education: From "Working in Third Space" to "Third Space Professionals"', in G. Strachan (ed.). *Research Handbook on Academic Labour Markets*. Cheltenham: Edward Elgar.

Whitchurch, C. (2023b [forthcoming]), 'Rehabilitating third space professionals in contemporary higher education institutions', *Workplace: A Journal for Academic Labor*.

Whitton, J., Parr, G., and Choate, J. (2021), 'Developing the Education Research Capability of Education-Focused Academics: Building Skills, Identities and Communities', *Higher Education Research and Development*, 41(6): 2122–36. doi: 10.1080/07294360.2021.1946016.

Wolf, A., and Jenkins, A. (2020), *Why Have Universities Transformed Their Staffing Practices? An Investigation of Changing Resource Allocation and Priorities in Higher Education*, London: Nuffield Foundation. https://www.kcl.ac.uk/policy-institute/assets/why-have-universities-transformed-their-staffing-practices.pdf. Accessed 3 November 2022.

Wolf, A., and Jenkins, A. (2021), *Managers and Academics in a Centralising Sector: The New Staffing Patterns of UK Higher Education*, London: The Policy Institute, King's College London.

Wooldridge, E. (2021), 'The Psychological Contract for Higher Education Beyond Covid', *WonkHE website*, 4 March. https://wonkhe.com/blogs/the-psychological-contract-for-higher-education-beyond-covid/. Accessed 3 November 2022.

Wootton-Cane, N. (2021), 'Thousands of Staff Made Redundant as UK Universities Struggle to Cope with Pandemic Fallout', 21 July, *Edvoy*. https://edvoy.com/articles/thousands-of-staff-made-redundant-as-uk-universities-struggle-to-cope-with-pandemic-fallout/. Accessed 3 November 2022.

Wray, S., and Kinman, G. (2021), *Supporting Staff Wellbeing in Higher Education*. https://www.educationsupport.org.uk/media/x4jdvxpl/es-supporting-staff-wellbeing-in-he-report.pdf. Accessed 3 November 2022.

Yale, A. (2020), 'What's the Deal? The Making, Shaping and Negotiating of First-Year Students' Psychological Contract with Their Personal Tutor in Higher Education', *Frontiers in Education*, 5: 60. doi: 10.3389/feduc.2020.00060.

Yamey, G., and Walensky, R. P. (2020), 'Covid-19: Re-Opening Universities Is High Risk,' *BMJ*, 370: m3365. https://www.bmj.com/content/370/bmj.m3365. Accessed 3 November 2022.

Ylijoki, O.-H. (2013), 'Boundary-Work Between Work and Life in the High-Speed University', *Studies in Higher Education*, 38(2): 242–55.

Ylijoki, O.-H., and Henriksson, L. (2017), 'Tribal, Proletarian and Entrepreneurial Career Stories: Junior Academics as a Case in Point', *Studies in Higher Education*, 42(7): 1292–308.

Ylijoki, O.-H., and Ursin, J. (2013), 'The Construction of Academic Identity in the Changes of Finnish Higher Education', *Studies in Higher Education*, 38(8): 1135–49.

Yudkevich, M., Altbach, P., and Rumbley, L. E. (2015), *Academic Inbreeding and Mobility in Higher Education*, London: Palgrave.

Zacher, H., Rudolph, C. W., Todorovic, T., and Ammann, D. (2019), 'Academic Career Development: A Review and Research Agenda', *Journal of Vocational Behaviour*, 110B: 357–73.

Zhou, Y., and Volkwein, J. (2004), 'Examining the Influences on Faculty Departure Intentions: A Comparison of Tenured Versus Nontenured Faculty at Research Universities Using NSOPF-99', *Research in Higher Education*, 45(2): 139–76.

Index

Note: Figures are indicated by page number followed by "f".
Tables are indicated by page number followed by "t".

Aarnikoivu, M. 107
academic
   academic-related 159, 160, 174
   activity(ies) 7, 12, 19, 20, 54, 60, 61, 66, 79, 80, 103, 107, 109, 127, 142–7, 149, 150, 156, 157, 187, 189
   atypical 24, 27f
   autonomy 3, 4, 145t, 147, 160, 161, 174
   balanced range of 92–3
   citizenship 117
   community 7, 8, 20, 24, 57, 61, 117, 138, 139, 168
   contract(s) 12, 28, 39, 98, 113, 114, 140
   division of labour 3, 24, 127
   employment functions 24–8, 33–5, 37, 38, 40, 42–4
   experience 46, 49
   faculty 1, 3, 6–12, 16–21, 23–5, 27–31, 34–7, 42, 48–52, 58, 60, 62, 64, 67, 74, 75, 86, 95, 107, 110, 115, 117–18, 126, 131, 135, 140, 145, 146, 150–1, 153, 154, 156–9, 165, 167–9, 172–4, 176
   formation 145t
   freedom 145t
   hinterland 19, 97, 151–2
   identity 12, 65, 74, 131
   interests 19, 120
   job(s) 44, 138, 158, 181
   labour market 3
   profession 1, 6–13, 16, 19, 21, 35, 53, 81, 131–77
   quasi- 139
   stage 33, 53
   transformational 145–6
   work 1–21, 5, 23–4, 33, 34, 44, 45, 49, 69, 90, 140, 151, 154, 156, 159, 161–2, 171–6
   workforce 6, 16, 21, 23–4, 33, 49, 69, 90, 151, 154, 156, 159, 171–6
   writing 95
activity(ies)
   academic 7, 12, 19, 20, 54, 60, 61, 66, 79, 80, 103, 107, 109, 127, 142–7, 149, 150, 156–8, 187, 189
   balance of 12–15, 34, 52–4, 70, 73, 111, 114, 143–4, 182
   clusters of 139
   cross-disciplinary 131
   developmental 66, 84, 96
   disciplinary 4, 18, 54, 131, 135, 139, 140, 150, 155
   emergent forms of 86
   expansion and contraction of 92
   exploratory 59t, 72t
   extended academic 61, 103, 107, 127, 142, 143, 144f, 147, 150
   favoured 71
   hidden components of 119
   new forms of 1, 15, 18, 20, 74, 75, 79, 89, 151, 155, 164, 172
   profession 71
   professional 18, 71, 187–9
   range of 5, 6, 9–10, 12, 17, 70, 92–3, 97, 118, 128, 138, 139, 154
   spaces 107
   theory 19, 109, 125–7, 155–6
   timescales 92, 107
   virtual 96
actors 67, 74, 75
adaptation 3, 5, 64, 122, 123, 142
advice
   and support 109, 121
agency
   active 61
   primary 16
   and structure 13, 69, 75, 87, 90, 146

agenda(s)
  emergent 128
agents
  primary 67, 74, 75, 151
AHEIA. *see* Australian Higher Education Industrial Association
Altbach, P. G. 10, 14, 35
Amundsen, C. 3, 8–10
Angervall, P. 148
Antonowicz, D. 8
apprenticeships 9, 135
approach(es)
  to careers 2, 15, 18, 56–7, 70, 71, 107, 151, 152, 158, 165–6
  flexible 86
  fluid 19, 156
  holistic 89, 95, 165
  interpretive 74
  mainstream 17, 18, 55, 58–61, 59t, 63–7, 154
  niche 17, 18, 56–7, 59t, 61–6, 154
  open-ended 48, 131, 145t, 152
  opt-in/opt out 82
  portfolio 17, 18, 55–6, 59t, 60–1, 63–7, 69, 154
  to roles 9, 10, 14, 17–19, 48, 49, 53, 55–8, 59t, 61–3, 66, 67, 89–90, 131, 145t, 154, 156
  speculative 144
  tactical 76
  team 140
Archer, L. 10, 55
Archer, M. 13, 15–16, 18, 67, 74, 75, 82, 151
Arthur, M. B. 15, 55, 146
Arvaja, M. 93
Ashwin, P. 10, 12
aspirations 6, 17, 19, 23–46, 50, 53, 54, 64, 75, 82, 104, 109, 114, 120, 126t, 127, 128, 154, 156, 175–6, 183, 187, 188
Athena Swan Charter 31
Australian Higher Education Industrial Association (AHEIA) 26–7

Baik, C. 26
Bäker, A. 174
Baker, V. L. 10
Balbachevsky, E. 11
Baré, L. 172

Barnes, L. L. B. 44
Barnett, R. 10
Baruch, Y. 10, 70
Becher, T. 7, 65, 143
Behari-Leak, K. 11
Belfield, C. J. 6
Bennion, A. 35, 63
Bhabha, H. K. 82
Blackmore, J. 172
Blackmore, P. 14
Bossu, C. 11
boundaries
  disciplinary 7, 59t, 133
  methodological 133
Bourdieu, P. 62, 148
Boyer, E. L. 35
brand 148
Braun, V. 57
Brew, A. 9, 62
Briner, R. 173
Broadbent, K. 26
Brown, N. 11, 26
Bryson, C. 25
business
  background(s) 141
  and industry 7, 15, 48, 70–1, 72t, 80, 99, 142, 183

Callender, C. 1
CAP. *see* Changing Academic Profession international study
career(s)
  advancement 12, 17, 23, 73, 75, 92, 98, 136, 154
  aspirations 19, 34, 38–9, 42, 120, 156, 175, 176, 183
  boundaried 13, 15–16, 55
  boundaryless 13, 15–16, 55, 70, 71, 154
  concertina 2, 13, 18, 91–107, 129, 146, 155, 166, 167, 176
  credit 18, 98, 107, 128
  designer 89
  development 11, 47–8, 50, 65, 87, 98, 110, 131
  drivers of 69
  frameworks 47, 48, 131
  guidance 79–80, 144f
  insecurity 6, 8, 71, 84
  intentions 12, 16–17, 23, 154

journey 75, 145
kaleidoscope 10
ladder 55, 64-6, 145
linear 2, 12, 53, 79, 91, 93, 106, 107, 123, 142
markers of achievement 91, 104, 109
milestones 2, 48, 55, 63, 106, 109
models 2, 12, 106, 107
non-linear 93
one-dimensional 69, 91
outcomes 72t
paths 1-4, 9, 12, 15, 16, 18, 19, 32, 36, 38, 46-8, 53, 56, 63, 72t, 74, 75, 79, 87, 89, 91, 92, 94, 100, 105, 107, 109, 115, 117, 118, 122, 128, 131, 142, 150, 154-6, 165, 183, 188
pathways 1-4, 12, 15, 18, 36, 47-8, 53, 63, 72t, 82, 117, 118, 128, 131, 155
positional 15, 48
progression 31-4, 49, 63-6, 72t, 74, 77, 78, 84, 109, 127, 128, 141, 158, 174
prospects 158, 160
re-booting of 92, 141
routes 78, 91, 100, 107
scripts 1, 14-16, 66, 69-92, 106, 131-2, 154-5
secure 65, 142
self-directed 82
service 98, 136, 164
structures 1, 10, 18, 63, 70, 75, 126t, 128, 154-5
targets 146
templates 2, 90, 107
timelines 105
timescale 8-9, 55, 58, 63, 91-2, 100, 107, 155
timetable 104
tracks 3, 15, 32, 33, 37, 39, 86, 183
trajectory(ies) 16-17, 23, 54, 74-5, 86, 89, 125, 154
zig zag 91-5
career-making
  fluid process of 90
  instrumental and transactional process of 145-6
career script(s)
  dominant 73t
  type of 72t, 75

caring
  responsibilities 5, 86, 92, 100, 125, 160, 175
Carli, G. 11
Carnegie Foundation for the Advancement of Teaching international survey 35
Carvalho, T. 10, 11, 48
case study institutions 16, 23, 26, 29, 34, 44, 50, 117
Cashmore, A. 32
casualization 8, 30, 154, 158, 162, 169
categories
  fixed 47, 57, 69, 90
Changing Academic Profession (CAP) international study 9, 11, 35
charities
  charitable giving 80
Chattopadhyay, S. 1
child protection 80
Chronicle of Higher Education. see The Chronicle of Higher Education
Churchill, B. 161
CIBER Research 158
citizenship
  good 13, 102, 145t, 149
Claeys-Kulik, A.-L. 6
Clarke, C. A. 5, 62
Clarke, V. 57
Clegg, S. 9
Clinton, M. 173
Coates, H. 10
collective
  good 140-1
collectivities 74, 75, 151
Collett, T. 45
commercial
  partners 125
commitments 1, 15, 18-20, 48, 58, 60, 69-73, 82, 84, 86, 93, 98-101, 103, 105, 106, 120, 126t, 127, 131, 135, 136, 138, 139, 146, 154-5, 173, 176, 181, 188
Commonwealth of Learning 163
community(ies)
  activism 138
  agendas 15, 70
  engagement 7, 8, 20, 48, 54, 58, 70, 84, 100, 117, 134, 138, 151

local 62, 140, 169, 174
outreach 15, 95, 96, 135, 136, 146, 150
underserved 102, 140, 150
confidence 76, 78, 81, 82, 94–5, 128, 142, 149–51
contact(s)
  informal 122, 126t
contract(s)(ed)(ual)
  casualised 100
  employees 126t
  employment 12, 41, 126t, 181
  fixed-term 25, 30, 31, 36, 52, 69, 83, 158, 159, 173
  full-time 41, 42
  hourly paid 31
  open-ended/permanent 27, 28f, 29, 36, 142
  part-time 25, 31, 69
  professional 112, 113, 133, 144
  psychological (*see* psychological contract)
  short-term 100
  social (*see* social)
  standard teaching and research 111
  status 26
  zero hours 31
contractual arrangements 8, 14, 18–19, 109–15, 126t, 155, 166
Conway, N. 173
Copeland, R. 26
Corbin, M. 4
cost benefit analysis 15, 55, 58, 59t, 72t, 76, 100–1, 131
COVID-19
  home schooling 160
  lockdowns 160, 161
  pandemic 6, 20, 23, 96, 101, 107, 145, 150, 153–77
  post-pandemic 107, 153–77
Crawford, C. 6
creative arts 93, 100, 105, 110, 115–17, 120, 144f
Creaton, J. 175
Creswell, J. 57
Crick, T. 157, 158
Crimmins, G. 25l
criteria
  progression 2, 4, 5, 8, 13, 14, 16, 18–20, 47–8, 55, 56, 70, 78, 90, 91, 93, 100, 107, 127–8, 153, 155

promotion 3, 9, 15, 55, 66, 67, 72t, 90, 107, 109–10, 115–18, 120, 121, 123, 124, 126, 128, 131, 155, 166
Crozier, D. 11
cultural reproduction 62, 148
Cummings, W. K. 9
Curtin, N. 8

Dagen, T. 11
Daly, C. J. 176
Danaher, P. A. 11
Dany, F. 11, 14–15, 70
Darab, S. 5
DBEIS. *see* Department for Business, Education, Innovation and Skills
Dean, L. 173
decision-making
  bodies 121
decisions
  micro- 87, 92, 106, 122, 125
Dee, J. R. 176
Deem, R. 5, 10
Degn, L. 9
Delanty, G. 15
de los Reyes, E. J. 167
department(al)
  head of 3, 39, 51, 52, 61, 102, 104–5, 111, 114, 117, 120, 126t, 128, 147–9, 151, 167–9, 174, 175, 181–3, 189
  home 109, 110
Department for Business, Education, Innovation and Skills (DBEIS) 29
Derrick, G. 161
Dewan, I. 25
de Weert, E. 10
digital environment 80, 165
Di Napoli, R. 10
discipline(s)(ary)
  affiliation 13, 18–20, 44, 109–10, 127, 153, 155, 166
  applications 61, 110, 142, 143, 144f, 145t
  applied 79
  bodies 126t
  boundaries 7, 55, 133, 150
  business-orientated 60–1, 79, 139
  cross-disciplinary 131, 140, 143, 144f
  extension 97, 132, 140, 142
  factors 136

focus 57, 143, 144f, 145t
hard 143, 150
hinterland 19, 141, 150
mutation 133
practice 97, 132, 136–40
soft 143
space 95–7
stretch 7, 131–6, 145t, 151–2
disconnections 109
discontinuities
  and breakdowns 119
disjunctures
  misalignments and 6, 12, 18–19, 21, 53, 107, 109–29, 155, 156, 166, 167
dislocation 107, 112, 121
dispositions 55, 56, 58
disruption(s) 2, 19, 20, 101, 105, 107, 121–2, 153, 155, 157, 161
diversification
  of academic workforce 69
diversity
  and inclusion 117, 136
Djerasimovic, S. 11
doctorate 4, 31, 37, 42, 93
domain
  disciplinary 57–8
  external/community 17, 47, 57–8, 59t, 154
  internal/motivational 17, 47, 57, 58, 59t, 154
  organisational 47, 57–8, 59t, 154
Dowd, K. O. 11, 15, 55, 70, 146
drivers
  personal 89, 105
  practice 97–100, 148
Duberley, J. 14, 15, 70

early career academics/faculty (ECAs). *see* faculty
ECAs. *see* faculty
economy
  formal economy 1–2, 13, 14, 20, 24, 33, 47, 60, 63, 81–2, 86, 116, 119, 121, 123, 126t, 127–8, 146, 147, 150, 153
  informal economy 1–2, 13–15, 48, 63, 67, 107, 126t, 127–8, 146–7
Edelman
  Trust Barometer 169
educational technology

blended learning 164
digital infrastructure 165
digital skills 161
hybrid learning 20, 153, 156, 164
lifelong education 166
online learning 38, 84, 94, 96, 100, 123–5, 128, 135, 139, 143f, 144, 151, 156, 163–4, 183
Edvoy 158
employability
  agendas 5, 70
  initiatives 95
  project 137
  skills 71
employee(s)
  contracted 126t
  engagement 5, 36
employment
  casual(isation) 169l
  category 51t
  fixed term 10
  framework(s) 3
  open-ended 10
  part-time 10, 69
  security/insecurity 167
  short-term 104
  status 69, 172
  trends 10
Enders, J. 10, 11, 80
engagement
  community 7, 8, 20, 48, 54, 58, 70, 84, 100, 117, 134, 138, 151
Engestrom, Y. 109, 125
Engwall, L. 169
entry points 12
equity
  and inclusion 132, 144f
Erickson, M. 5, 159
European Union (EU) 6, 28
exit
  plan 59t, 60, 72t, 73, 79, 99, 124, 141
  points 7, 12, 110
  strategy 81

faculty
  atypical (*see* academic)
  early career 2, 10, 26, 31, 36, 49, 100–1
  fixed-term (*see* contracts)
  full-time (*see* contracts)

lone 140
member(s) 26, 36, 132, 151, 171
mid-career 12, 42, 97, 174
neither teaching nor research 25t, 38t, 40t, 181
open-ended/permanent (*see* contracts)
part-time (*see* contracts)
reductions in 101, 172
'research-active' 29
research-only 24, 29, 33, 34t, 37, 39, 45, 51t, 159, 172
teaching and research 27, 29, 33, 36, 37, 39, 41, 45, 51t, 171–2
teaching-only 24–9, 32, 37, 39, 51t, 171–2
women 31
Faculty Bargaining Services (FBS) 26–7
family
  commitments 82, 93, 103, 106
  responsibilities 9, 52–3, 71, 78
Fanghanel, J. 8
FBS. *see* Faculty Bargaining Services
Finkelstein, M. J. 9, 26, 33–4
Fink-Hafner, D. 11
Firth, V. 170
flexible working 36, 107, 161, 162
formal
  parameters 8, 19, 63
  structures 79, 146, 169, 188
Franco-Santos, M. 6, 10, 45
Freeman, R. 7–9, 11, 31, 32, 34, 48
Freidson, E. 2
Fritsch, N. S. 65
Frølich, N. 11
Fumasoli, T. 11, 45

Galaz-Fontes, J. F. 9, 10, 14, 35
Gandy, R. 36, 44, 175
Garbe, E. 15, 70
gender
  balance 52
Gibbs, P. 106, 169
Giddens, A. 58
Glaser, J. 11
Goastellec, G. 11
Goedegebuure, L. 10, 161
Gold, J. 36, 44, 175
González Ramos, A. M. 65
Goodall, A. 174

Goodman, J. 26
Gordon, G. 7, 10, 11, 48, 169, 173
Gormley, D. K. 44
Gornall, L. 10
Graham, A. T. 45
Granovetter, M. 99
Grant, J. 97, 174
Green, D. A. 11
Green, H. 31
Groark, C. J. 11
Guest, D. E. 173
Gupta, S. 9

Harland, T. 5
Harrison, P. 36, 44, 175
Hartman, Y. 5
Hazelkorn, E. 164
HEA. *see* Higher Education Academy
head(s) of department 3, 39, 51, 52, 61, 102, 104–5, 111, 114, 117, 120, 126, 128, 147–8, 151, 167, 168, 174, 175, 181–3, 189
health
  professions 8, 51
  and social care 15, 70, 79–80, 95, 132
Heard-Laureote, K. 175
hedging bets 59
Heffernan, A. 176
Heffernan, T. A. 176
Henkel, M. 7, 8, 15, 65, 106
Henriksson, L. 10
Herriot, P. 173
HESA. *see* Higher Education Statistics Agency
heuristic
  device 58
higher education 1–9, 11, 12, 15, 17, 18, 23–8, 31–45, 48, 50–2, 54, 57, 60–1, 63, 76, 78, 79, 81, 82, 85, 89–91, 93, 94, 96, 99, 100, 103, 106, 110, 112–13, 117, 118, 132, 141, 142, 144, 150, 152–76, 179, 183, 184, 190
Higher Education Academy
  Fellowship 36, 89, 117
  National Teaching Fellowship 36
Higher Education Statistics Agency (HESA) 7, 8, 16, 23, 25, 27, 28, 31, 34–5, 37, 45, 48, 91, 113, 144, 145, 159

Hodges, C. 163–4
Holcombe, E. 11–12
Horvath, A. 1
Hosch-Dayican, B. 11
Houses of Parliament
　House of Commons 158
Huberman, M. 55
Hughes, A. 170
humanities xiv, 15, 31, 37, 51, 58, 65, 70–1, 76, 78–81, 85, 95, 97–9, 101, 102, 110, 113, 114, 119, 121, 123, 132, 140, 146–9, 180
human resources 12, 28, 29, 36, 50, 172, 173, 182

impact
　agendas 60, 98, 139
implementation capability 116
individual
　approaches 2, 14, 18, 49, 53, 107, 131, 149, 151
　aspirations 50, 54, 126, 187
　commitments 131, 173
　interests 61, 87
　practice 16, 49, 92
　predilections 6, 128
　preferences 13, 14, 143
　relationships 19, 126t, 131
　strengths 83, 128
　values 13, 71
individualism 147
industry 7, 15, 39, 48, 65, 70–1, 72t, 76, 78, 80, 81, 99, 114, 125, 137, 142, 183, 189
information technology 94
innovation 26, 29, 32, 59t, 115, 123, 127, 132, 135, 146–7
institution(al)
　boundaries 55, 60, 150
　career pathways 18, 63, 72, 105, 117, 131
　case study 16, 23, 26, 29, 34, 44, 50, 117
　civic 170
　descriptors 70
　expectations 4, 94, 112, 159
　job profiles 47, 111, 127
　locale 9, 143
　management team 29, 50, 63, 144, 168–9
　missions 13, 50, 135, 143–4, 187
　policy 5, 12, 18, 29, 32, 42, 48, 49, 53, 75, 115, 150, 152

pre-requisites 70, 114, 147
processes 1, 54, 66, 154
requirements 6, 53, 69, 89
Russell Group 28, 30, 43–4, 50, 51, 58, 61, 62, 64, 76, 79, 81, 82, 85, 92, 93, 97, 99, 101–3, 110–12, 114–17, 119–21, 123, 125, 132, 134, 135, 139–42, 146, 148, 149
scripts 1, 13, 15–18, 20, 70, 71, 73t, 74–9, 81–7, 89–92, 98, 100–2, 106, 110, 113, 114, 116–18, 120, 122, 123, 125, 126t, 128, 131, 135, 137, 138, 145–6, 149–51, 155, 165, 167–8
strategy 139
structures 10, 11, 15, 18, 24, 46, 54–5, 57–8, 64, 66, 90, 139, 150–1, 155
system 76
type 16, 17, 44, 50, 64, 154
interests
　extended 81–2
　personal 46, 47, 56, 72t, 76
internal
　dialogue(s) 74, 90, 151
　scripts(s) 1, 10, 15, 17–18, 67, 69–71, 72t, 73t, 74, 75, 78, 79, 82–90, 96, 100, 105–7, 109, 114, 122, 125, 126t, 128–9, 131, 135, 138, 154–5, 162, 165, 176–7
international(isation) 121
interview(s)
　first round of 47, 50, 51t, 52t, 53–7, 63–4, 66, 187–8
　questionnaire(s) 42
　questions 42, 53, 121
　second round of 51t, 52t, 53, 56, 57, 67, 69–71, 73t, 189–90
investment 13–14, 28, 36, 100, 131, 137, 164, 165, 171

Jacobs, K. 174
Janke, E. M. 11
Jenkins, A. 23, 25, 28, 29, 172
JISC. *see* Joint Information Systems Committee
job(s)
　description(s) 9, 12, 16, 33, 47–8, 53, 55, 56, 65, 67, 70, 74, 90, 111, 112, 114, 133, 189

profiles 14, 18–19, 47, 109–15, 127, 155, 166
security 60, 77, 124, 157, 158
Joint Information Systems Committee (JISC) 160, 161, 163, 165
Jones, D. 5, 10
journalism 79–80

Kallio, K.-M. 6
Kallio, T. J. 6
Kaplan, D. M. 11, 15, 55, 70, 146
Karlsen, J.-E. 166
Kaulisch, M. 11
KEF. *see* Knowledge Exchange Framework
Kehm, B. 11, 31–2
Kennerly, S. 44
Kenny, J. 6
Keohane, N. 6
key relationships 41–3, 41t, 48, 54, 182, 189
Kezar, A. 12
Kibbe, M. J. 161
Kinman, G. 45, 158–60, 171, 200
Kitson, M. 170
Knights, D. 5, 62
knowledge
  circulation 170
  co-creation of 145t
  economy 10
  exchange 20, 32, 33, 39, 56, 62, 63, 111, 117, 126t, 132, 170, 171, 181, 183
Knowledge Exchange Framework (KEF) 32
Kolsaker, A. 9
Kwiek, M. 8, 10, 11

Laudel, G. 11
law 45, 51, 70–1, 79, 110, 143, 144f, 169, 170
Law, S. F. 169, 170
leadership
  and innovation 32, 115, 123
League of European Research Universities (LERU) 4
learning
  blended 164
  distance 96, 118, 124–5
  lifelong 139

online 38, 84, 94, 96, 100, 123, 125, 128, 135, 139, 144f, 151, 156, 163, 164, 167–8, 183
skills 95, 135
student 30, 32, 50, 112–13, 118, 165
support 48, 50, 51, 117
support professionals 51t, 160
teaching and 7–8, 20, 32, 38t, 50, 59t, 94, 96, 98, 112, 133, 135, 139, 140, 142, 143, 144f, 153, 163, 164
leavers 40–2, 45
lecturer. *see* positions
Leisyte, L. 5, 11, 15
Le Roux, M. N. 11
lifestyle
  considerations 82, 83, 90
  patchwork 97
line manager(s) 75–7, 85–6, 90, 103, 109, 111, 112, 119–20, 126, 128, 137, 145, 147, 149, 150, 159, 167, 181, 187–9
Little, D. 11
lived
  experience 12, 18, 48, 107, 155
  reality 20, 62–3, 150, 153, 156
Locke, W. 2, 4, 6–9, 11, 17, 23–6, 28, 31–5, 48, 49, 55, 62–4, 73, 82, 91, 100, 106, 164, 165, 169, 170
longitudinal dimension 2, 6, 13, 16, 17, 51, 90
Lopes, A. 25
Loveday, V. 25

Machado-Taylor, M. 12
Mainiero, L. A. 10
mainstream
  approach to role 55, 58–60, 59t, 65, 66
management
  and administration 78, 181
  middle 5, 39, 40t, 174
  position(s) 24, 35, 39, 51, 114, 123
  role 12, 17, 23, 50–2, 77, 87, 101, 102, 112, 114–15, 154, 174
  senior 12, 17, 23, 29, 39, 50, 51, 63, 123, 124, 126, 144, 154, 168–9, 171
managers
  institutional 90, 109
  line 75–7, 85–6, 90, 103, 109, 111, 112, 119–20, 126t, 128, 137, 145,

147, 149, 150, 159, 167, 181, 187, 188, 189
  local 3, 19, 114, 120, 155–6
  middle 40, 42, 51, 128
  senior 37, 40t, 48, 121, 182
Marginson, S. 1
Marini, G. 2, 5–7, 10–12, 17, 31, 45, 48, 49, 55, 91
marketisation 28, 157
Mashile, D. A. 176
Masten, A. 167
McAlpine, L. 2, 3, 8–10
McCall, R. B. 11
McComb, V. 26
McGaughey, F. 157, 161, 168, 171
McIntosh, E. 11
McKie, A. 159
media 3, 13, 15, 45, 51, 70–1, 79–80, 95, 126, 148
mediating artefacts 126t
medicine 29, 37, 79, 144, 180
Medina, E. 176
Meek, L. 161
mental health
  psychosocial hazards/safety 159
  stress 59t, 85, 101, 106, 111, 133, 158–60, 166–8
  wellbeing 36, 105, 145t, 157–9, 162, 165, 168, 171
mentor(s)
  mentorship 13, 151
metrics 119
Miles, M. 55
Mingers, J. 5
misalignments
  and disjunctures 6, 12, 18–19, 21, 53, 107, 109–29, 155, 156, 166, 167
Montauti, M. 6
morphogenesis
  morphogenetic 20, 74, 126
  morphostasis 16, 74
Morrish, L. 45
Musselin, C. 3, 5, 10, 14, 70
Myers, K. R. 161

Nash, M. 161
National Student Survey (NSS) 28
network(s)
  external 19, 42, 60, 152

lateral 81–2
vertical 59t, 148
niche
  approach to role 62–3
non-governmental organisations 7, 9, 59t, 80, 81, 99
Noor, K. M. 44
Noordegraaf, M. 2
North America 31
NSS. *see* National Student Survey
Nutt, D. 11
Nyland, J., 170

OECD. *see* Organisation for Economic Co-operation and Development
online
  learning 38, 84, 94, 96, 100, 123, 128, 135, 139, 144, 144f, 151, 156, 163, 164
  media 148
  platforms 96
opportunities
  serendipitous 122
opportunism 149
option(s)
  alternative 85
  bespoke 145t
  future 71
  to leave 125
  to opt out 138, 141–2
Organisation for Economic Co-operation and Development (OECD) 159, 165
organisational
  culture(s) 33, 176
  processes 118
  restructuring 110
  systems 118
  understandings 118
Ortlieb, R. 10–11, 15
output
  types of 116
outreach
  activity 112–13, 134

pastoral care 58, 62, 95, 102, 103, 143f, 149–50
patronage 148
pay. *see* salary

Pen Portrait
  Pen Portrait 1 77–8, 84
  Pen Portrait 2 80–1
  Pen Portrait 3 87–9
  Pen Portrait 4 93–4
  Pen Portrait 5 104–5
  Pen Portrait 6 113–14
  Pen Portrait 7 116–17
  Pen Portrait 8 123–5
  Pen Portrait 9 134–5
  Pen Portrait 10 137
  Pen Portrait 11 138–9
Pensions 6, 71, 84
performance
  management 9, 13, 174
  public 148
  review 5, 10, 20, 70, 153, 166, 170
  unscripted 151
personal
  circumstances 92, 107, 127
  comfort zone 72t
  commitments 1, 15, 20, 58, 70, 73, 100, 105, 106, 127, 131, 154–5
  development plan(s) 13
  drivers 89, 97–100, 105, 148
  enrichment 146
  inclinations 76
  interests 1, 12, 16, 46, 47, 56, 61, 67, 70, 71, 72t, 73, 76, 83, 85, 154–5
  responsibilities 155
  strengths 1, 12, 15, 18, 56, 61, 67, 70, 71, 73, 85, 154–5
  values 58, 72t
Peters, M. A. 106
Petrie, K. 6
Pietilä, M. 4, 5, 10
Pifer, M. J. 10
Pinheiro, R. 5, 10
policing 79–80, 144f
policy
  development 132
  environment 53
  individual 5, 9, 49, 53, 70, 132, 150
  institutional 5, 12, 18, 29, 32, 42, 48, 49, 53, 75, 115, 150, 152
  university 132
portfolio
  approach to role 62
  of experience 31

position(s)
  assistant professor 30–1
  associate professor 4, 30–1
  dean 3, 39, 41–2, 51, 52, 102, 149, 168
  department chair 174
  enterprise professor 32
  head of department 39, 51, 52, 61, 102, 104–5, 114, 117, 120, 148, 174, 175
  lecturer 4, 29–3, 34t, 37, 52, 52t, 62, 63, 65, 66, 73, 77, 81, 85–7, 89, 92, 94, 95, 96, 98, 99, 103, 105, 111–22, 132, 133, 136, 140–2, 148
  post-doctoral 4, 8, 9, 31–2, 48, 95
  principal investigator 139, 160
  principal lecturer 30–1
  principal research fellow 30–1
  pro-vice-chancellor 39, 50, 117, 124, 144, 169
  professor 4, 30–3, 34t, 37, 39t, 52t, 58, 61, 62, 66, 77, 85, 86, 92, 97, 99, 101–5, 110–12, 115, 116, 121, 123, 124, 125, 132, 135–7, 146–9
  senior academic 24, 33, 42
  senior lecturer 29–3, 34t, 37, 52t, 63, 66, 73, 77, 81, 85, 86, 89, 92, 94–6, 98, 99, 103, 105, 113–17, 120, 133, 140–2
  reader 29, 32, 34t, 37, 39, 52t, 61, 66, 76, 83, 88, 89, 92, 93, 99, 100, 105, 116, 119, 121, 125, 133, 141, 147, 149
  research assistant 30, 33, 34t, 132
  research fellow 30–1, 37, 52, 52t, 62, 81, 82, 84, 86, 99, 103, 119, 120, 148
  teaching assistant 30, 34t
  teaching fellow 24, 30–2, 61, 84–6, 101, 119, 120, 137–8, 140, 149
  teaching specialist 24
  vice-chancellor 124, 169
practice
  based 64, 73
  day-to-day 5, 48, 119
  disciplines 95, 118, 136
  discipline-informed 95, 118, 139
  drivers 97–100, 148
  environments 69, 70, 90
  evidence-based 118
  networks 126t, 147
  scripts 1, 2, 13, 15, 17, 18, 70, 71, 73, 73t, 74, 75, 79–82, 86–91, 93, 100,

106, 107, 109, 118, 122, 125, 126t, 127, 128, 136, 137, 139, 144, 146, 150, 151, 155, 169–71, 175
transformation of 18, 74, 151
practitioner
   allegiances 131
   background(s) 110, 141
   settings 126t, 136
predilections 6, 86, 128, 131
pressure points 119
Pritchard, R. 166
private sector 17–18, 37, 38t, 39, 45, 81, 99, 138, 141, 173
profession(s)
   academic 1, 6–13, 16, 19, 21, 35, 53, 71, 81, 104, 131–52, 156, 157, 161, 166
   caring 70–1
   classic 15, 79
   health 8, 51, 137
   late entrants 100, 141
   law 45, 51, 70, 79
   media 51, 70
   social care 15, 79–80
professional
   allegiances 15, 18, 49, 74, 155
   background(s), 98, 141
   bodies 7, 9, 59t, 126t
   capital 60, 79
   collective 139
   development 4–5, 25, 26, 36, 48, 120, 128, 170, 176
   formation 19, 151, 156
   identities 136
   loyalties 86
   networked 63, 174
   paradigms 133
   practice 1, 3, 7, 8, 12, 19, 48, 58, 72t, 90, 97, 98, 117, 118, 127, 131, 142, 147, 150–2, 155
   practitioners 70
   responsibilities 18, 48
   services 50, 98, 125, 139, 159, 165, 168, 172–4
   staff 3–4, 20, 48, 115, 126t, 140, 144–5, 168
   supra-professional 90
professionalism
   extended 147
professor. *see* position
profile
   self- 145t
   teaching and research 4, 61
   unique 148, 149, 152
programme
   development 113
   leadership 149–50
   teaching 93, 126t
progression
   criteria 2, 4, 5, 8, 13, 14, 16, 18–20, 47, 55, 56, 70, 78, 90, 91, 93, 100, 107, 127, 153, 155
   pathways 15, 72t, 82, 109–10, 115–18, 166
project
   flagship 112
   management role 112
   management skills 135
promotion
   committee 76, 79, 115
   criteria 3, 9, 15, 55, 66, 67, 72t, 90, 109–10, 115–18, 121, 123, 124, 126t, 128, 131, 155, 166
   processes 4, 162, 171
psychological contract
   breach 173
public
   engagement 5, 11, 39, 132, 144f, 145t
   good 140, 146, 152, 170
   sector 38t, 39, 137
Putnam, R. D. 148

RAE. *see* Research Assessment Exercise
rankings
   global 30
RE. *see* Research England
reader. *see* positions
Reale, E. 5, 6
Recovery 62–3, 123, 162, 165, 167
redundancy(ies)
   compulsory 158
   voluntary 158
REF. *see* Research Excellence Framework
refugee education 80
regional 15, 20, 50, 59t, 79, 134, 145t
relationships
   permeable 170
   supportive 120
Renfrew, K. 31

research
  allocations of 26
  databases 71, 103, 115
  educational 94, 115
  evaluation 9, 28
  excellence framework 5, 24, 32, 64, 70, 71, 79, 89, 96, 113, 114, 134, 149, 172
  fellow 30, 37, 52, 52t, 62, 81, 82, 84, 86, 99, 103, 119, 120, 123, 148
  funding 29, 36, 50, 84, 85, 88, 96, 101, 111–13, 138, 157, 160, 170, 172
  grant capture 126
  grants(s) 60, 102, 103, 111, 126t, 139, 161
  pedagogical 7–8, 60, 115–17, 125
  project 27, 29, 84, 87, 88, 117, 126t
  research-only 4, 8, 17, 23–5, 25t, 27, 29, 30, 32, 33, 36–9, 40t, 44, 45, 50, 51t, 69, 111, 159–60, 172
  senior research fellow 32, 52t, 123
Research Assessment Exercise (RAE) 28
Research England (RE) 32
Research Excellence Framework (REF) 5, 10, 14, 24, 28–30, 64, 71, 78–9, 89, 96, 113, 114, 134, 149, 172
  scores 113
resilience
  adversity 157, 163, 167, 176
  collective/individual 157
  as a learning process 167, 168
resources
  under resourced 134
responsibilities
  caring 5, 86, 92, 100, 125, 160, 175
retention 36, 51, 135, 175
revenue stream 123
Robinson, S. 5
Rodgers, P. 5
role(s)
  education-focused 156
  management 12, 17, 23, 50–3, 77, 87, 102, 112, 114–15, 154, 174
  mentor(s) 126t
  neither teaching nor research (*see* faculty)
  research-only (*see* faculty)
  specialization 7, 158, 162
  teaching-only (*see* faculty)
  teaching and research (*see* faculty)

Rose, A. 7–12, 31, 32, 34, 48
Rosewell, K. 10, 12
Ross, J. 159
Ross, P. M. R. 166, 167
Rosser, V. J. 44
Rothwell, A. 32
Rothwell, F. 32
Rousseau, D. M. 15, 55, 146, 173
Rubrics 2, 3, 119, 126t
rules and resources 58
Russell Group. *see* universities
Ryan, J. F. 44, 175

Salary 36, 77, 137
Sang, K. 45
Santoalha, A. 14
satisfaction
  intrinsic 84
satisficing 59t, 84
scholarship
  teaching and 7–8, 87, 112, 132
schools
  liaison 136
Schuck, S. 11
science
  applied 78, 80, 81, 84–9, 92, 99, 101–4, 110–12, 114, 121, 123–5, 133, 137, 140, 142, 147, 149
  teaching 134
Scott, P. 9, 152, 160, 169
Scott Metcalfe, A. 9
scripts
  accommodation with 91
  institutional 1, 13, 15–17, 70–9, 73t, 81–4, 86, 87, 89–92, 98, 100–2, 106, 110, 113, 114, 116–18, 120, 122, 123, 125, 126t, 128, 131, 135, 137, 138, 145–6, 150, 151, 155, 165, 168–9
  internal 1, 10, 15, 17, 18, 67, 69–71, 72t, 73t, 74, 75, 78, 79, 82–90, 96, 100, 105, 106, 107, 109, 114, 122, 125, 126t, 129, 131, 135, 138, 155, 162, 165, 176–7
  practice 1, 2, 13, 15, 17, 18, 70, 71, 73, 73t, 74, 75, 79–82, 86–91, 93, 100, 106, 107, 109, 118, 122, 125, 126t, 127, 128, 136, 137, 139, 143–4, 146, 150, 151, 155, 169, 170, 171, 175

sector
  private 17–18, 37, 38t, 45, 81, 99, 138, 141, 173
security
  financial 60
  material 73
  personal 49, 72t
  sense of 14, 61, 65, 83
Seeber, M. 6
self-
  profiling 13, 15, 145t, 148, 156
  marketing 51, 135
  reliance 147
senior lecturer 29–33, 34t, 37, 52t, 63, 66, 73, 77, 81, 85, 86, 89, 92, 94–6, 98, 99, 103, 105, 113–17, 120, 133, 140–2
senior manage(r)(rs)(ment) 12, 17, 23, 29, 37, 39, 40t, 48, 50, 51, 63, 121, 123, 124, 126t, 144, 154, 168, 171
senior management teams 29, 63, 126t, 144, 168–9, 171
service(s)
  agreements 126t
  careers 164
  to community 59t
  contributions 78
  probation 87
  public 110, 141
  social 70–1
  to students 62, 146
Sewpersad, R. 173, 174
Shams, F. 5
Shankar, K. 157–61, 168, 171, 172
Shattock, M. 1
Siekkinen, T. 10, 11
skills
  agendas 137
  employability 71
  project management 135
  skillset(s) 19, 94, 120, 136, 155–6
  'soft' 19, 152
social
  capital 126
  contract 150–1, 153, 157, 172–5
  media 3, 13, 126t
  outcomes 84
  responsibility 174
  sciences 31
  scientists 115

(external) stakeholders 174
solutions
  bespoke 114, 125, 127t
Sousa, C. A. 6
space(s)
  commercial 99
  discretionary 61
  disruption of 107
  lateral 97
  safe 19, 85, 155
  space/time nexus 92–3
spatial
  dimensions 2
  parameters 18, 97
  stretch 99
splitting 82
Squazzoni, F. 161
Staton, B. 158
STEM (Science, Technology, Engineering and Mathematics) subjects 51, 135
Stern, Nicholas (Lord) 29
Stevenson, J. 6
Stoltenkamp, J. 11
strengths
  personal 1, 12, 15, 18, 56, 61, 67, 70, 71, 73, 85, 154–5
Strike, A. 10
strike action 78–9
structure(s)
  and agency 13, 69, 75, 87, 90, 146
student(s)
  admissions 149–50
  as co-creators of knowledge 145t, 171
  attainment 135
  experience 20, 28, 60, 62, 70, 71, 72t, 95, 126t, 132, 135–6, 143, 145t
  outcomes framework 71
  pastoral care of 58, 143f, 149–50
  psychological contract 173–4
  retention 135
  skill sets 19, 94, 120, 136, 155–6
Sullivan, S. E. 10, 44, 175
Super, D. E. 52–3
survey
  instrument(s) 10, 35, 46
  questionnaire(s) 34, 179–85
Sutherland, G. 158–61
Sutherland, K. A. 8
sweet spot 88, 92

synergy 50, 58, 59t, 112, 123, 140, 150, 187–9

Tagliaventi, M. R. 11
Taylor, J. 12
teaching
  enhancement 95, 97
  hybrid teaching 20, 153, 164
  online teaching 96, 118, 159–61, 163, 167–8
  teaching excellence framework 5, 32, 70
  teaching-only (*see* contracts)
  teaching programme 93, 126t
  teaching/research nexus 83
  track 116
Teaching Excellence Framework (TEF) 5, 32, 70
Technology 29, 51, 80, 87, 88, 94, 95, 115, 119, 124, 135, 142, 165
TEF. *see* Teaching Excellence Framework
Teichler, U. 9, 10, 12
temporal dimensions 2, 21, 90, 91, 167–8
tenure
  tenure track 4, 10, 100
The Chronicle of Higher Education 158–60, 171
think tank 82
third mission. *see* knowledge (exchange)
third world
  countries 80–1, 84, 88–9
time
  blocks of 102
  calculations 104
  clock 100, 101, 106
  compression 92, 100, 107
  control of 103
  deferred 150
  disruption of 2, 107
  extended 2, 92
  extension 31
  future 63, 103–4, 106
  hidden 101–3
  juggling of 101, 102
  real 164
  as a resource 100–1
timescales
  stretching and compression of 92, 100
tipping point 86–7, 102

Tomlinson, M. 10
Trowler, P. 7, 65, 143
Trung, T. V. 176
trust
  erosion of 168–9
  public trust 169
typology
  one-dimensional 69

UCEA. *see* Universities and Colleges Employers' Association
UCL. *see* University College London
UCU. *see* University and College Union
UK Coalition Government 28
UKRI. *see* United Kingdom Research and Innovation
uniform subjects 95
United Kingdom Research and Innovation (UKRI) Fellows 132
United States (US) 4, 26, 158, 160, 163, 171, 174
university(ies)
  culture 171
  decision-making 172
  post-1992 29, 30, 34, 50, 51, 60, 62–4, 73, 86, 92, 93, 96, 98, 100, 104, 105, 116, 119, 133–6, 140, 147, 149
  post-2004 34, 50, 51, 64, 81, 83, 93–5, 99, 141
  pre-1992 24, 29, 30, 33, 34, 36, 51, 60, 64, 78, 81, 84, 86, 89, 92, 94, 96, 98, 99, 101–3, 112, 115, 118–22, 132, 133, 136, 137, 140, 141, 147, 149
  pre-1992 Russell Group 51, 58, 61, 62, 76, 79, 81, 82, 85, 92, 93, 97, 99, 101–3, 110–12, 114, 115, 116, 117, 119–21, 123, 125, 132, 134, 135, 139–42, 146, 148, 149
  research intensive 24, 25, 28, 30–1, 42, 50
Universities and Colleges Employers' Association (UCEA) 3–4, 26–7, 29, 30, 32, 34, 36
Universities UK (UUK) 6
University and College Union (UCU) 3–4, 26, 71, 158, 160, 171
University College London (UCL) 1, 30
University of Lincoln 170
University of Tennessee. *see* Knoxville 158
UCU Scotland 158, 160, 171

Ursin, J. 10
US. *see* United States
UUK. *see* Universities UK

value
  added 144
variables
  career stage 64–6
  discipline 64, 65
  gender 17, 64, 65
  institutional type 16, 64
Veles, N. 11
Videira, P. 48
Vocation 59t, 62, 140–1
Volkwein, J. 176
Vostal, F. 106
vulnerability 149

Waaijer C. J. F. 9
Walensky, R. P. 171
Watermeyer, R. 10, 157, 158, 171
Watson, D. 157–8
Webber, K. 12
Weiss, S. 10, 11, 15
Wellcome Trust 159
Whitchurch, C. 2, 7, 10, 11, 17, 31, 48, 49, 53, 55, 91, 144–5, 169, 173
Whitton, J. 26
widening participation 38, 59t, 90, 96, 102, 134–7, 140
Willmott, H. 5
Wolf, A. 23–5, 28, 29, 172
Wooldridge, E. 173
Wootton-Cane, N. 158
work(ing)
  allocation 13, 20, 118, 119, 126t, 133, 153
  boundary 135, 140
  collaborative 126t, 137
  community-based 139
  conditions 9, 25, 35, 48, 85, 145, 146, 159

  environment 86
  humanitarian 15, 80
  innovative 19, 20, 118, 128, 150, 153, 156
  pathfinding 128
  remote 159, 161
  sabbaticals/study leave 175
  unacknowledged 62
  unpaid 62
  workforce 1, 6, 8, 10, 12, 16, 20, 23, 24, 33, 36, 49, 90, 110, 117, 127, 151, 153, 154, 156, 158, 159, 166, 171, 172, 174, 176
  workforce diversification 6, 10, 12, 21, 69, 90, 110, 127, 151
  work-life balance/conflict 5, 9, 13–15, 43, 59t, 61, 65, 71, 72t, 73, 86–9, 101, 123, 125, 127, 145t
  workload model(s) 9, 19, 103, 109, 110, 118–20, 127, 155, 166
  workloads 6, 7, 25, 30, 71, 84, 111, 119, 158, 159, 167, 171, 172
workforce
  diversifying 21
  profiles 117
work-life balance
  acceptable 15, 65, 123
  improved 72t
  optimal 71
Wray, S. 45, 158–60, 171
Wright, M. O. 167

Xu, X. 1

Yale, A. 174
Yamey, G. 171
Ylijoki, O-H. 10–12, 15
Yudkevich, M. 10, 14

Zacher, H. 12, 53
Zhou, Y. 176

www.ingramcontent.com/pod-product-compliance
Lightning Source LLC
Chambersburg PA
CBHW071829300426
44116CB00009B/1484